Succeeding with Use Cases

Succeeding with Use Cases

Working Smart to Deliver Quality

Richard Denney

♦♦ Addison-Wesley

Upper Saddle River, NJ • Boston • Indianapolis • San Francisco
New York • Toronto • Montreal • London • Munich • Paris • Madrid
Capetown • Sydney • Tokyo • Singapore • Mexico City

The publisher offers excellent discounts on this book when ordered in quantity for bulk purchases or special sales, which may include electronic versions and/or custom covers and content particular to your business, training goals, marketing focus, and branding interests. For more information, please contact:

U. S. Corporate and Government Sales
(800) 382-3419
corpsales@pearsontechgroup.com

For sales outside the U. S., please contact:

International Sales
international@pearsoned.com

Visit us on the Web: www.awprofessional.com

Library of Congress Catalog Number: 205920918

ISBN 0-321-31643-6

Text printed in the United States on recycled paper at R.R. Donnelley and Sons Company in Crawfordsville, Indiana.

First printing, May 2005

Contents

Preface

If the Unified Software Development Process (USDP) were a coloring book, I'm afraid I'd be characterized as one of those kids who just can't color within the lines. I've been using use-case-like "things" for quite some time, although they may have been called something else: *workflows*, *scenarios* when Object Modeling Technique (OMT) came out, and then eventually *use cases*. But the funny thing is, more often than not I wasn't using them like the USDP described them being used. Rather, I was combining them first with this technique, and then that one. It's not that I was trying to be a rebel; use cases just seemed to fit in nicely with other techniques to solve a problem. Eventually, as the USDP matured, I began to notice that others were starting to mention QFD in conjunction with use cases and discuss operational profiles of use cases. Scott Ambler added project portfolio management to his Enterprise Unified Process, an extension to USDP; and preconditions and postconditions actually became an official part of use cases. It finally occurred to me: *other people were coloring outside the lines too*! The motivation for this: problems that were best solved with techniques that were not a part of USDP proper; problems for which other disciplines already had solutions.

It was this realization that led to this book: that my experiences with disciplines, such as QFD, Software Reliability Engineering, Model-based Specification (preconditions, postconditions, and invariants), Requirements

Configuration Management, and Project Portfolio Management *combined with use cases* might benefit others in the use case development community.

This book presents what I hope you will agree is a whole new set of perspectives on use case-driven development. Innovation, solutions to problems, and *ways of working smarter* often arise when ideas from multiple areas are combined. As use cases continue to mature, future improvements in use case-driven development are likely to arise from just such cross-pollination of use cases with other disciplines of software engineering. This book looks at four areas that focus on quality engineering.

1. Quality Function Deployment (QFD)

2. Software Reliability Engineering

3. Model-Based Specification (Preconditions, Postconditions, and Invariants)

4. Requirements Configuration Management/Project Portfolio Management

From each discipline, the book pulls practical, 20/80, "high bang for the buck" ideas that help you and your organization *work smart to deliver quality products* in use case-driven development.[1]

Overview of Parts and Chapters

The book is organized into four parts—one per quality engineering discipline—with two chapters each. Here's an overview of what you'll find in each part of the book.

---

[1] "Quality" as used in this book is the project stakeholders' (especially customers') relative valuation of scope (functions and features), schedule (speed of delivery to the customer), cost and degree of defect-free operation (i.e. reliability). This is the same definition used by Jim Highsmith (2000) and others in the software quality arena.

Part 1—Quality Function Deployment

Like it or not, software development is increasingly becoming a *team sport*! And it's a game being played on a "two dimensional field." Chapter 1, "An Introduction to QFD: Driving Vision *Vertically* Through the Project," introduces QFD, *a team-oriented product-planning tool* that is used to translate business drivers into the technical requirements and design aspects of a product. You will learn how to use QFD in use case-driven development as a mechanism for *moving vision vertically—the first dimension of the playing field—through projects* starting at the senior management/marketing level, where vision is hatched and business priorities are being set, downward to the development team level, so that the product that is released is true to the original vision and business priorities.

The second dimension in which the "team sport" of use case-driven development is played out in a company is horizontally. Chapter 2, "Aligning Decision Making and Synchronizing Distributed Development *Horizontally* in the Organization," looks at the factors that make use case-driven distributed development difficult and the combined use of QFD and use cases to align decisions and synchronize use case-driven development *horizontally* across multiple component or product teams, or business groups in a company. You'll learn how to use QFD and simple optimization problem-solving tools to find the optimum duration for a development iteration and the optimum set of high-priority use cases that can be implemented in that time across distributed teams.

Part 2—Software Reliability Engineering

Software Reliability Engineering (SRE) is about *increasing customer satisfaction by delivering a reliable product, while minimizing engineering costs*. Use case-driven development and SRE are a natural match, both being usage-driven styles of product development. What SRE brings to the party is a discipline for focusing time, effort, and resources on use cases in proportion to their estimated frequency of use or criticality, called an *operational profile*. In Chapter 3, "Operational Profiles: Quantifying Frequency of Use of Use Cases," you'll learn how to build an operational profile for the scenarios that make up a single use case and for a package of use cases. Examples are provided to illustrate the use of operational profiles to enable you to work intelligently in how you plan the activities that affect your product reliability. The chapter concludes by showing how to extend operational profiles to address risk profiling of use case packages.

Your product has been in final system test for days—or has it been weeks? Surely it must be time to stop testing and release it! Chapter 4, "Reliability and Knowing When to Stop Testing," looks at another important concept that Software Reliability Engineering brings to use case development: A concrete way to talk about "reliability." This includes how to define it, measure it, set goals in terms of it, and track it in testing. In this chapter, you will learn how to set *quantitative* reliability goals in the form of a *failure intensity objective*. The development and testing group then tracks product reliability in system tests against this objective providing a sound method to determine when the reliability goal has been reached, testing can terminate, and the product can be released.

Part 3—Model-Based Specification (Preconditions, Postconditions, and Invariants)

In Chapter 5, "Preconditions, Postconditions, and Invariants: What They Didn't Tell You, But You Need to Know!" you are introduced to a time-tested technique for specifying the expected behavior of abstract data types and objects—*model-based specification*—and learn how to apply it in a fresh way to pose sharp questions in *use case failure analysis*: the analysis of potential ways a system, specified by a use case, might fail. In doing so, you'll learn some things about preconditions and postconditions they forgot to mention in "Use Case 101." The chapter concludes with ideas on how to work smartly in applying model-based specification, including the section "The Absolute Least You Need to Know: One Fundamental Lesson and Three Simple Rules," which, if you get nothing else from the chapter, will give you a take away you can apply to any and all use cases right away. The goal of this chapter is nothing less than providing you a whole new perspective on use case preconditions and postconditions.

Not only does the model-based specification with its preconditions, postconditions, and invariants provide an integrated basis for use case failure analysis, taken as a unit they are a veritable *triple threat test case*. In Chapter 6, "Triple Threat Test Design for Use Cases," you'll learn how to take the preconditions, postconditions, and invariants generated from failure analysis in the previous chapter and design test cases from them using Robert Binder's *Extended Use Case Test Design Pattern.*

Part 4—Use Case Configuration Management

There is no question that a commercial requirements management tool is useful for use case management; but can it pay for itself at your company? Chapter 7, "Calculating Your Company's ROI in Use Case Configuration Management," looks at a model to help you *calculate the Return On Investment (ROI) on requirements management tools for use case management.* Not only will it help you decide if such tools make sense for your company, it also helps illustrate some of the types of problems configuration management of use cases is meant to address.

In Chapter 8, "Leveraging Your Investment in Use Case CM in Project Portfolio Management," you'll learn how to leverage your company's investment in use case CM to provide metrics and reports for what could well be *the most far-reaching, single process improvement possible in your company: Project Portfolio Management.* Project Portfolio Management is the measured allocation of development resources according to some strategic plan. You'll learn how to leverage use case-based metrics and reports to evaluate the mix of strategic project types in the project portfolio and evaluate if projects are executable in the times specified by the portfolio, an approach called *pipeline management.*

Part 5—Appendices

Appendices A through D provide further supporting materials. They provide more detailed, how-to information that should prove useful as you read the chapters.

Who Should Read What

This book is for anyone doing use case-driven development who wants to think outside the box a little to try some new ideas. Here's some guidance on who should read what parts and chapters of the book, and what background you are assumed to have.

Table P.1 provides a guide to the parts and chapters of the book likely to be of greatest interest based on the role you play in product development. As is clear from this table, this book has something of interest for just about every role in product development. A check indicates a topic that is core to a team role: this is the role that would likely be applying that topic. A plus sign indicates that understanding of topic is a "plus" for a team role (e.g., your role interfaces with team members that would be using that technique, so your understanding would be beneficial).

Table P.1   *Recommended parts and chapters based on your role in product development. A checkmark indicates that a topic is core to role. A plus sign indicates that understanding of topic is a "plus."*

	QFD		Software Reliability Engineering		Model-based Specification		Configuration/ Portfolio Management	
Chapter	1	2	3	4	5	6	7	8
Project Managers & Program Managers	✓	✓	✓	✓			✓	✓
Product Managers	✓	+	✓	+	+		✓	✓
Project/Product Portfolio Managers	✓	+					✓	✓
Senior Managers/ Upper Management	✓	+					✓	✓
Marketing	✓		+				+	✓
Testers	+		✓	✓	✓	✓	+	
Test Managers	+	+	✓	✓	+	+	+	+
Software Engineers	✓	+	✓	✓	✓	✓	+	
Requirements Engineers/ System Analysts	✓	+	✓	✓	✓	✓	✓	+
Anyone doing safety/ mission/business critical systems	+	+	✓	✓	✓	✓	+	

	QFD		Software Reliability Engineering		Model-based Specification		Configuration/ Portfolio Management	
Chapter	**1**	**2**	**3**	**4**	**5**	**6**	**7**	**8**
Anyone doing "Design by Contract"			+	+	✓	✓		
Anyone facilitating team meetings	✓	✓						
Academics teaching class in Software Engineering	✓	✓	✓	✓	✓	✓	✓	✓

Knowledge About Use Cases

The only assumption made about your background as a reader is that you are already familiar with use cases. The scope of the book does not include an introduction to use cases, UML, Unified Software Development Process, and so on. Many excellent books already cover these topics.

Knowledge About the Other Software Engineering Disciplines

Previous knowledge of the other software engineering disciplines discussed in this book is *not* necessary. Do keep in mind that whole quality engineering disciplines have been condensed down to two chapters each. These are disciplines that merit whole books, and have large conferences and research and development communities, so what you will see is only a small part of what are large disciplines, but they are parts that yield a good bang for the buck for the use case community. Ample references have been provided to allow you to explore topics in more depth if you desire. A goal of this book is to increase the visibility of these other disciplines to the use case community, and I think references are key to this goal.

For Those Who Hate Math

Two parts of the book—Part 2, "Software Reliability Engineering," and Part 3, "Model-Based Specification"—have a little math in them.

Part 2 involves a little probability and an equation or two, all of which you will be walked through carefully, so no prior background in probability is needed.

Part 3—especially the first chapter—may be the book's most challenging technically, more due to the concepts than the math. The only assumption made is that you are familiar with arithmetic and simple algebra.

Unified Software Development Process

All the ideas in this book can be applied whether or not you are following the Unified Software Development Process (USDP). If you are, however, following USDP you might find Table P.2 useful: It provides guidance on phases of the USDP in which you will find the application of the techniques of each chapter most beneficial. A checkmark indicates the phase in which the techniques as exemplified in the chapter would likely occur. A plus sign indicates other phases in which the techniques could be applied, but which are not specifically illustrated in the chapter.

Table P.2   *Suggested phase of Unified Software Development Process for application in each chapter. A checkmark indicates use as described in chapter. A plus sign indicates additional uses not specifically covered in the chapter.*

	Chapter	Inception	Elaboration	Construction	Transition
QFD	1	✓	+	+	+
	2		✓	✓	
Software Reliability Engineering	3		✓	✓	✓
	4		✓	✓	✓
Model-Based Specification	5		✓	+	
	6		✓	✓	✓
Configuration / Portfolio Mngt.	7	N/A	N/A	N/A	N/A
	8	N/A	N/A	N/A	N/A

To review Table P.2, moving top to bottom, QFD is a technique that by design is capable of being applied in all phases of a project. The example provided in Chapter 1 illustrates its use during inception in helping a team decide the focus of a release. The application of QFD in Chapter 2 is focused on planning and coordinating use case distributed development and would be used in elaboration and/or construction.

Chapter 3 is concerned with operational profiles that would be created during elaboration, then their results used in all subsequent phases for prioritization of effort and resource. The setting of reliability goals discussed in Chapter 4 would occur as part of planning done in elaboration. The use of those reliability goals would then be used in tracking reliability growth of the product during testing in construction and transition.

Having used QFD or operational profiles to identify use cases that were frequently used, critical and/or important to business drivers, the model-based specification techniques of Chapter 5 would be used in elaboration for failure analysis of the system as described by those key use cases. In construction, those same techniques could also be used in specifying class or component interfaces using design by contract. In Chapter 6, test planning based on the work of Chapter 5 would be done as part of late elaboration or early construction. The test cases would be used in all subsequent phases as a basis for testing.

Finally, the calculation of ROI on a requirements configuration management tool, covered in Chapter 7, and project portfolio management, covered in Chapter 8, would occur as separate programs apart from any single software product release and so are not applicable to specific phases per se. The results of project portfolio management would of course be used as part of the input to the inception phase of all projects.

How Parts of This Book Relate

Each of the four parts of this book—like the disciplines they pull from—are standalone and can be read and used independently of one another. A few of the techniques can, however, be leveraged off of one another.

Project portfolio management (Part 4, Chapter 8) is over-arching in relationship to all other topics in this book in that stresses in a company due to "too much work, too little time" affect virtually every other aspect of software development and the quality of products produced. A company that has not sorted its vital few projects from the trivial many is likely to have staff with neither the interest nor time for new innovative ideas.

The biggest bang for the buck in applying the ideas of Part 3, "Model-Based Specification," will come from application to use cases that are frequently used and/or are critical in nature. The techniques on describing operational profiles in Part 2, "Software Reliability Engineering," are ideal for identifying such use cases, as are the prioritization techniques of Part 1, "Quality Function Deployment."

It is also possible to use frequency of use information or criticality information obtained from an operational profile (Part 2, "Software Reliability Engineering") as one of many business drivers used to prioritize use cases with QFD. An example of this is provided in Chapter 2, "Aligning Decision Making and Synchronizing Distributed Development Horizontally in the Organization."

Conversely, you may find that a QFD matrix (Part 1, "Quality Function Deployment") is an ideal tool for building informal operational profiles for a product (Part 2, "Software Reliability Engineering").

What This Book Is Not

As with the scope of software projects, it's probably as important to be clear about what this book is *not* as it is *what it is*. I've touched on a couple things already, but they are worth reiterating.

The book does *not* provide an introduction on use cases: what they are, their benefit, or how to write them.

Nor will this book provide an overview of UML or the Unified Software Development Process. In general, this book is largely software development life-cycle neutral. Some of the ideas presented in the book actually work just as well with Extreme Programming's (XP) Stories as they do with use cases, and these will be pointed out.

While you will be getting a good impression of what the other disciplines are about—QFD, Software Reliability Engineering, Model-Based Specification, CM/Project Portfolio Management—the intent is not to present a definitive tutorial on any of these topics. Having said that, what you do get in this book from a use case-driven development standpoint may be all you ever need.

Richard Denney
Austin, Texas
www.software-quality-consulting.com

Acknowledgments

I'd like to thank Mary O'Brien, Chris Zahn, Brenda Mulligan, Christy Hackerd, and the rest of the team at Addison-Wesley Professional for the opportunity and their support in publishing this book.

I'd also like to acknowledge the members of the review team for their valuable feedback as the book was being written. It's a better book because of them. In alphabetical order, they are: Daryl Kulak, Dean Leffingwell, Granville Miller, Sam Supakkul, Lauren Thayer, Geri Schneider Winters, and Lian Zerafa.

Part 1

Quality Function Deployment

Managing Use Case-Driven Development in "2D"

"Even if you have the right people in the right jobs, unless you synchronize their efforts, and link them to the business priorities, you do not have an edge in execution. The money making doesn't happen..."

—Ram Charan, What the CEO Wants You to Know (Charan 2001)

There is today a problem which characterizes, or maybe I should say *complicates*, software development. It would be convenient if this problem were technical in nature: We as software engineers are good at tackling those. But, unfortunately, it is a problem that many software engineers fear: It is a *people problem*. It is the problem of how to get people aligned, seeing a common vision, thinking alike, and synchronizing their efforts. Like it or not, software development is increasingly becoming a *team sport* (Leffingwell and Widrig 2003).

And if software development is a team sport, the game is being played on a two-dimensional field[1]:

- *Vertically*, companies must be able to move product vision at the senior management/marketing level, where business priorities are being set, downward to the team level, so that the product that is released is true to the original vision and business priorities.

- *Horizontally*, companies must be able to synchronize multiple project teams, each representing separate components or even whole products, so that they work on the same use cases, in the same order of priority, and with the same vision. In short, distributed software development.

In these chapters, we will look at the pivotal role use cases play in addressing this problem of developing software as a team sport and introduce the use of Quality Function Deployment (QFD) as a tool for prioritizing, aligning, and synchronizing use case-driven development in these two dimensions.

QFD is a product-planning tool that is used to translate business drivers into the technical requirements and design aspects of a product. QFD's roots reach back to Japan's shipbuilding and automotive manufacturing industries in the late 1960s as part of a broader interest in improved quality control by pioneers such as Yoji Akao.[2]

The interest in QFD in the West was stimulated by reports of the achievements made by Toyota through its application between 1977 and 1984, which included a reduction in product development costs, cycle time, and rework problems—and, most importantly, *the delivery of products that*

---

[1] There is a third dimension in which the game is played, but which we won't address here, and that is time. Given that few systems are built "big bang" in one release, companies must learn to manage product vision, requirements, and decisions through time ("Does anyone remember why we designed it this way?!"), across staff changes and company reorganizations, mergers, and acquisitions. In a very literal sense, the team and company that released version 1.0 of a product can be completely different from the one that releases version 5.0.

[2] If you are interested in reading more about the history of QFD, see Akao (1997).

customers wanted. Of those taking note of Toyota's success were the big three U.S. automakers. Their interest in QFD in the 1980s as part of a larger program to improve product quality helped spread interest in the U.S.

Today, though originally developed for manufacturing industries, QFD-like ideas are being used successfully throughout the world for all sorts of applications, including software development, the services industry, and process management, and is considered an essential part of the quality improvement toolkit.

As with the other disciplines in the other parts of this book, QFD is a topic for a book on its own. In fact, based on the number of available titles, it is a topic worth *hundreds* of books. But while the QFD process is standardized and documented for manufacturing, there is no standard for its application in software development,[3] much less use cases specifically.[4] So while yet another book on QFD is probably not needed—and as Karl Wiegers has noted, few software development organizations seem willing to undertake the *full rigor* of QFD, anyway—some insights into the 20% that yields 80% of the benefit in conjunction with use case driven development is very much needed.

Chapter 1, "An Introduction to QFD: Driving Vision *Vertically* Through the Project," introduces you to QFD in general and focuses on the vertical dimension of software development as a team sport. In it, you

- Are introduced to the basic mechanics of QFD.

- Learn the difference between business drivers, user requirements, and system requirements, and the use of QFD to link and prioritize them vertically in the company.

- Get a lesson from QFD on the importance of *prioritized* business drivers and why simply identifying business drivers *isn't* enough.

---

[3] Cohen (1995) provides a good starting place for a brief overview of its application to software. Haag et al. (1996) survey several software vendors' use of QFD in their system development life cycle. Details on actual application, however, are not given.

[4] Lamia (1995) looks at a variety of possibilities for incorporating QFD into OO design, including use cases.

- Learn how to analyze use cases and quality requirements (nonfunctional requirements) in terms of how they correlate with one another, positively or negatively.

- Learn how to run a QFD workshop; although an individual can certainly use QFD as a tool, its biggest value is as a tool for team product planning and vision alignment.

Chapter 2, "Aligning Decision Making and Synchronizing Distributed Development *Horizontally* in the Organization," addresses the horizontal dimension of software development as a team sport (i.e., use case-driven distributed development across multiple component or product teams).

In this chapter, you will:

- See QFD applied to two software development examples from the oil and gas industry, again reinforcing the theme of QFD as a team problem solving/decision-making tool.

- Work through an example of QFD used as a mechanism for aligning decision making horizontally cross-company. This example will also illustrate a QFD process that *begins* with use cases and works *backward* to identify the business drivers (not a part of "standard" manufacturing-based QFD, but something you may need to do in real-life software development).

- Learn the value added by QFD to the nonfunctional requirements of a suite of fully dressed use cases.

- Learn three factors that make use case-driven distributed development difficult.

- Discover how to use QFD to synchronize use case-driven distributed development and how to find an *optimum* duration for a development iteration with an *optimum* set of high-priority use cases that can be implemented in that time across distributed teams.

1

An Introduction to QFD: Driving Vision *Vertically* Through the Project

One good thing about small, one-person software development efforts is that the person with the ideas and the product's vision is the same person that specs out the product and writes the code. There was a time when I fancied that the big problems in software development were the technical problems; problems that involved specs, design, and code. At some point, my opinion on this started to change as I began to notice that the thorny problems folks encounter in projects are quite frequently *people problems.* Given that few projects are one-person shows anymore, how do you point a group of people in the same direction, help them envision a problem in the same way, and synchronize and coordinate their efforts toward a common vision? *That,* it finally occurred to me, was the *real* problem in software development.

One form of this "people problem" that large projects face is how to move product vision and its associated business drivers, hatched at the senior management/marketing level, vertically downward to the project team level so that the product that is built, tested, and released is true to that original vision and business drivers.

The Language Gap

If you've ever been in a room where both upper management/marketing types and technical geeks are present at the same time, you know there is often a language gap. While one is talking about the need to grow revenue for this and that customer segment, the other is saying, *"Just tell me what to build!!"*

A way to understand this problem is by applying Karl Wiegers' levels of requirements types. In his article, "10 Requirements Traps to Avoid," Karl Wiegers argues that a fair amount of confusion comes about in projects because of the failure to recognize the existence of "several types of requirements, all legitimate and all necessary." To paraphrase, these requirements types are *business drivers[1]*, *user requirements*, and *system requirements* (i.e., functional and quality/non-functional requirements of the system's software and hardware).

Business drivers emanate from the point of view of the developing organization and provide a clear sense of *why* a project is being undertaken and the value the product will provide. User requirements, on the other hand, reflect the point of view of the user, describing what the user requires in terms of tasks or goals to be accomplished.[2] Finally, system requirements represent the product from the point of view of the system itself and what is required of its software and hardware to support the user's requirements.

---

[1] Wiegers (1999) actually uses the term "business requirements," but I've found this term has a different meaning for some people than what I think Wiegers intends: for some it is akin to business rules used in databases (i.e., a business requirement describes some real-world constraint on the business). I now use the term business drivers as a substitute for business requirements as most people clearly connect with this ("What is driving this project?").

[2] No distinction will be made here between users and customers, though it is an important distinction of which to be aware. When customer and user are not one and the same, meeting the customer's requirements is a necessary, but not sufficient goal, for unhappy users will likely sour future sales. Gauss and Weinberg (1989) illustrate this point with toy sales: if either the parent (the paying customer) or the child (the user) is dissatisfied, a toy will not succeed in the market place. For a software example of this, in the oil and gas industry, IT departments are often customers for, but typically not users of, products designed for oil and gas exploration. In such cases, there is a win-win situation that must be achieved of meeting the customer's requirements while also meeting the requirements of the user. QFD can be a useful tool for helping identify which of a host of product features or designs best provides a win-win situation for customer and user alike.

This transition in focus from business to user to system is illustrated in Figure 1.1, which shows a simplified form of Wiegers' requirements levels.

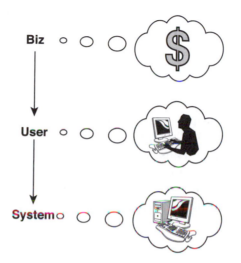

Figure 1.1   *Wiegers' levels of requirements illustrate the transition in focus in a software project from thinking about the business, to the user, to the system.*

Beyond a classification of requirements types, the hierarchy of Figure 1.1 is also a good model for understanding the communication gap that exists vertically in projects. It's not that upper management is *wrong* when they talk in "biz" speak or that technical geeks are *wrong* when they just want someone to tell them the component interface to implement. It is just that each is dealing with different requirement types of the project, "all legitimate and all necessary."

Use cases—and their equally low-tech cousins, such as storyboards, XP stories, workflows—have helped with this problem by providing a lingua franca for at least the user requirements that are understandable by upper management, marketing types and technical geeks alike. Looking at Figure 1.1, we see that use cases—as a means of stating a user's requirements—are in a pivotal position in the hierarchy, serving as a vertical bridge on the transition down from the sometimes lofty and vague business perspective to the sometimes very "down in the weeds" detail of the system perspective. But sometimes more is needed to help manage this transition from business to user to system. That's where Quality Function Deployment (QFD) can come in.

QFD in Use Case-Driven Projects

QFD is a tool that can certainly be used by an individual, but its real value is as a structured approach for team prioritization and decision making. A team that uses QFD for product planning will emerge with a common vision of the business drivers, priorities, assumptions, issues, and questions that need to be addressed.

While the QFD process is fairly standardized for manufacturing, there is no standard for its application in software development in general, much less use cases specifically. QFD has received some discussion in the use case community as a means of prioritizing use cases.[3] Used in this fashion, QFD serves as a tool for linking business drivers to use cases by identifying those use cases that are *best aligned to the business drivers* of the project: in QFD lingo, "deploying" the business drivers to the user requirement level.

What has received less attention in the use case community, however, is the subsequent use of QFD coupled with prioritized use cases to prioritize other aspects of software development, such as alternate design approaches. This is the second transition of Figure 1.1, from what the user requires to what is required of the system to support the user. Used in this way, QFD serves as a tool to identify those *aspects of product design best aligned to the use cases, which are in turn aligned to the business drivers.*

Again, while there is no standard, I have found the following combination of QFD, coupled with the hierarchy of Figure 1.1, to be of value:

1. QFD used as a framework to move vision and its associated business drivers vertically through the project to the user requirement level as a prioritized set of use cases.

2. QFD, coupled with prioritized use cases, as a framework for prioritizing and decision making in terms of what is required of the system.

This approach is illustrated in Figure 1.2, in which QFD is used as the mechanism to transition vertically from thinking about the business, to

---

[3] Wiegers (1999) references QFD as a means of prioritizing use cases. Wyder (1996) also provides an example.

thinking about the user, to thinking about the system, a la the hierarchy of Figure 1.1.

In the diagram of Figure 1.2, arrows show the business drivers of a project as input to the first QFD matrix whose output—a prioritized list of use cases—serves as the subsequent input to other QFD matrices, for example, to prioritize alternate designs for a product.

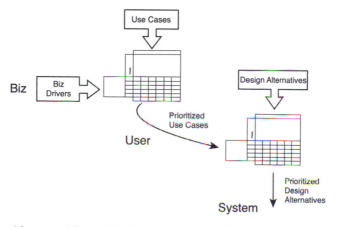

Figure 1.2   *A general framework for applying QFD to use case-driven projects.*

We are going to look at an example of how QFD is used as a tool for product planning, helping a team to make this vertical transition as part of that planning, but first we'll talk about business drivers a bit more. Given that the adage "garbage-in, garbage-out" applies to QFD, it's worth spending some time talking a bit more about that first, initial input to the QFD process of Figure 1.2: the business drivers.

Business Drivers in QFD

In standard manufacturing-based QFD, the process starts with the *Voice Of The Customer* or *Customer Needs*, couched as what are often called quality requirements; hence, the origin of the "Q" in QFD. These "customer needs" often sound like the ambiguous non-functional requirements we are warned against in software engineering:

- System must be easy to use

- System must be reliable

- System must respond quickly to inputs

In QFD, however, these ambiguous sounding quality requirements eventually evolve into very technical, non-ambiguous requirements. It's all part of the process.

As Figure 1.2 shows, however, the QFD process as described in this chapter starts with business drivers; it is based on the use of QFD as a mechanism for working vertically through Wiegers' levels of requirement types, from business drivers, to user requirements, to system requirements, and even design. My experience is that a software project is typically driven by a combination of factors, only some of which are customer needs. For example, I've seen projects where the prime objective was to explore technology the company did not understand well as a way to increase understanding and minimize risk in the long term. That approach is very much associated with the risk-driven development style of the Unified Software Development Process or the "Agile" methodologies and is not something one would typically see in a standard manufacturing QFD example as a "customer need." On the other hand, if the business drivers for a project are strictly limited to making the customer happy, the business drivers will be a standard QFD "voice of the customer."

A business driver is something that provides a clear sense of *why* a project is being undertaken and the ultimate *value* it will provide; it's a force to which businesses must respond and drives a business's direction. A business driver could be a customer need (system must be reliable) or an internal company objective (minimize risk by exploring technology not well understood). Ideally, business drivers are win-win in nature, providing value for both you *and* the customer. A business driver that makes money for you but produces a product the customer is unwilling to pay for is not terribly useful, and a customer need that does not line up with your profitability is a money-losing situation for you.

Business drivers as used in QFD are a way to make a project's vision tangible and provide a basis for prioritizing virtually every activity of the project. In a way—and this is very important—in QFD *the prioritization of the business drivers is in a sense a business driver itself.* As the prioritization of business drives is the crucial beginning of the QFD process (mistakes made here will propagate forward through the rest of the process) it is worth a closer look.

The "Chaos" of Projects and the Importance of Prioritization

QFD boiled down to simple mechanics is in large part about establishing links between things (QFD is an ideal tool for traceability)—in our software project model the links are from business drivers, to use cases, to aspects and parts of the system—and about prioritizing those links.

Prioritization is so ubiquitous to project management that it's easy to overlook its importance. We prioritize because we can't do it all (we have time for X or Y, but not both) or because a product can't be all things (it can be X, or it can be Y, but it can't be both simultaneously). We prioritize as a way of deciding to follow one path or another.

You may be aware that some systems, both natural and man-made, produce radically different outcomes when started with just slightly different initial conditions. In the relatively new field of chaos theory this is called *deterministic chaos.* These systems are deterministic: given the same starting state and inputs they produce the same result every time. It is just that even very slight changes in the starting state and inputs can result in radically different results. This is what makes weather prediction so difficult; the weather is chaotic in this very sense.

I'm convinced that software projects are chaotic systems too, and you may well agree! If you could take a software project, clone it, and start the copies with the same business drivers, but with *different* priorities, you might find the projects producing significantly different products.

Let's take a very concrete example of this that will set us up for our QFD example. How many of you have bought a car because it is ugly? Raise your hand. I don't see any hands. OK, how many of you have bought a car because it is fuel *in*-efficient…uses too much gas? Still no hands. How about cost…have you ever bought a car because it cost too much money? Safety…have you ever bought a car because it's un-safe? By and large we all buy cars using the same business drivers: we look at the gas mileage, how much it costs, what it looks like, safety, and so on. If we all buy cars using the same business drivers, why don't we all drive the same car? Priorities. We place different priorities on the business drivers, and those priorities result in radically different decisions about the cars we own and drive.

While it may be OK for us all to drive around in different cars, if we are an engineering team designing next year's new model car, we must work from the same set of business drivers and with the same priorities.

I was helping facilitate a working session once for a cross-company program composed of several separate product teams working in concert. The group was made up of project managers, product managers and/or technical leads from each product line. I had the group start by listing the business drivers for the program. In just a few minutes the group was able to produce a handful of drivers for the project. Quick agreement. Slam dunk. They were ready to get going with project planning issues! But before letting the group move ahead, I asked them to take just a moment more to *prioritize* the list of business drivers in rank order. I had each person work alone in silence, then come to the front and write the business drivers on the board in priority order. While the group readily agreed on the business drivers, their priority level was another matter. Nearly an hour later, the group was still trying to reach agreement on this matter of priorities. It had become apparent that unless a consensus was reached, it was unclear whether this program was going to wind up building a Hum Vee, a Harley, or something in between (metaphorically speaking, that is; this was in the oil and gas industry).

Running a QFD Workshop: Mega Motors Example

Unless you are already somewhat familiar with QFD, all this probably sounds a bit nebulous, so it's time for an example. While QFD can certainly be used as a tool by an individual, its biggest value is as a tool for team product planning, so our example follows a development team in a workshop setting. For our example, we'll take a use case and QFD-driven approach to thinking about the design of an automobile; actually, a *video storyboard* about an automobile.

Storyboarding is a great requirements engineering technique for eliciting what Leffingwell and Widrig call "Yes, but..." reactions from a customer.[4] The effectiveness of storyboards was demonstrated for me by a colleague who successfully used them in the oil and gas industry on a reinvent-the-paradigm project that proposed to change radically how the user approached their job.[5] A storyboard was used as an effective tool to communicate both to the customer and the project team what life would look like in this new vision of the world.

There are a number of goals for this example of which I'd like you to be aware. First and foremost, I want to illustrate QFD's use as a tool for *planning the focus of a release*. What better way to demonstrate this than with an example from the industry that helped popularize QFD, allowing companies like Toyota to plan for products customers would want to purchase.

The example also needs to demonstrate the basic parts and process of working with the QFD matrix without the domain of the problem getting in the way. This example—creation of a storyboard for a new vehicle—has the benefit that most people are familiar enough with automobiles to recognize whether the QFD process is producing results that really make sense or not. And it is simple enough to avoid getting bogged down in or distracted by the complexities and realities of creating a software system, allowing you to focus on learning QFD. The same goal could have been achieved with familiar examples, such as an ATM system or banking system, but they are already *high mileage* examples in the use case literature (pun definitely intended).

And finally, whereas we may be accustomed to associating use case-driven development with software, there is certainly no reason it cannot be applied elsewhere, such as in the design of hard-goods and services. This example will be novel in that respect.

---

[4] See Leffingwell and Widrig's (2003) chapter on storyboarding.

[5] Thanks go out to Edward Pierce and his usability team.

For a real life example of use cases applied to the development of drive-by-wire cars at Volvo, see Johannessen et al.'s *Hazard Analysis in Object Oriented Design of Dependable Systems.*

After we've looked at QFD in action, we'll look at examples of QFD applied to more "standard" software development projects in Chapter 2, "Aligning Decision Making and Synchronizing Distributed Development *Horizontally* in the Organization."

Workshop Overview

Mega Motors is planning the focus of their next release of their flagship vehicle. Before full development begins, a project team composed of both marketing and engineers has been given the task of determining what key features of the vehicle will be most attractive to the customer. After these key features have been identified, a video-based storyboard shot with a mockup will be produced that focuses on these key features in use in a fashion typical of the customer. The video storyboard will be used with focus groups to get early impressions and reactions to the proposed new vehicle features and enhancements.

You have been asked to facilitate an offsite QFD workshop to jump start and align the thinking of the project team members.

Before the Workshop

As workshop facilitator you meet with hosts of the workshop—Vice President of Marketing and Vice President of Engineering—the day before the workshop is to begin. You start by working with them to draft an initial objective statement for the workshop:

> *"Determine what key features of the Mega Motors vehicle will be most attractive to the customer, along with a key use case that will be used as the basis for a video-based storyboard shot with a mockup to advertise these key features being used in typical fashion by a typical customer."*

Next, you give a brief overview of the QFD process, and in particular review the basic components of a QFD matrix (see Figure 1.3).

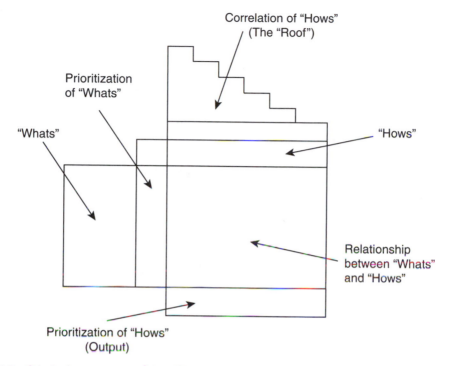

Figure 1.3   *Principal components of the QFD matrix, sometimes referred to as the "House of Quality."*

Walking through the diagram of Figure 1.3, you explain to the VPs that QFD stands for Quality Function Deployment. To make sense of the name, try this: The "F" in QFD stands for the features and functions of the product. The goal of QFD is to find the best set of "F" to meet—or *deploy* (that's the "D")—the goals "Q."

The QFD matrix is the central tool in QFD; it is sometimes called the "House of Quality." The matrix is a tool for establishing links between goals (the "Q, "which is referred to as **Whats** in the matrix) and ways to meet or *deploy* those goals (the "F," which is referred to as **Hows** in the matrix). These links are captured in the matrix as **Relationships between Whats and Hows** (the central part of the matrix).

You also explain that what constitutes the **Whats** and **Hows** can change as you work through the QFD process: the outputs from one matrix (i.e., the **Hows**) can become the inputs to another matrix (i.e., the **Whats**) as illustrated in Figure 1.2.

The **Correlation** section of the matrix—sometimes called the "roof"[6] of the House of Quality—provides a means of capturing information about **Hows** that may interact with one another—either in a positive, reinforcing way, or negatively, working against one another.

The output of the QFD matrix is a **Prioritization of Hows**, calculated as a function of the prioritization of **Whats** and the strength of relationships between **Whats** and **Hows**.

Finally, you lay out a tentative game plan for working with the project team (see Figure 1.4).

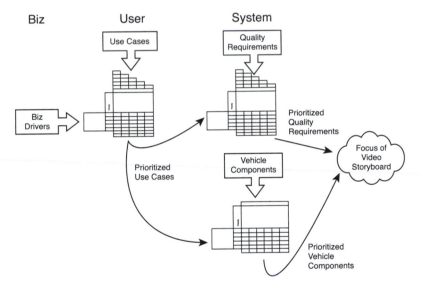

Figure 1.4   *Road map for the Mega Motors QFD workshop.*

Working through Figure 1.4, note the following:

1. The workshop will begin by determining a prioritized set of business drivers for the project (video production).

---

[6] In a traditional QFD "House of Quality" this is drawn to look more like a roof, hence the name. The slanted look here is an artifact of the matrix implementation in a spreadsheet, a common method of implementing a QFD matrix.

2. The development team will brainstorm use cases that could be used as the basis for a storyboard of the vehicle being used in a manner typical of the customer.

3. The use cases will then be analyzed and prioritized to identify those that most closely align with the business drivers.

4. Those prioritized use cases will then be used to analyze quality requirements, such as reliability, safety, and vehicle look and feel, to see which quality requirements best align with the prioritized use cases.

5. The same will be done with components of the vehicle—engine, transmission, body, and so on—to identify those components that best align with the prioritized use cases.

6. The workshop will conclude with the results of the prioritized quality requirements and vehicle components being used to sketch out a video that shows the vehicle in use—as per the highest priority use case—showcasing the high-priority quality aspects of the high-priority components of the vehicle (e.g., reliability of the engine, safety of the interior, sporty feel of the steering, and so on).

Specify Business Drivers

The next day, you begin the QFD session with the usual introductions and explain to the team that QFD is a type of Joint Application Development (JAD) session, where ideally you have representatives for each of the roles that need to be filled in the development of a product: in this case, a team made up of marketing and engineering, representing the two ends of the hierarchy of Figure 1.1. You emphasize to the team that while QFD can be done by a single person, the real value is in the team alignment that occurs and increased problem solving from the "two heads are better than one" phenomenon.

You have prepared a QFD "road map" to help the team better visualize the overall QFD process for the workshop and will use it throughout to orient the team as to where they are at any given time (see Figure 1.5).

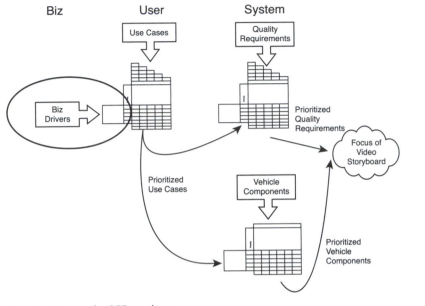

Figure 1.5 *Your location on the QFD road map.*

With intros and overview out of the way, you review the workshop objective statement drafted with the VPs of Marketing and Engineering. In order to make sure that everyone really buys into this objective statement, you ask the team for pros and cons on the objective as stated; in doing so you may bring to the surface tacit issues that have been missed. With minor modifications in place and a "thumbs up" vote to signify sign-off from all team members, you are ready to proceed.

What Is Driving the Project?

OK, you ask: what is *driving* this project (i.e., production of the video storyboard)? The marketing group has done its homework and has identified a profile of customer types it plans to bring into the focus group. The team suggests that the business driver for the project is to produce a focus group video that targets the interests of the following customer profile:

- Young single male

- Young single female

- Married couple with young children

- Double income couple, no kids

- Older, retired couple

Addressing the engineers in the group, you ask if they are comfortable with this customer profile as a means to drive the project. One question they have is how do you know these are the right business drivers?

Good question. You reply that in some sense the QFD workshop *is* a way to determine if the business drivers are right. Engineers build prototypes all the time to test ideas. You ask them to think of QFD as a way of prototyping a *project*, allowing you to run through a complete product development cycle quickly, from start (thinking about the business drivers) to end (thinking about the final product that results from the business drivers). In fact, with QFD, *what-if* analysis is pretty easy, allowing you to essentially simulate different projects from start to end, exploring the consequences of different priorities at the business driver or use case levels. In doing this, you may well learn along the way that the initial business drivers are leading to results you intuitively feel are not what they should be, in which case, a reexamination of the business drivers may be in order. As with any prototype, the real value of QFD may not necessarily be the artifacts produced but with the discovery process that takes place. And one discovery could well be that your business drivers aren't right.

This prototyping concept appeals to the engineers in the workshop, and they agree that as a first iteration they can't think of any better business drivers.

Prioritize Business Drivers

One last critical step remains: prioritizing the list of customer profiles. As it turns out, this is also a very good way to test if you have the right business drivers.

---

[7] Additional details available in Chapter 8, "Leveraging Your Investment in Use Case CM in Project Portfolio Management."

For this, you explain you will be using a technique called *Wideband Delphi.*[7] This is a group problem-solving technique that is often applied to project schedule and effort estimation; here you will apply it to prioritizing the business drivers. You explain that it is an iterative process of first making anonymous prioritizations individually or in small groups. This is then followed by "show-and-tell" of individual results, and then group discussion of any divergence ("This is why I prioritized differently from you..."). In this process, tacit assumptions and information held by individuals are brought to the surface for the group as a whole to see. With a couple of iterations of this process, the group will hopefully converge on an answer that is better than any individual would have come up with alone.

To start the Wideband Delphi prioritization, you break the team into several small groups, place them in separate corners of the room, and tell each they have $100 of virtual money to spend on the customer profiles, allocating the money in proportion to the relative importance of the customer. This is a standard prioritization technique used by meeting facilitators and has been suggested by Todd Wyder for use with QFD in ranking use cases. This approach has the benefit that it ranks the business drivers via a ratio scale. The problem with the use of 1-5 or 1-10 type rating scales, which are traditionally used in QFD,[8] is that they are ordinal scales: is a business driver assigned a 5 *really* five times more important than one assigned 1?[9] It has the added benefit of preventing the ranking of every business driver high-priority; something marketing folk—indeed all of us—are often wont to do!

After a period of time, each separate group has completed allocation of their $100 across each of the customer types. You re-assemble the team and have each group present their results on a flip chart at the front of the room. Each presentation is followed by discussion, and you also ask the group to brainstorm the pros and cons of each prioritization as they are presented. Pro/con analysis is a great tool for surfacing hidden assumptions and decision-making criteria at work.[10] At the end of the first iteration, three key issues have emerged:

---

[8] There is a movement afoot to replace the use of ordinal scales traditionally used in QFD with ratio scales. The QFD Institute is a source of information on this topic.

[9] In QFD prioritization is done from high to low: a score of 5 is better than a score of 1. This is done to accommodate the arithmetic used in QFD.

[10] A meeting facilitation trick I owe to a colleague, Michael Begeman.

1. One group has rated **Older, Retired Couple** quite high on the list.

   - **Pro cited**: "This group represents a significant portion of the future demographics."

   - **Con cited**: "**Older, Retired Couple** may potentially have less disposable income in upcoming years."

2. Another group has placed **Married Couple with Young Children** high on their list.

   - **Pro cited**: "This group has traditionally been the strongest in terms of brand loyalty to Mega Motors."

3. Another group has placed **Double Income Couple, No Kids** at the top of their list.

   - **Pro cited**: "This group has lots of disposable income for buying vehicles."

The Wideband Delphi prioritization process has brought to the surface what the team quickly realizes are actually business drivers in their own right (i.e., the customer profile for the new Mega Motors vehicle needs to take into account *market size*, *brand loyalty*, and *disposable income* of each customer type). As this discovery illustrates, part of the value of QFD is that it helps bring to light tacit assumptions, hidden agendas, and misconceptions as a team works through a problem. In doing this, information previously held by individuals surfaces to become part of the team collective consciousness. This is the process at work, and it's important to keep a record of team discoveries as you go.

Enter Business Drivers into QFD Matrix

With this bit of alignment in place, each small group once again goes to its corner of the room to re-prioritize the customer profile. After reviewing each group's results of the second round, they are finally able to agree on an allocation of dollars across the list of customer types (see Table 1.1). This split, they all are willing to agree, is a decent compromise of the new business drivers underlying the customer profile (i.e., *market size, brand loyalty*, and *disposable income*).[11]

Table 1.1 *$100 in virtual money is allocated in proportion to importance of each customer type based on the market size, brand loyalty, and disposable income of each customer type.*

Customer Type	Dollar Amount
Young Single Male	$1
Young Single Female	$4
Married Couple with Young Children	$70
Double Income Couple, No Kids	$15
Older, Retired Couple	$10
TOTAL	$100

At this point, the team has successfully turned a vision and objective statement into a concrete set of prioritized business drivers that can be used for prioritization and for making trade offs. The business drivers are entered into the QFD matrix along with the priorities converted to percentages (see Figure 1.6).

While representatives of all the customer types will be included in the focus group, type **Married Couple with Young Children**, the customer type of greatest importance, has been selected by the team as the focal point for the video storyboard showing the vehicle being used in a fashion typical of the customer. This selection is reflected in Figure 1.6 as highlighted text.

---

[11] QFD could actually be used at this point to prioritize the customer types in terms of the newly discovered business drivers. As the purpose of the example is to explain QFD, however, that would only make things more confusing.

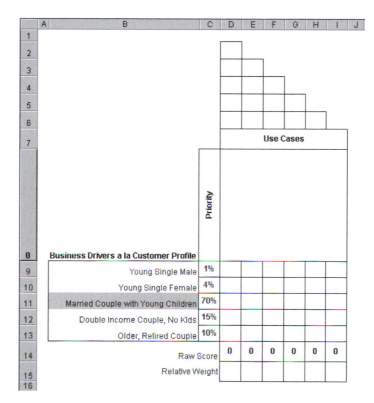

Figure 1.6   *Prioritized customer types are entered into the QFD matrix as business drivers. Highlighting shows highest priority type and focal point for the video storyboard.*

Identify Use Cases

In "traditional" manufacturing-based QFD, after the customer needs are identified (also called *voice of the customer*, or business drivers), the next step is to identify what are variously called *technical performance measures* or *technical requirements*. This latter term in particular does not mean what it would in a software engineering context. Technical requirements in QFD lingo are actually *measures* that can be made on a manufactured product to judge how well it satisfies the customer needs. As Lou Cohen has pointed out, for QFD applied to software, it is common for this measurement phase to be skipped over, moving directly to the identification of features and functions of the software; that is what we'll do here.

The "F" in QFD stands for functions. The goal of QFD is to find the best set of "F" that meets or *deploys* the goal "Q." As we are dealing with use case-driven development projects, the "F" will stand for use cases. In our Mega Motors QFD workshop, the goal is to identify the set of use cases that can best be used to meet our business drivers.

Brainstorm Use Cases to Meet Business Drivers

In this next step of the Mega Motors workshop, the team brainstorms a list of use cases that reflect the use of the vehicle by the customer types that have been identified (refer to Figure 1.6). Figure 1.7 shows where you are in the overall QFD process at this point.

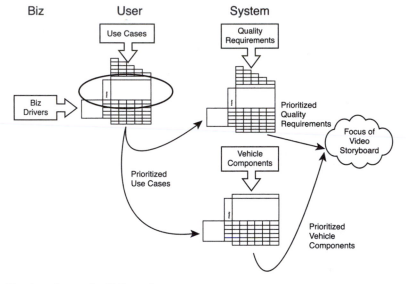

Figure 1.7   *Your location on the QFD road map.*

Because the business drivers of our Mega Motors example are couched in terms of a customer profile that closely resembles actors in use case development, the team is able to quickly develop a set of use cases that reflect different uses of the vehicle. The team also selects the use cases to emphasize different features and functions and to stress different components of the vehicle. For example, the **Drive through Mountains** use case was selected because mountain driving is notoriously difficult on the engine going uphill, brakes going downhill, and relies heavily upon good steering for hairpin turns; in all, a thorough use of three components in a manner distinct from the other use cases.

The use cases identified by the team are:

- Carpool in Stop and Go Traffic

- Drive Long Road Trip

- Go Off-roading

- Take/Pick Up Kids at School

- Romantic Night on the Town

- Drive through Mountains

In the previous step of the workshop, you worked with the team to identify **Married Couple with Young Children** as the focal point for the focus group video storyboard. From this set of uses cases just identified, one will eventually be selected (in the next step) as the basis for the storyboard itself, showing a married couple with children using a mockup of the Mega Motors vehicle. In addition, the set of prioritized use cases as a whole will be used to analyze and prioritize quality requirements and components (in the step after next). These will be featured in the video.

Enter Use Cases into QFD Matrix

After the list of use cases is identified, the use cases are entered into the QFD matrix (see Figure 1.8).

Keep in mind that the business drivers for a project will not always bear such a resemblance to use case actors. Neither is it the case that the QFD process always starts with business drivers. There may be occasions in which the use cases come first, followed by the search for business drivers with which to prioritize them.

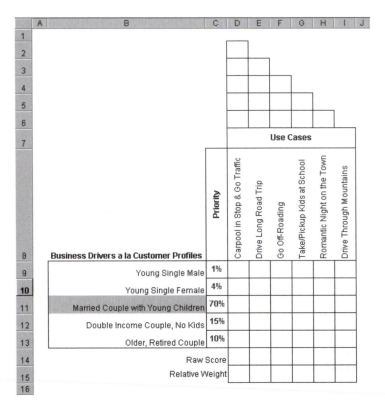

Figure 1.8   *Use cases to be analyzed and prioritized are entered into columns of matrix.*

Analyze Relationship of Use Cases to Business Drivers

To this point in the Mega Motors workshop, you have worked with the team of engineers and marketing reps to identify a prioritized set of business drivers and a set of use cases (not yet prioritized). In this next step of the QFD workshop (see Figure 1.9), the team analyzes and prioritizes each use case in terms of each business driver. This provides:

1. A prioritization of the use cases in terms of how well each lines up with the business drivers

2. One use case singled out as the basis for the storyboard itself, which will show a married couple with young children using a mockup of the Mega Motors vehicle as per the use case that is selected

There are generally two ways to proceed on analyzing use cases (columns) in terms of business drivers (rows). One approach is to proceed by column, analyzing one use case against all business drivers, then moving to the next use case, and so on. This column-wise approach is advocated by Ronald Day in *Quality Function Deployment: Linking a Company to Its Customer,* stating that if the team works row-wise, they can often find a relationship between almost any customer need (business driver) and technical requirement (use case).

On the other hand, when the QFD matrix is being used to select the best choice(s) from a set of alternatives, I'm inclined to argue that row-wise works best, taking a business driver and analyzing it in terms of all the use cases, then moving to the next business driver. Working row-wise lends itself better to asking the question: Which of these use cases *best* meets a given business driver? Because part of the goal of the workshop is to identify the *best* use case for a video storyboard, this is the strategy you decide to use with the team.

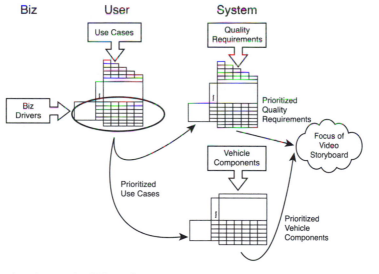

Figure 1.9 *Your location on the QFD road map.*

Which Use Cases Best "Deploy" Each Business Driver?

From this stage of the QFD workshop forward, you have arranged to have a projector in the room, attached to a computer setup with the QFD matrix.

This provides a common display for the whole team to see and work from. Working row-wise, you start with the first business driver, **Young Single Male** (i.e., video storyboard must target this customer) and walk the team through asking this question: *Which of the following use cases is a young single male most likely to be interested in?*

- Carpool in Stop and Go Traffic

- Drive Long Road Trip

- Go Off-roading

- Take/Pick Up Kids at School

- Romantic Night on the Town

- Drive through Mountains

You instruct the team to rate interest using this scale common to QFD:

- 9 (nine)—Very Interested

- 3 (three)—Interested

- 1 (one)—A little interest

- 0 (blank)—Not enough interest to mention

To further aid the prioritization of the use cases and address the concern expressed by Ronald Day about working row-wise, you instruct the team that as a *guideline*, try not to assign more than two use cases a nine. (This is just a suggestion, and is based on trying to identify that proverbial 20% of the use cases that delivers 80% of the bang for the buck. Because there are six use cases, 20% would be approximately one or two use cases that you are restricting to receive a "9".)[12]

---

[12] In Chapter 2, "Aligning Decision Making and Synchronizing Distributed Development Horizontally in the Organization," you'll see an example where you probably would not want to restrict the number of high scores ("9s") on a row.

Figure 1.10 shows the QFD matrix after row one—**Young Single Male**—has been completed.

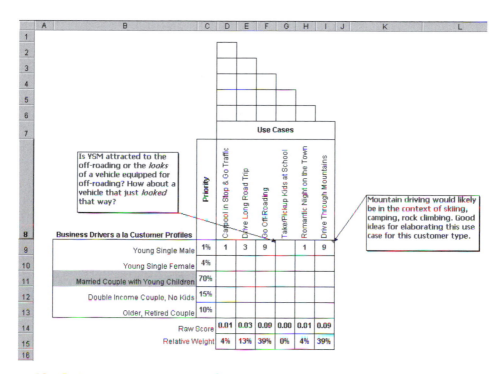

Figure 1.10   *Each use case is rated in terms of interest to Young Single Male. Assumptions, ideas, issues, and questions are recorded as the analysis proceeds, shown here as comments made in cells of the matrix.*

A very important part of QFD is the discovery and brainstorming that occurs while a team is thinking about the correlation of business drivers to use cases. As a facilitator, you are prepared to capture ideas, issues, assumptions, notes, and questions on a flip chart at the front of the room. You also have the person working the QFD matrix record this information as notes in the appropriate cells of the matrix (refer to Figure 1.10).

For example, as the team discusses the interest of young single males in the use case **Go Off-roading,** there is discussion as to whether they are really attracted to off-roading per se, or more to the looks of a vehicle that is *equipped* for off-roading (i.e., big tires, high ground clearance, and so on). This is an important insight the team feels worth capturing (a vehicle that *looks* like an off-road vehicle is cheaper to build than one actually capable of off-roading).

Another question, as the team discusses the possible interest of young single males in use case **Drive through Mountains,** is what about the mountains would draw the attention of a young single male? The answer: skiing, camping, rock climbing, and so on. This information could well be used in future elaboration of the use case for this particular customer type if that becomes necessary; again, this is information the team felt worth capturing. QFD is not only a powerful tool for prioritizing use cases, but also for harnessing team brainstorming in a structured, systematic way.

As the team scores each use case in terms of the business driver (interest in use case by young single male), the results are instantly calculated at the bottom of the QFD matrix implemented as a spreadsheet. The row **Raw Score** sums for each column are the products of business driver priority times the score given to the use case (blank, 1, 3, or 9). The row **Relative Weight** then calculates the relative percent for each use case's raw score. Excel formulas for use case **Drive through Mountains** are shown in Figure 1.11.

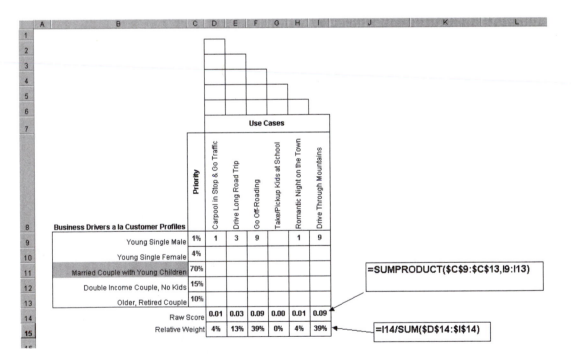

Figure 1.11   *Excel formulas for calculating Raw Score and Relative Weight for each use case. Your favorite spreadsheet will have similar functionality.*

Results

After about an hour and a half, the team has completed a review of each use case in terms of each business driver.[13] Each use case has received a rating of 0 (blank), 1, 3, or 9, indicating the strength of its relationship to the business driver (the higher the number, the stronger the relationship). Just as important as the score, however, are the team discussions that transpire; this is team alignment to a common understanding of the problem taking place. Some of the various ideas, assumptions, and notes recorded as part of the discovery process are shown in Figure 1.12.

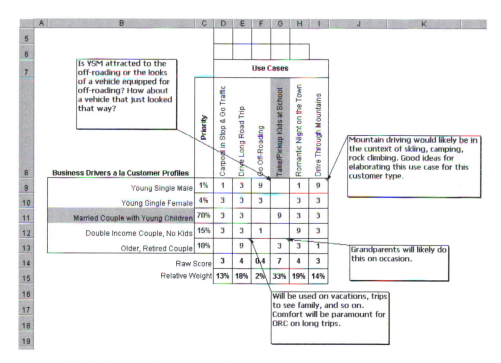

Figure 1.12   *Relationship part of matrix completed showing strength of relationship between use cases and business drivers (i.e. focus group customer types).*

---

[13] As a facilitator, you can estimate approximate times needed by calculating the number of cells to be worked through (e.g., five business drivers times six use cases = 30 cells) then allowing some amount of time per cell for the team discussion. Pick an amount of time per cell that allows discussion to occur but still gets the team through the entire matrix in a reasonable amount of time.

The final prioritization of use cases is summarized in Table 1.2, with use case **Take/Pick Up Kids at School** being the highest ranking use case. This use case is selected by the team as the basis for the focus group video storyboard in which a married couple with young children (the high-ranking customer type) will be shown using a mockup of the Mega Motors vehicle taking and picking up the kids at school. Customer type **Married Couple with Young Children** and use case **Take/Pick Up Kids at School** are highlighted in the QFD matrix to indicate this (see Figure 1.12).

Table 1.2   *Relative importance of each use case in terms of business drivers*

Use Case	Raw Score	Relative Weight
Carpool in Stop and Go Traffic	3	13%
Drive Long Road Trip	4	18%
Go Off-roading	0.4	2%
Take/Pick Up Kids at School	7	33%
Romantic Night on the Town	4	19%
Drive through Mountains	3	14%

In addition to providing a basis for prioritizing use cases, analyzing the relationship between business drivers and use cases can also help identify missing use cases. If you have a business driver for which no use case seems to correlate very well, you may well be missing a use case or use cases; in QFD lingo, the customer need or business driver has no function (use case) through which to be deployed.

Analyze Correlations Between Use Cases

The next and final step for this particular QFD matrix is to analyze the correlation between the use cases (see Figure 1.13).

In "standard" QFD, this step is usually done with non-functional requirements or design goals that can sometimes work against one another. For example, in software the design goal to build a component that is highly portable from one platform to another may work against the design goal of optimum speed. The code you have to write to be portable may not be the same code you would write to take advantage of hardware acceleration tricks on a given, single platform. The idea is to apply this same concept to use cases, looking for ones that the team anticipates are going to *negatively* correlate, where aspects of the product required for one use case work against aspects of the product required by another use case.

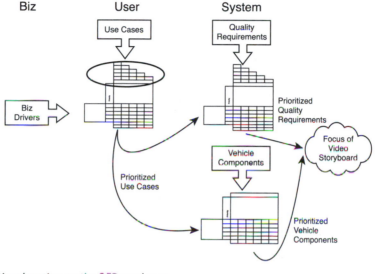

Figure 1.13   *Your location on the QFD road map.*

In this step, you have the team fill in the top, correlation part of the QFD matrix (see Figure 1.14).

The correlation part of the matrix is set up such that there is a cell for each pair-wise combination of use cases. Figure 1.14 shows that the team has identified a negative correlation (denoted with a minus sign) between use case **Go Off-roading** and use case **Drive Long Road Trip**: they anticipate that the characteristics of a vehicle designed for off-roading (tight suspension, short wheel base for going over bumps, knobby off-road tires) are opposites of the design characteristics of a vehicle built for comfort on long road trips. In the correlation part of the matrix, use cases that work against one another are shown with a negative sign. Likewise, the team has identified a negative correlation between the use case **Go Off-roading** and the use case **Take/Pick Up Kids at School**: a key design characteristic of a vehicle built for off-road driving is high ground clearance. This is seen to impede the activities of use case **Take/Pick Up Kids at School,** namely easy loading and unloading of cargo and putting kids in, and taking kids out of, a car seat.

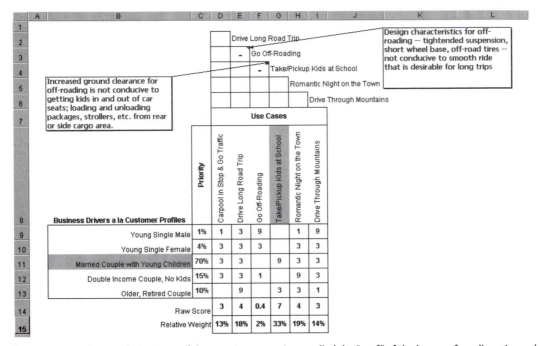

Figure 1.14 *The correlation part of the matrix—sometimes called the "roof" of the house of quality—is used to make note of use cases that may work against one another.*

First Matrix Complete; QFD Workshop Status Check

The Mega Motors QFD workshop team has made good progress, so you decide to review the results thus far:

- A set of business drivers has been identified in the form of a customer profile (that is to say, types of customers that will be attending the focus group).

- The customer types were prioritized using a variant of Wideband Delphi. In addition to producing a prioritized set of customer types, the process also helped bring to the surface tacit assumptions and information held by individuals for the group as a whole to see. Three additional underlying business drivers were identified: *market size, brand loyalty,* and *disposable income* of each customer type.

- From the prioritized list of customer types, **Married Couple with Young Children** scored highest and was identified as the focus of the video storyboard.

- Use cases were identified that would be of interest to all the customer types. The use cases were then prioritized by analyzing the relationship between each business driver and use case, scoring that relationship with a scale of 0 (blank), 1, 3, or 9 (highest score).

- The high-ranking use case—**Take/Pick Up Kids at School**—was then selected by the team to serve as the basis for the storyboard's storyline.

- Correlations between use cases were analyzed to identify negative correlations (i.e., use cases that might work against one another). Use case **Go Off-roading** was identified as having a negative correlation with use cases **Take Long Road Trip** and **Take/Pick Up Kids at School**.

In the next step of the QFD workshop, the prioritized use cases will be used to move the business drivers down into aspects of system design to analyze quality requirements and vehicle components that should be featured in the focus group video storyboard.

"Flipping the Matrix": Deployment to Quality Requirements

As noted earlier, QFD has received some attention in the use case community as a means of prioritizing use cases. What has received less attention, however, is the subsequent use of prioritized use cases as input to QFD to prioritize *other* aspects of software development (e.g., alternate design approaches). That is the goal of the Mega Motors QFD workshop team in the next step.

Recall that the "D" in QFD stands for "Deployment." In a previous workshop step, the team analyzed the relationship between business drivers and use cases to identify the priorities over the use cases that would best *deploy* the business drivers. In this next step, the business drivers will be deployed *deeper* into design aspects of the product by use of the prioritized list of use cases.

The prioritized use cases will be used to analyze quality requirements, such as reliability, safety, and vehicle look and feel, to see which quality requirements best align with the prioritized use cases and, in turn, the business drivers. The same will be done with components of the vehicle: engine, transmission, body, and so on.

These results will then be used to finish the outline for a video storyboard showcasing the high priority quality aspects of the high priority components of the vehicle (e.g., reliability of the engine, safety of door locks, and so on) while in use by the high priority customer type—married couple with young children—taking and picking up their kids at school (the high-priority use case).

In this step of the workshop (see Figure 1.15), the team will prioritize quality requirements for the Mega Motors vehicle in terms of the prioritized use cases from the QFD matrix (columns of Figure 1.14). This involves building a new QFD matrix in which the output of Figure 1.14 becomes the input of the new matrix. This is sometimes called "flipping the matrix" because columns of the first QFD matrix will now become the rows of the next matrix (see Figure 1.16).

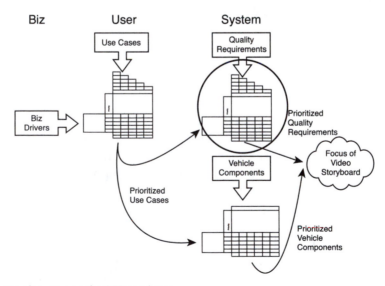

Figure 1.15   *Your location on the QFD road map.*

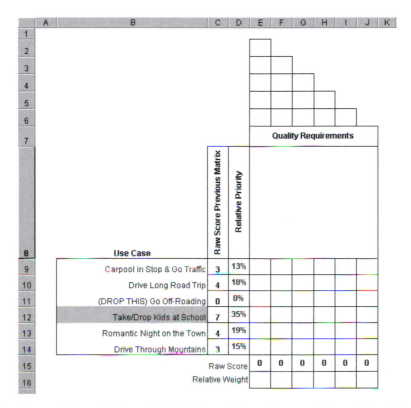

Figure 1.16   *The matrix for analyzing and prioritizing quality requirements takes as its input the output from the matrix shown in Figure 1.14.*

Resolve Negative Correlation Between Use Cases

One issue that must be addressed at this point is what to do about the results of the analysis of use case correlations (see Figure 1.14): use case **Go Off-roading** was identified as having a negative correlation with use cases **Take Long Road Trip** and **Take/Pick Up Kids at School**. Such negative correlation can sometimes be an opportunity for new radical product design as a team brainstorms for innovative ways to turn what appears to be a negative into a positive.

For example, thinking outside the box a bit, a team might decide to build a vehicle with adjustable suspension allowing for high ground clearance for off-roading, low ground clearance for easy passenger and cargo loading and unloading, and adjustable stiffness for a soft, smooth ride on long road trips and tight, controlled ride on the trail. Voilà! Markets that were once separated—the off-roaders and the luxury/family/road-trippers—are now united! And in fact, that is *just* what Land Rover did in 1993 with their Electronic Air Suspension (EAS) system, dubbed the "magic carpet ride," combining the luxury car market with the off-road market.

In the case of the Mega Motors team, however, because the **Go Off-roading** use case ranked so low in relative weight, the decision of the team is to drop that use case as a driver in the project. In the flipped-matrix of Figure 1.16, this is accomplished by zeroing out the raw score in the new matrix. This effectively cancels out this use case as a factor in subsequent analysis based on prioritized use cases. This identifies another strength of QFD: it is fairly easy to do *what-if* analysis to explore the consequence of different priorities at the business driver or use case levels.

Brainstorm List of Quality Requirements

To brainstorm, the team begins by compiling a list of quality requirements in which the identified customer types are typically interested. Between a common set of requirements used on most Mega Motors vehicles and review of ideas and notes collected thus far in the workshop (e.g., those in Figure 1.12), the team is able to quickly identify a half dozen quality requirements:

- Reliability

- Good Looks

- Safety

- Fuel Economy

- Sporty Power and Steering

- Seating and Cargo Capacity

The quality requirements are entered into the new QFD matrix as columns, as shown in Figure 1.17.

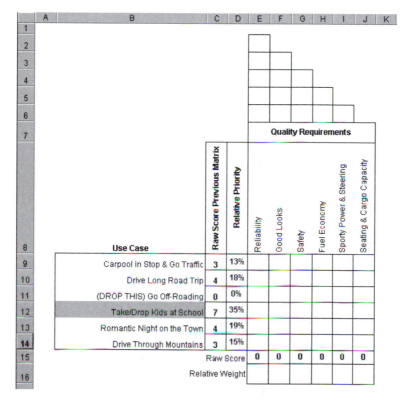

Use Case	Raw Score Previous Matrix	Relative Priority	Reliability	Good Looks	Safety	Fuel Economy	Sporty Power & Steering	Seating & Cargo Capacity
Carpool in Stop & Go Traffic	3	13%						
Drive Long Road Trip	4	18%						
(DROP THIS) Go Off-Roading	0	0%						
Take/Drop Kids at School	7	35%						
Romantic Night on the Town	4	19%						
Drive Through Mountains	3	15%						
Raw Score			0	0	0	0	0	0
Relative Weight								

Figure 1.17   *Quality requirements to be analyzed and prioritized are entered as columns in the matrix.*

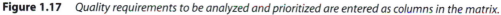

Which Quality Requirements Are Most Important for Each Use Case?

Next, you work with the team to analyze and prioritize each quality requirement (columns) in terms of each use case (rows). The goal is to identify a few key quality requirements that are most important to the prioritized use cases. You instruct the team to rate the quality requirements in terms of their importance to each use case:

- 9 (nine)—Very important to the use case

- 3 (three)—Important to the use case

- 1 (one)—Somewhat important to the use case

- 0 (blank)—Has little or no importance to the use case

As before, you have the team work row-wise. For each use case they will review each quality requirement, and then move to the next use case. You instruct them that as a guideline they should try not to allocate more than two 9s per use case; this forces the team to think in terms of what is the biggest bang for the buck in quality requirements per use case.

The results of the team's efforts are shown in Figure 1.18. In addition to scoring each quality requirement in terms of importance to the use cases, the team also makes notes on assumptions upon which the scoring was based: ideas, questions, and so on. These are entered on the flip chart at the front of the room and into the appropriate cells of the QFD matrix, which is being projected on the screen at the front of the room.

The scoring of quality requirements in terms of use cases has identified **Reliability** and **Seating and Cargo Capacity** as the two high scoring use cases; this is indicated by the highlighting in Figure 1.18.

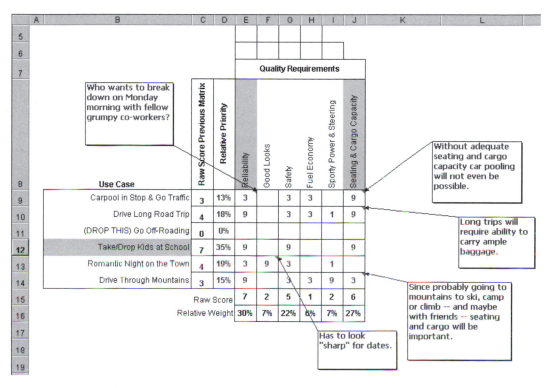

Figure 1.18   *Completed matrix showing importance of quality requirements to use cases. The two high-scoring quality requirements, Reliability and Seating and Cargo Capacity, are highlighted.*

Analyze Correlations Between Quality Requirements

The final step of analysis on this matrix is to have the team analyze the quality requirements in terms of how they correlate with one another, identifying ones that work positively in support of one another and ones that work against one another negatively. The quality requirements are entered in the correlation part of the matrix—the "roof" of the matrix—then analyzed pair-wise. The results of the team's analysis of the correlation of quality requirements are shown in Figure 1.19. To summarize, **Reliability** and **Safety** were found to be positively correlated: a vehicle that was unreliable was likely to also be unsafe. Given that safety was highly ranked as a quality requirement to start with, marketing felt it might be worthwhile to pursue reliability and safety in tandem as part of the video storyboard. This addition of **Safety** to the list of quality requirements to focus on in the video storyboard is indicated by highlighting in the matrix (see Figure 1.19).

Quality requirement **Fuel Economy** was found to be negatively correlated with **Sporty Power and Steering** (the more power, the more gas it burns), and also with **Seating and Cargo Capacity** (the more carrying capacity, the bigger the vehicle, the more gas it burns). Even though **Fuel Economy** was not rated very important to the use cases, the team decided it was wise to make note to be alert for potential drops in the fuel efficiency of the vehicle that might result from increases in seating and/or cargo capacity (a high-ranking quality requirement). This is a typical use of the correlation information in QFD: while you may decide that a given quality requirement is not to be the focus of a new release, you also don't want it to regress in response to some other change. In software, performance is a quality requirement that often suffers this fate.

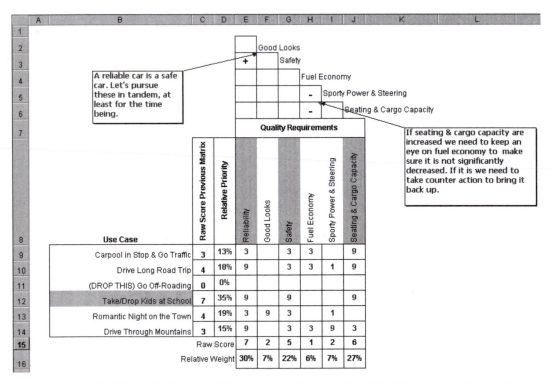

Figure 1.19   *Reliability and Safety were found to be positively correlated. Fuel Economy was found to be negatively correlated with both Sporty Power & Steering and Seating & Cargo Capacity.*

Flipping the Matrix: Deployment to Vehicle Components

One last QFD matrix is needed to complete the analysis of the Mega Motors team. In this final QFD step (see Figure 1.20) the prioritized use cases are used to analyze components of the vehicle—engine, transmission, body, and so on—to determine which best align with the prioritized use cases and, in turn, the business drivers.

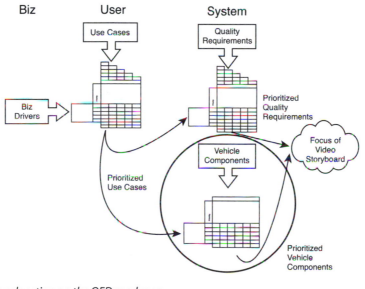

Figure 1.20   *Your location on the QFD road map.*

Working with the team, you work through the same process as in the previous section, "Flipping the Matrix: Deployment to Quality Requirements," but rather than addressing quality requirements, it is done for the following components of the Mega Motors vehicle:

- Brakes

- Steering

- Engine

- Transmission

- Body

- Interior

- Suspension

The results of this step are shown in Figure 1.21; the team did not feel it necessary to do analysis of the correlation of components, so there is no "roof" to the matrix.

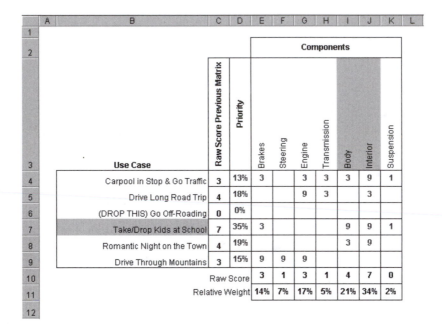

Use Case	Raw Score Previous Matrix	Priority	Components						
			Brakes	Steering	Engine	Transmission	Body	Interior	Suspension
Carpool in Stop & Go Traffic	3	13%	3		3	3	3	9	1
Drive Long Road Trip	4	18%			9	3		3	
(DROP THIS) Go Off-Roading	0	0%							
Take/Drop Kids at School	7	35%	3				9	9	1
Romantic Night on the Town	4	19%					3	9	
Drive Through Mountains	3	15%	9	9	9				
Raw Score			3	1	3	1	4	7	0
Relative Weight			14%	7%	17%	5%	21%	34%	2%

Figure 1.21   *Matrix showing relationship of vehicle components with use cases.*

To summarize the results of this last step, components **Body** and **Interior** were identified by the Mega Motors team as having the greatest correlation to the prioritized use cases. They are shown highlighted in Figure 1.21 to indicate that they will be the featured components of the video storyboard.

Workshop Conclusion and Summary

With the completion of the third and final QFD matrix, the team is ready to wrap-up its findings (see Figure 1.22).

To review, the objective statement of the workshop was to:

> *Determine what key features of the Mega Motors vehicle will be most attractive to the customer, along with a key use case that will be used as the basis for a video-based storyboard shot with a mockup to advertise these key features being used in typical fashion by a typical customer.*

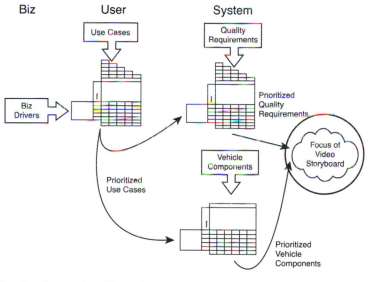

Figure 1.22   *Your location on the QFD road map.*

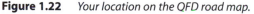

From the workshop, the following has been identified as the basis for the focus group video storyboard:

> *The video will follow a married couple with young children as they drive the new Mega Motors vehicle to take and pick up their children from school. Featured in the video will be the vehicle's interior and body, focusing on safety, reliability, and ample seating and cargo capacity.*

One good thing about QFD is its support of traceability. When results are presented after the workshop to the VP of Engineering and Marketing, it will be possible to explain the trail of thought leading to the recommendation. QFD also allows the VPs to do follow-up *what-if* analysis on alternate business driver priorities, exploring other possible outcomes, if they choose to do so.

Finally, while this workshop has successfully identified the overall focus of the video storyboard, a further QFD workshop is probably needed to drill down into more detail,[14] this time extending participants to include someone from the team that will actually produce the video. The goal of that workshop will be to:

- Use QFD to identify and prioritize specific parts of the interior and body that play key roles in the scenarios that make up the **Take/Drop Kids at School** use case.

- Select the highest priority parts from the prioritized list to brainstorm and prioritize design ideas to make them reliable, safe, and facilitate expanded seating and cargo capacity.

A QFD road map for such a follow-up workshop is given in Figure 1.23.

To close the workshop, you review assigned action items and then conduct a brief "postmortem," looking for things participants thought worked well in this workshop and should be repeated in subsequent workshops and for things that could be done better next time. That task completed, the workshop comes to a close.

---

[14] This two-phase approach is a common, practical application of QFD in which a quick pass is made over a product at a coarse level of granularity to identify the product hot spots, here the key components of the vehicle most critical to Take/Pick Up Kids at School use case. A second pass is subsequently made drilling-down into more detail on just those critical components. See Cohen (1995).

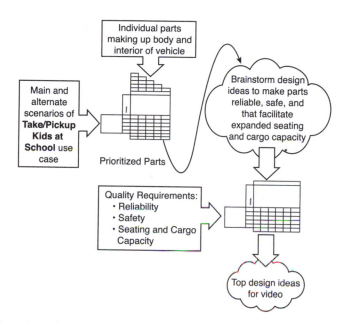

Figure 1.23   *QFD roadmap for subsequent workshop to drill down deeper in identifying design ideas for specific parts of body and interior to make them reliable, safe, and facilitate increased seating and cargo capacity.*

Chapter Review

Let's review what we've discussed about QFD in this chapter:

- QFD is a product-planning tool that is used to translate business drivers (such as market size, brand loyalty, and disposable income of a customer segment) into the technical requirements of a product (such as seating & cargo capacity of vehicle interior).

- Although QFD can certainly be used as a tool by an individual, its biggest value is as a tool used by a team. A team that works through product planning with QFD will emerge with a common vision of business drivers, priorities, assumptions and issues and questions to be resolved.

- While the application of QFD to manufacturing is fairly standardized, no such standard exists for its application to use case-driven development. The general approach described in this chapter is to use QFD to transition from what the business requires, to what the user requires (stated with use cases), to what is required of the system. This transition is based on Wiegers' levels of requirement types.

- The use case community has given some attention to QFD as a tool for prioritizing use cases. But prioritized use cases can in turn also provide a means of prioritizing other aspects of software development (e.g., alternate product designs).

- A useful way to think of QFD is as method of *prototyping a project*, allowing a team to run through a complete product development cycle quickly, from start (thinking about the business) to end (thinking about the final product that results from the business drivers). *What-if* analysis with QFD allows a team to explore the consequence of different priorities at the business driver or use case levels.

2

Aligning Decision Making and Synchronizing Distributed Development *Horizontally* in the Organization

In the previous chapter, we looked at the combined use of QFD and use cases to link business drivers to user requirements, and user requirements to system requirements and design decisions: the *vertical* dimension of requirements management. In this chapter, we turn to the second dimension of requirements management: using QFD and use cases to align decisions and synchronize use case-driven development *horizontally* across multiple component, product, or business groups in a company (i.e., use case-driven distributed development).

Two examples will be used in this chapter, both centered on a hypothetical company, Oil & Gas Exploration Systems. The examples first utilize QFD to analyze Oil & Gas Exploration Systems' needs for a company-wide developer's kit for shared earth modeling (we'll get to this in the section titled, "The Problem: Selecting a Shared Earth Modeling Development Kit") and then to synchronize use case-driven development across the company as their product line is migrated over to the new developer's kit. While Oil & Gas Exploration Systems is a hypothetical company, the examples are based on actual experiences and illustrate real product development issues faced by software development companies in the industry.

Using QFD to Align Decision Making Horizontally Across a Company

We begin this chapter by looking at an example of QFD applied to cross-company decision making. This example is based on an actual program[1] in which I helped get the team going in its use of QFD, but the *real* work was done by a sharp team of geoscientists and developers and coordinated largely by a colleague.[2] This example has been simplified and tweaked a bit to better convey the QFD process; results of analysis and decisions reached are kept somewhat vague to protect proprietary information.

A Brief Overview of Oil and Gas Exploration

Searching for oil, an activity that started in the 1850s as a hit or miss, by the seat-of-the-pants outing, has today grown into a big industry that employs big science. Big *geoscience* and *computer science*, to be specific. At the risk of oversimplifying, the search for oil and gas today can be said to involve building elaborate computer models of the surface and sub-surface of the area where you think oil exists, then drilling exploratory wells where the models indicate the greatest probability for oil that can be recovered in a profitable fashion.

A number of different disciplines have evolved through the years for searching for oil, each with its own use cases ("workflows" in geoscience lingo) and approach to modeling the earth. Three key disciplines used in oil and gas exploration are geology, geophysics, and petrophysics. Each provides a piece of a large puzzle that must be assembled in order to determine what may lie beneath the surface of the earth. Let's look briefly at these three disciplines.

---

[1] I learned many years ago that developing examples for training material is a "damned if you do, damned if you don't" situation. If you use a "toy problem," you may err with a problem that is so easy that it doesn't illustrate the application of a technique to "real life" situations. And if you use a "real life" example, you may err with a problem domain that distracts teaching the technique. While this is a "real life" example of the use of QFD, keep in mind that an understanding of the geoscience is not necessary nor the issue. The essential point to focus on is the mechanics of QFD for deciding between alternatives, which could well have been labeled Alternative-1, Alternative-2, Alternative-3, and so on, but then I would have erred with an example that wasn't very interesting!

[2] Thanks to Dale Davis for a great example of QFD in action in the oil and gas industry.

Geology, the oldest of the geoscience disciplines, utilizes models built on what we know about the earth's strata, or distinctive layers of rock, such as the Permian, Triassic, Jurassic, Cretaceous, and Tertiary. The goal with these models is to find a convergence of the geologic elements we know from empirical observation are needed to form and trap oil and gas.

Geophysics, on the other hand, is a more recent discipline, being applied to oil exploration for the first time in the early 1920s. Geophysics utilizes models based on seismic data of the earth obtained by "thumping" the earth and listening for the return of sound energy reflected off the earth's subsurface structures—rocks, salt domes—to produce an image of the earth's subsurface.

Petrophysics builds models of the earth based on direct measurement of the subsurface made from the boreholes of wells drilled into the earth, a process called well-logging. Well-logging got its start in 1912 when a Frenchman, Conrad Schlumberger, hit upon the idea of lowering tools into a borehole to make electrical measurements of the subsurface rocks. Today, a variety of measurements such as electrical resistivity, nuclear properties and sonic travel times provide empirical evidence of the makeup of the earth's subsurface where a well has been drilled.

In our next example, we look at a hypothetical company—Oil & Gas Exploration Systems (O&G for short)—that builds software systems that oil companies buy or lease for earth modeling as part of their exploration for oil and gas. In the example, O&G turns to QFD to plan the next big evolution in their product line: a multi-disciplinary approach to oil and gas exploration.

The Problem: Selecting A Shared Earth Modeling Development Kit

O&G has different products, made of a variety of components, for each of the disciplines—geology, geophysics, and petrophysics. For a variety of reasons, the product lines developed independently as part of separate business divisions. As the need to improve the efficiency of oil and gas exploration grows, O&G (and the industry in general) has come to recognize the importance of integrating these products and their respective disciplines so that information is quickly and easily shared between them in near real-time, a concept that in the industry is called *shared earth modeling*.

In order to accomplish this level of integration in its product suite, O&G has decided to invest in the development of a developer's toolkit—or dev kit—for earth modeling that can be shared company-wide across all components of its product suite. Rather than starting from scratch, O&G will use the source from an existing dev kit as a starting place and then customize and extend it as needed to support the breadth of the O&G product suite.

O&G has decided to use QFD to analyze their needs for such a dev kit, then select from among a variety of candidate dev kits available internally (e.g., as part of existing products and research efforts) and externally from various consortia.

O&G's QFD Road Map

Figure 2.1 shows the QFD road map that O&G plans to use to analyze their needs for a dev kit; let's walk through the process quickly. The QFD process uses four QFD matrices:

1. In the first step, Matrix 1, the business drivers for selecting a dev kit are used to prioritize the collective set of use cases from each of the three products of the three disciplines: geological use cases, geophysical use cases, and petrophysical use cases.

2. In step two, Matrix 2, the prioritized use cases are used to prioritize non-functional requirements for the dev kit.

3. In the third step, Matrix 3, the prioritized use cases *combined* with the prioritized non-functional requirements of step two are used to identify various modeling techniques that best support O&G's needs for a dev kit.

4. In the final step, Matrix 4, the prioritized set of modeling techniques is used to prioritize the candidate dev kits from which a winner will be selected.

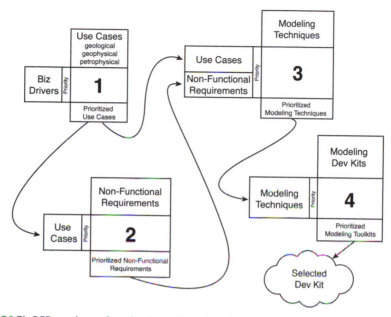

Figure 2.1   *O&G's QFD road map for selecting a shared earth modeling dev kit.*

Working from Figure 2.1, let's walk through the QFD process in more detail. O&G will use a workshop much like the one described in the previous Mega Motors example, but details of the workshop itself will not be elaborated upon. Also, actual results of each of the four matrices of Figure 2.1 are not provided but are described in terms of their general inputs, analysis done on them by the O&G team, and their outputs. This is done in part to protect proprietary results of the actual program this example is based upon. This also helps you focus on the main point of the example, the mechanics of QFD as a decision-making tool, by avoiding overly detailed examples from geoscience and earth modeling (a domain many readers may not be familiar with).

No two applications of QFD are likely to be quite the same, so differences in the Mega Motors and O&G example will be highlighted to illustrate just some of the variations that can occur.

Matrix 1: Prioritize Use Cases

The O&G QFD team has been selected to include geoscientists and developers from each of the disciplines that the dev kit must support: geology, geophysics, and petrophysics. The QFD process begins with Matrix 1.

Identify Use Cases

Whereas the Mega Motors QFD process began with the team thinking about business drivers, the O&G team begins by thinking about the essential use cases that must be supported by an earth modeling dev kit. Use cases come naturally to geoscientists because the process of oil and gas exploration has traditionally been described in terms of what they call *workflows*, which are essentially the steps in a use case.

The use case of Appendix A, "Sample Use Case," named **Create 2D Cross-Section**, is an example of the type of use case the O&G team identifies, and it illustrates the combined use of three disciplines—geology, geophysics, and petrophysics—for oil and gas exploration. (Understanding this use case is *not* essential to this QFD example and is provided solely for informational purposes.)

After the O&G QFD team has identified all the essential use cases for all the products, they are entered as columns of Matrix 1 (refer to Figure 2.1).

Identify Business Drivers to Prioritize Use Cases

Next, the team turns its attention to what criteria form a basis for prioritizing their use cases. As already noted, this is different from the Mega Motors example where the team started with the business drivers. While this may be out of the norm from a "standard" manufacturing QFD perspective, it reflects the real-life diversity you are likely to experience in using QFD. Used in this fashion—use cases first, business drivers second—the question that the team asks themselves is: *What is it that makes one use case more important than another in terms of this project (i.e., selection of a shared earth modeling dev kit)?* In doing this, the team works backwards to an agreement on what the business drivers for the project are. Either way—working forward as in the Mega Motors example, or backwards as the O&G team is doing—the end result is the same: team alignment.

The O&G team uses pros and cons analysis of the use cases to help understand as a group what criteria makes one use case more important than another and arrives at the business drivers shown in Table 2.1. These are entered as rows in Matrix 1 (refer to Figure 2.1).

Table 2.1   *O&G's Business Drivers for Prioritizing Use Cases of Matrix 1 Figure 2.1*

Business Driver	Description	Priority
Benefit Derived	The benefit derived by having a use case's results readily available to other geoscience disciplines via a shared earth model. Use cases ranked on a scale of	75%
	9—Highly beneficial to most or all other disciplines	
	3—Highly beneficial to a few other disciplines	
	1—Somewhat beneficial to a few other disciplines	
	0 (blank)—Little or no benefit to the other disciplines	
Frequency of Use	Based on product's operational profile[3], use cases are divided into three broad categories and ranked on a scale of	25%
	9—High frequency of use	
	3—Medium frequency of use	
	1—Low frequency of use	

Analyze Relationship of Business Drivers to Use Cases

Given a prioritized set of business drivers and essential use cases for each of the three O&G disciplines, the QFD team scores each use case in terms of the business drivers, resulting in a set of *prioritized use cases* (refer to bottom of Matrix 1 in Figure 2.1).

There is a subtle difference between this process for the O&G team and that used by the Mega Motors team. Recall that the Mega Motors team was asked to identify the use cases that *best* met a given business driver by restricting the number of high scores (i.e., a 9) they allocated on a row. While the Mega Motors team was trying to find the *best* use case for a video storyboard, the O&G team is trying to factually record the relationship

---

[3] Details of describing an operational profile for a suite of use cases are covered in Part 2, "Software Reliability Engineering."

between business drivers and use cases. So for a given business driver, such as **Benefit Derived** (refer to Table 2.1), it could in principle be that every use case does indeed deserve a high score for this business driver (i.e., a 9).

Here's a heuristic you can use to try to tell if you should restrict the number of high scores on a row when working row-wise: *Are you trying to find the best choice(s) on the row, or are you trying to weed out the ones that don't apply?* If you are trying to find the best choice—say, the best use case—from among a number of candidates, restrict use of high scores to force the team to make the difficult decision of identifying the best of the best. If, however, you are trying to simply weed out the ones that don't apply, in principle all could very well receive high scores. How do you know which you are trying to do: find the best or weed out the non-applicable? That just depends on the problem at hand, and answering that question is part of the team alignment that takes place as part of the QFD process.

With the completion of Matrix 1, the O&G QFD team moves on to Matrix 2 (refer to Figure 2.1).

Matrix 2: Prioritize Non-Functional Requirements

Next, the team turns its attention to the quality requirements or, as we'll call them here, the *non-functional requirements*, of the dev kit. They begin with a new matrix—Matrix 2—and populate the rows with the prioritized use cases from Matrix 1.

Identify Non-Functional Requirements

The Mega Motors team had a standard set of non-functional requirements they used for the automotive industry (e.g., reliability, safety, and so on). The O&G team decides to take a little more analytical approach and reviews each use case by asking, *What non-functional requirements are pertinent to this use case?* And, in fact, non-functional requirements are fairly standard attire for what Alistair Cockburn calls the fully dressed use case (Cockburn 2000), so the team is accustomed to this as part of their normal use case-driven development. The difference now, however, is that the *non-functional requirements will be prioritized with respect to the suite of use cases as a whole.* This is an example of the value added by QFD to use case development.

Following is a sample of some of the non-functional requirements identified by the O&G team as being pertinent to their use cases:

- **Construction speed (faster is better):** Given a model of a specified spatial resolution, time required to build the model from its constituent elements (e.g., horizons and fault surfaces).

- **Display speed (faster is better):** Speed at which the model can be drawn in 3D.

- **Query speed (faster is better):** The user selects a point on or in the model and makes a query: speed at which associated data structures return the values for this query.

- **Memory size (smaller is better):** Amount of memory required to store a model of a particular spatial resolution.

Notice that the O&G team is careful to specify for each non-functional requirement the desired "direction" (e.g., for something like *speed*, faster is better). This is, in fact, standard practice in QFD and is just one more step in making sure that a team is aligned in their thinking.

To complete this step, the non-functional requirements identified by the team are placed in the columns of Matrix 2 (refer to Figure 2.1).

Analyze the Relationship of Use Cases to Non-Functional Requirements

As just noted, while non-functional requirements are a part of the fully dressed use case, QFD adds an additional bit to this relationship by helping identify non-functional requirements that are *highest priority to a suite of use cases as a whole*.

Given a prioritized set of use cases (rows) and non-functional requirements (columns), the QFD team scores each non-functional requirement in terms of its importance to each use case. The result: a *prioritized set of non-functional requirements* (refer to the bottom of Matrix 2 in Figure 2.1).

With Matrix 2 complete, the O&G QFD team moves to Matrix 3 (refer to Figure 2.1).

Matrix 3: Prioritize Earth Modeling Techniques

The team has arrived at what is, in some sense, the heart of the decision about which shared earth modeling dev kit they will use: the prioritization of modeling techniques in terms of use cases and non-functional requirements. In techniques for modeling, simulating, and analyzing the earth is where Big Geoscience meets up with Big Computer Science, combining mathematics, physics, the geosciences, computer aided design (CAD), computer simulation, and decision analysis.

Again, the team begins with a new matrix—Matrix 3—and populates the rows with both the prioritized use cases of Matrix 1 and prioritized non-functional requirements of Matrix 2.

Identify Modeling Techniques

From their knowledge of the modeling techniques used in O&G's own product suite, plus those known to be supported in competitor's products and those supported in open source dev kits, the team puts together a set of modeling techniques they believe should be considered as a basis for shared earth modeling.

Here are a few examples the team feels are important to consider:[4]

- **XYZ Orthogonal**: This simple approach to earth modeling involves dividing space into orthogonal cells by equally spaced orthogonal planes in the three coordinate directions.

- **XY Orthogonal**: In this approach to earth modeling, each surface (e.g., horizons, faults, and so on) is defined as an XY-orthogonal grid. Each surface is single-valued (i.e., each XY point has a single value).

---

[4] These are provided solely to give you an idea of the design decisions that are being made at this point. A detailed understanding of each modeling technique is not needed.

- **Triangular/Tetrahedral:** An approach common in computer aided design (CAD); surfaces are modeled as triangular grids. Volumes (e.g., of a sub-surface salt dome) are modeled as tetrahedra,[5] congruent to the bounding triangles.

Now that the team has identified the list of modeling techniques for consideration, they are entered into the columns of Matrix 3 (refer to Figure 2.1).

Analyze Relationship of Use Cases and Non-Functional Requirements to Modeling Techniques

Given a prioritized set of use cases and non-functional requirements, the QFD team scores each modeling technique in terms of how well it supports each use case and how well it meets each non-functional requirement. The result is a *prioritized set of modeling techniques* (refer to the bottom of Matrix 3 in Figure 2.1).

Matrix 4: Prioritize Shared Earth Modeling Dev Kits

The O&G QFD process concludes with a final matrix, Matrix 4 (refer to Figure 2.1). The team populates the rows of Matrix 4 with the prioritized modeling techniques from Matrix 3. The list of candidate dev kits being considered by O&G are then put in the columns of Matrix 4. These candidates include dev kits available internally as part of existing products and research efforts and externally, such as gOcad (Geo Computer Aided Design), a dev kit developed and maintained by a consortium of companies and universities sponsoring research in 3D earth modeling.[6]

The QFD team then scores each dev kit in terms of how well it supports each modeling technique. The final result of the O&G QFD process is a *prioritized set of dev kits* (refer to the bottom of Matrix 4 in Figure 2.1).

---

[5] A tetrahedron (singular) is a pyramid with three sides, resulting in four faces counting the bottom. "Tetrahedra" is plural. Tetrahedral means having the form of a tetrahedron.

[6] To learn more about shared earth modeling, visit the gOcad research consortium Web site at http://www.gocad.org or the consortium's spin-off company that maintains the gOcad developer's kit at http://www.earthdecision.com.

Example Conclusion and Summary

With the completion of Matrix 4 in Figure 2.1, the O&G QFD process is complete. The process has produced not only a prioritized set of dev kits but also a list of questions that need to be answered and assumptions that must be validated. When addressed, however, the team will be ready to make a recommendation on the winning dev kit as the future basis for shared earth modeling for the O&G product suite.

As in the case of Mega Motors, after the O&G QFD team makes its final recommendation it will be possible to explain the train of thought leading to the recommendation, and additional *what-if* analysis can be performed by examining alternate priorities on use cases, non-functional requirements, modeling techniques, and so on.

The O&G example is not only an example of how QFD can be used to align decision making horizontally across a company, it also reiterates the theme from the previous chapter of QFD as a means of driving vision vertically through a project or, in this case, a cross-company program. Starting with use cases and business drivers used to prioritize them, the O&G team has used QFD to translate them into decisions about which modeling techniques work best for the company and eventually into the selection of a dev kit for shared earth modeling.

In Chapter 1, the point was made that although QFD is a tool that can certainly be used by an individual, its real value is as an approach for team product planning, prioritization, and decision making. It is a way to get a team "on the same page" and with the same vision of where a product needs to go. The O&G example you've just seen demonstrates this idea when the "team" is a *company*.

In fact, the bigger the team, the greater the leverage afforded by QFD. In the actual case study which the O&G example represents, participants noted as part of a review of the overall process that a primary value of having used QFD was that the elements of the *decision making process were made very explicit* and *communication enhanced among the cross-company players*. In the politically charged atmosphere of a company, those two things alone may be enough to justify QFD!

Using QFD to Synchronize Distributed Development Horizontally Across Component Teams

In our previous example, Oil & Gas Exploration Systems (O&G) used a combination of QFD and use cases to help align cross-company decision making about their requirements for a shared earth modeling developer's kit (dev kit). In this, our final example, O&G has completed selection of a dev kit and completed necessary customizations and extensions to support the breadth of the O&G product suite. Now O&G looks to the task of planning the port of products over to the use of the new dev kit.

Again, O&G will use a combination of use cases and QFD, this time to coordinate the development. This decision is motivated by problems O&G has experienced in the past working with distributed development (i.e., development that requires the coordination between a large number of component teams spread across its three business divisions: geology, geophysics, and petrophysics). This problem is further compounded by geographical separation of the teams in four cities spread across two countries.[7] One problem that can arise in such development is making sure that the vision is clear as to what needs to be worked on by each team and *in what order* (i.e., how to synchronize the work that is to be done). The problem is best illustrated by looking at the solution.

Entropy Happens in Distributed Software Development

Figure 2.2 shows a matrix similar in concept to that described by Schneider and Winters: rows of the matrix are prioritized use cases, and columns component teams (the use case of Appendix A is the first row of this matrix).[8] An "X" in a cell indicates that the corresponding component team has work to do in implementing the corresponding use case. One way to

---

[7] This is a problem many large software development companies in the oil and gas industry face. Reality is often stranger than fiction.

[8] See Schneider and Winters (1998), the section "Use Cases Versus Architectural View."

construct such a matrix is to draw a sequence diagram for each use case with components as columns in the sequence diagram. All components that play in the sequence diagram receive an "X" in the matrix.

This matrix is a great way to do a summary rollup of a collection of sequence diagrams. Scanning the matrix horizontally you can quickly see all the components that play in a use case, and scanning vertically you can see all the use cases in which a component plays. A matrix like this is a valuable tool for communicating to component or product teams how their "piece" fits into the larger picture.

Use Cases	Priority	Base Mapping	Data Management	Geologic Interpretation	Petrophysical Interpretation	Reservoir Simulation	Seismic 2D Interpretation	Seismic 3D Interpretation	Seismic Data Management	Seismic Processing	Statistical Analysis Engine
Create 2D Cross-Section	11%	X	X	X	X			X	X		
Manage Reservoir Model	9%	X	X	X	X						
Search Data Projects With Filter	9%		X		X	X	X	X	X	X	X
Construct Geo-Framework	8%	X	X	X	X	X	X	X	X		
Load Seismic Data	8%			X				X	X	X	
Construct Fluid Property Model	8%	X	X	X	X			X	X	X	
Interpret With Multi-Valued Horizon	7%		X	X	X	X	X	X	X		X
Evaluate Geo-Statistics	7%	X		X			X	X	X	X	
Manage Well Log Data	5%						X	X	X	X	
Build Wellbore Model	5%	X	X	X	X	X	X	X	X	X	
Geostatistical Evaluation	4%	X	X	X	X						
Manage Map Files/Data	4%	X	X	X	X	X		X			
Drill Horizontal Well	4%		X	X	X	X		X			X
View Wellbore in 3D	3%	X	X	X	X			X	X	X	
Interpret With Flattened Volumes	3%		X				X				X
Display Horizons in 3D Viewer	3%	X		X	X						X
Run Reservoir Simulation	2%		X	X	X	X	X	X			X
Manage Corporate Data	1%		X	X				X	X	X	X

Figure 2.2   *Matrix showing which component teams (columns) will participate in the implementation of each use case (rows).*

The planning problem such a matrix is meant to obviate is illustrated in Figure 2.3, where circles indicate what each component team is working on at an instance in time. In this admittedly extreme example, though everyone is hard at work, when complete the bits won't plug together to form any meaningful functionality.

While the problem with this approach is evident when looking at Figure 2.3, without use cases to provide a basis for knowing what a meaningful chunk of functionality *is*, and without a matrix such as this to provide a common visual roadmap for planning and coordination, distributed development can readily drift into situations similar to that illustrated in Figure 2.3, especially when teams span business groups or are separated geographically. There's a kind of a second law of thermodynamics that applies to software development: *Entropy happens in distributed software development!*

Use Cases	Priority	Base Mapping	Data Management	Geologic Interpretation	Petrophysical Interpretation	Reservoir Simulation	Seismic 2D Interpretation	Seismic 3D Interpretation	Seismic Data Management	Seismic Processing	Statistical Analysis Engine
Create 2D Cross-Section	11%	(X)	X	X	X		X	X			
Manage Reservoir Model	9%	X	(X)	X	X						
Search Data Projects With Filter	9%		X		X	X	X	X	X	(X)	X
Construct Geo-Framework	8%	X	X	(X)	X	X	X	X			
Load Seismic Data	8%		X				X	X	(X)		
Construct Fluid Property Model	8%	X	(X)	X	X		X	X	X		
Interpret With Multi-Valued Horizon	7%		X	X	X	X	X	(X)	X		X
Evaluate Geo-Statistics	7%	X		(X)			X	X	X	X	
Manage Well Log Data	5%						(X)	X	X	X	
Build Wellbore Model	5%	X	X	X	(X)	X	X	X	X	X	
Geostatistical Evaluation	4%	(X)	X	X	X						
Manage Map Files/Data	4%	X	X	X	X	X		(X)			
Drill Horizontal Well	4%		(X)	X	X	X		X			X
View Wellbore in 3D	3%	X	X	X	(X)		X	X	X		
Interpret With Flattened Volumes	3%		X				X				(X)
Display Horizons in 3D Viewer	3%	X		(X)	X						X
Run Reservoir Simulation	2%		X	X	X	(X)	X	X			X
Manage Corporate Data	1%		X	X			X	X	X	(X)	

Component Teams

Figure 2.3 *Circles indicate work that each component team is doing at a given instance in time. Though everyone is hard at work, when complete the bits won't plug together to form any meaningful functionality.*

To be fair, "software development entropy" is not the only reason you might find yourself in a situation such as that shown in Figure 2.3. In the "Big Bang Integration" style of software development (i.e., wait until all bits are done, then integrate them and test) the order in which you do component work really doesn't matter, in theory at least. For companies that utilized this philosophy but are now trying to move over to the iterative, incremental development philosophy of the Unified Software Development Process, Extreme Programming, or the Agile community in general, old habits can die hard.

For whatever reason it happens, the solution to the problem shown in Figure 2.3 is obvious: make sure that the component teams coordinate and synchronize to work on the same use cases in the same priority order, with QFD providing the means to *determine* that priority according to a given set of business drivers.[9]

Planning the Length of Iterations and Number of Use Cases per Iteration in Distributed Software Development

There is another aspect of distributed software development that has presented problems for O&G in the past: planning the length of development iterations and the number of use cases to deliver per iteration. While this may be straightforward for use cases that are to be implemented by a single team, distributed development of use cases introduces some twists, namely:

1. Given a use case, *not all component teams are affected equally* in terms of the effort required of them. Some teams will have a lot of work to do, others just a little.

2. *Not all component teams are staffed equally*, so their capacity for how much work they can take on varies.

---

[9] This approach is compatible with the Unified Software Development Process' risk-driven planning for iterations, as long as risk is adequately represented in the business drivers used to prioritize the use cases via QFD. In such a case, high priority translates to high risk.

3. The implementation of use cases is rarely distributed across the *same* set of component teams for any two use cases. This is evident from looking at the matrix of Figure 2.4.[10]

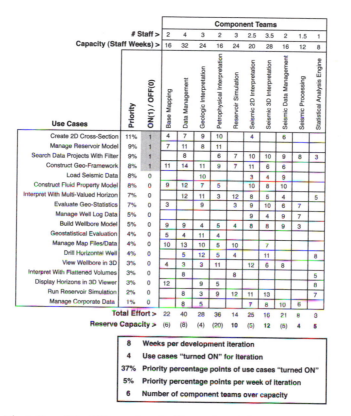

Figure 2.4   *Adaptation of the QFD matrix to facilitate what-if planning of number of use cases per iteration in distributed software development.*[11]

---

[10] To understand why this is an issue, imagine a matrix like that of Figure 2.2 where all use cases were implemented by the very same teams. To select the number of use cases for an iteration, simply start picking the highest priority use cases until some team's capacity for development is exceeded (i.e., they have more work to do than they have staff to do it in the time allotted by the iteration). It is the lack of this uniformity that makes the problem trickier; selecting use cases in strict priority order simply does not work.

[11] While the components associated with use cases are fairly realistic, use case priorities and efforts to implement use cases are hypothetical.

Taken together, these three factors can represent a non-trivial planning problem for use case-driven distributed development. To address these issues, O&G has developed an adaptation of the QFD matrix (see Figure 2.4; Figure 2.5 shows formulas for implementation as an Excel spreadsheet).

The next six sections walk you through the mechanics of the matrix in Figure 2.4 as a planning tool for use case-driven distributed development. The matrix is used to plan one iteration at a time: iteration duration (here in weeks) and scope (use cases). As the planning for one iteration is completed, the use cases for that iteration are "removed" (zeroing their priority removes them from consideration) and the matrix is reused to plan the next iteration. This process is repeated until all use cases have been allocated to an iteration.

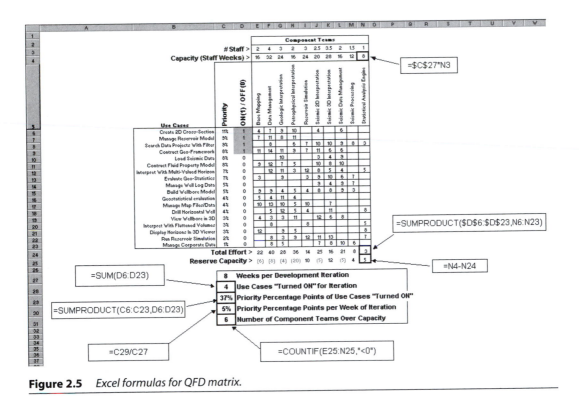

Figure 2.5   *Excel formulas for QFD matrix.*

Estimating Effort Required per Component Team to Implement Use Cases

The first requirement for the O&G planning is to estimate the effort required to implement a use case on a component team basis. For this, the "Xs" of Figure 2.2 have been replaced in the matrix of Figure 2.4 with estimates of effort, here expressed in terms of staff weeks (e.g., 2 staff working 4 weeks = 8 staff weeks of effort).[12] Taking the sum of all effort in a column provides the total effort required of a component team *if* all use cases are implemented.[13]

But O&G wants to be able to play *what-if* games with the length and scope of a development iteration, including and excluding use cases to see what the total impact is on each component team in terms of required effort for different sets of use cases. To do this, a new column is added to the matrix: **ON(1) / OFF(0)**. This column lets the O&G planning team turn use cases "ON" or "OFF" for an iteration (i.e., be part of the next iteration or not). Row **Total Effort** at the bottom of the matrix then tallies the effort, per component team, for *just* the use cases that have been turned "ON".

Estimating Capacity of Each Component Team for Work

As the O&G planning team does *what-if* analysis adding use cases to an iteration, they need some way to tell whether each of the component teams has been pushed over its limit in terms of how much work it can take on. To address this, O&G planners first need to estimate the work of which each team is capable. For this, two new rows are added to the top of the matrix; refer to Figure 2.5. The first, **# of Staff**, is used to specify the number of staff that is available for work on each component. Part time availability of staff is represented as a fraction (e.g., component teams **2D** and **3D Seismic**

---

[12] For ideas on estimating the effort required to implement a use case, see the "Techniques for Estimating Effort" section in Chapter 8, "Leveraging Your Investment in Use Case CM in Project Portfolio Management."

[13] Taking the sum of effort in a row provides the total effort needed across component teams to implement a use case. This value can be used as a sanity check of effort required to implement the use case versus its importance. A similar example of this is presented in this book: see the "Air Bags and Hawaiian Shirts" section in Chapter 3, "Operational Profiles: Quantifying Frequency of Use of Use Cases." See also Cohen's (1995) section on cost deployment.

Interpretation have one member that splits their time equally between the two teams; hence, 2.5 and 3.5 available staff, respectively).

The second new row at the top of the matrix is **Capacity**, which is measured in staff weeks of effort. The cells of this row are calculated by taking the number of staff that are available to work on each component—previous row, **# Staff**—times the number of weeks planned for the iteration (see **Weeks per Development Iteration** at the bottom of the matrix in Figure 2.4). For example, the capacity for the Data Management component team is 4 staff times 8 weeks of development, which equals 32 staff weeks of work.

Determining Component Teams that Are Over Allocated

With these new rows, the O&G planning team is now able to determine when component teams have exceeded their limit in terms of how much work they can take on. A row at the bottom of the matrix (refer to Figure 2.4)—**Reserve Capacity**—calculates the difference between available capacity of component teams (row **Capacity**) and what is required of them by the set of use cases that have been turned "ON" (**Total Effort**). Negative values for **Reserve Capacity** (shown in parenthesis) indicate a team that is being asked to do more work than they have capacity for. For example, notice that in the matrix with the top four ranking use cases selected, the capacity of six component teams to deliver has already been exceeded.

Keeping Score of What-If Scenarios

Just below the matrix in Figure 2.4, a number of measures are grouped into a box to allow the O&G planning team to "keep score" of the *what-if* analysis, comparing the results of one *what-if* scenario to the results of the next. The scoreboard includes simple measures, such as:

- Iteration length in weeks.

- Number of use cases included in the iteration (i.e., the number with a "1" in their ON/OFF column).

- Sum of priority percentage points from the priority column for those use cases that are "ON" (i.e., have a "1").

- The priority percentage points *per week* of development (i.e. sum of priority percentage points divided by the number of weeks in the iteration). Use of this measure will be illustrated soon.

- Number of component teams that are over allocated (i.e., those teams with a negative value in row **Reserve Capacity**).

Maximizing the Bang for the Buck

All that remains is for the O&G planning team to find a set of use cases that maximizes the bang for the buck for the iteration, while staying within the capacity of each of the component teams. This is certainly something that can be done by trial and error manually. As luck would have it, however, the problem of planning the number of use cases per iteration that a distributed development team can implement fits pretty well into the mold of what is called an optimization problem for which relatively inexpensive tool support is available, for example, as add-ins to Excel. This is fortunate for O&G, whose large cross-company programs sometimes have QFD matrices two and three times the size of Figure 2.4.

An *optimization problem* is one that can be cast in a form like the following:

1. Select values for some set of parameters

2. Such that some "thing" (e.g., profits, cost, risk) is maximized or minimized

3. All the while making sure certain constraint(s) are met

Using a matrix like that of Figure 2.5, you can couch the planning of use cases for an iteration as an optimization problem like this:[14]

---

[14] Again, as long as risk is adequately represented in the business drivers used to prioritize the use cases via QFD, this approach is compatible with the Unified Software Development Process' risk-driven planning for iterations: high priority translates to high risk. In such a case, the optimization problem becomes one of maximizing the set of risky use cases that can be developed by the distributed teams.

1. Select:

    a. A *set of use cases* for the iteration (i.e., turn them on in the
        matrix)

    b. And a *duration* for the iteration (weeks)

2. Such that the *priority percentage points per week* of iteration is maxi-
    mized (this is the sum of priority percentage points for all use cases
    selected for the iteration, divided by the number of weeks in the
    iteration)[15]

3. All the while making sure no component team is over allocated

Figure 2.6 shows an optimized matrix produced using Evolver, an optimization problem solver add-in for Excel.[16] Figure 2.7 illustrates the Evolver
setup used to produce the matrix of Figure 2.6. In this case, Evolver was set
to consider development iterations lasting between 4 to 8 weeks, a constraint imposed by the business needs of O&G.[17]

---

[15] Using a value like priority percentage points per week as the value to be maximized ensures that
the solution the optimization tool finds keeps the iteration length as short as possible. If you were
to maximize strictly based on total priority percent points of use cases delivered, the best way to
maximize that number is to simply increase the length of the iteration so that all use cases can be
implemented in one iteration; not a very useful answer.

[16] Evolver has a variety of problem-solving methods; the "recipe" method is used here and assumes
implementation of one use case does not depend on another. If you have use cases whose implementation is dependent upon one another you can either bundle them as a single entry in the
matrix and adjust the effort for implementation accordingly (easiest solution) or extend the matrix
to allow notation of dependencies and utilize a different solving method in which certain use cases
are required to precede others.

[17] My purpose in providing this screen shot is not to explain how to use Evolver, but rather convey
the "flavor" of such a tool and to illustrate it's not "rocket science"; one setup interface was all that
was needed for this example.

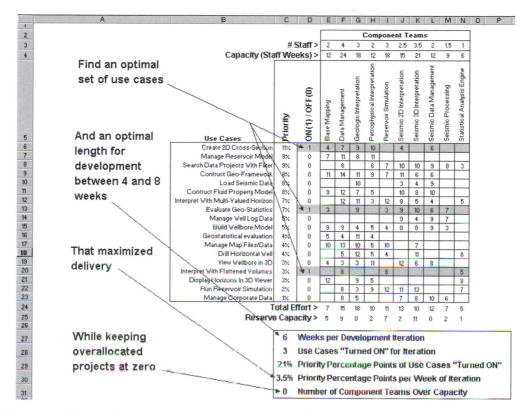

Figure 2.6 *Planning the number of use cases per iteration in distributed software development cast as an optimization problem.*

Figure 2.7 *Evolver is an optimization problem solver add-in for Excel. The setup shown here was used to produce the optimized QFD matrix of Figure 2.6.*

First Iteration Planned: Plan Subsequent Iterations

To summarize the results of Figure 2.6, the answer to the optimization problem produced by Evolver is for an initial development iteration of 6 weeks with delivery of three use cases (in gray) which average to 3.5% priority percentage points per week of development (sum of priority percentage points of use cases to be delivered divided by six weeks). In doing this, several teams are down to a reserve capacity of zero, and several more close to capacity (i.e., they have all the work they can handle).

With that, the planning for the *first* iteration of development in O&G's port of its products to the new shared earth model is complete. To plan the second iteration, O&G repeats the process with the use cases identified from the first iteration removed from the matrix (setting their priority to zero will do the trick). This process is repeated until all use cases have been allocated to an iteration. The result will be a schedule that delivers the highest-priority use cases per iteration and utilizes component teams as well as can be expected while not over-allocating any.

Chapter Review

Let's review the chapter. Here are key points you've learned:

- The theme of QFD as a *team* planning/decision-making tool was re-emphasized with two examples from the oil and gas industry, first as a tool for synchronizing company-wide decision making, then as a tool for planning and synchronizing use case-driven distributed development.

- While not "standard" manufacturing-based QFD, you may find that in some instances it is more natural to work with use cases first, business drivers second. In this case, the question the QFD team asks themselves is: *What is it that makes one use case more important than another in terms of a project?* In doing so, you work backward to arrive at a team agreement on what are the business drivers for the project. Whether working frontward or backwards, the end result is team alignment on the business drivers.

- While non-functional requirements are part of the fully dressed use case, QFD adds additional value helping identify non-functional requirements that are *highest priority to a suite of use cases as a whole.* This was illustrated with an example in which prioritized use cases were used to prioritize non-functional requirements, and then the two *combined—* use cases plus non-functional requirements—were used to prioritize system design decisions.

- Use case-driven distributed development—development involving implementation by multiple component or product teams—presents a number of challenges for an organization. One problem is that of making sure the vision is clear as to what needs to be worked on by each team and *in what order.* A QFD matrix of prioritized use cases (rows) and component teams involved in implementation (columns) is an effective tool for communicating the game plan.

- A second problem associated with use case-driven distributed development is that of planning the length of development iterations and the number of use cases to deliver per iteration. This problem has three contributing factors: not all component teams have the same amount of work to do in implementing a use case; not all component teams are staffed equally; and each use case may very well have a unique set of component teams implementing it. Luckily, the problem fits well into the mold of an *optimization problem,* and a QFD matrix can easily be run through an optimization tool to help a team determine an optimal length of time for an iteration and the set of highest-priority use cases that can be implemented in that time across the distributed teams.

Part 2

Software Reliability Engineering

Working Smart to Deliver Reliability in Use Case Development

> *"Software Reliability Engineering: More Reliable Software, Faster and Cheaper"*
>
> —*the slogan of SRE, John Musa*

Software Reliability Engineering (SRE) is about increasing customer satisfaction by delivering a reliable product while minimizing engineering costs. Use case-driven development and SRE are a natural match, both being usage-driven styles of product development.[1] What SRE brings to the party is a discipline for focusing time, effort, and resources on use cases in proportion to their estimated frequency of use, or criticality, to maximize reliability while minimizing development costs. Consider this: Is it really necessary to apply the same level of rigor to the engineering—analysis, inspection, development and testing—of all use cases? By understanding how a product is really going to be used by the user, the engineering team

---

[1] For a comparison of the two disciplines, see Runeson and Regnell (1998), *Derivation of an Integrated Operational Profile and Use Case Model.*

can focus its efforts on those use cases most likely to have defects in operational use by the customer. The result: Higher reliability as experienced by the customer, while minimizing development and test costs. Or as John Musa says, "More reliable software, faster and cheaper."

The field of SRE traces its roots back to work being done at AT&T Bell Labs, Murray Hill, in the early 1970s by pioneers such as John Musa. SRE contains two ideas that, after the fact, leave you wondering why somebody didn't pioneer the subject earlier. The first is to quantify frequency of product use by the user. Use cases and scenarios already provide a discrete unit for describing product use; SRE provides the means to quantify that use with what is called an *operational profile*.

In Chapter 3, "Operational Profiles: Quantifying Frequency of Use of Use Cases," we'll look at building operational profiles for the scenarios that make up a single use case and for a package of use cases.[2] Examples are provided to illustrate the use of operational profiles to work smart in how you plan the activities that affect your product reliability. The chapter will conclude by showing how to extend operational profiles to address risk profiling of use case packages.

The second idea SRE brings to use case development is a concrete way to talk about "reliability," including how to define it, measure it, set goals in terms of it, and track it in testing. This is the focus of Chapter 4, "Reliability and Knowing When to Stop Testing."

---

[2] In UML, a use case package is a logical grouping of use cases and/or other use case packages. An operational profile can be built for a package, for the use cases of multiple packages, or for all the use cases of a system. To keep things simple, operational profiles will be discussed in terms of a "package" (singular), but just keep in mind it may in fact be a package pulling some or all of the use cases from a number of other packages.

3

Operational Profiles: Quantifying Frequency of Use of Use Cases

A use case with many bugs can seem reliable if the user spends so little time running it that none of the many bugs are found. Conversely, a use case that has few bugs can seem unreliable if the user spends so much time running it that all those few bugs are found. This is the concept of perceived reliability: it is the reliability the user experiences, as opposed to a reliability measure in terms of, say, defect density. SRE begins by defining the *operational profile* of a product: a description of the product's usage patterns that includes *frequency of use*. This allows the engineering team to optimize development and testing, concentrating on the most frequently used use cases, and hence having a greater chance of failure in the hands of the user.

By taking such an approach, project teams work smarter—not harder—to deliver a reliable product.

In this chapter, we'll start by looking at building operational profiles for the scenarios that make up a single use case, followed by building operational profiles for a package of use cases. This chapter will conclude by showing you how to extend operational profiles to address risk profiling of use case packages.

Operational Profile of Use Case Scenarios

Let's begin with the operational profile for the scenarios that make up a single use case. Figure 3.1 shows a stylized use case with numbered blocks representing steps in the use case. This use case is made of six scenarios that represent different paths through the use case.

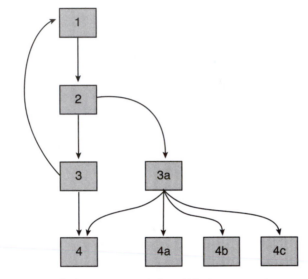

Figure 3.1   *Stylized use case with six scenarios. Numbered blocks are steps in use case.*

The scenarios for the use case in Figure 3.1 can be described in terms of the steps that make each up; they are:

- 1, 2, 3, 4

- 1, 2, 3, 1

- 1, 2, 3a, 4

- 1, 2, 3a, 4a

- 1, 2, 3a, 4b

- 1, 2, 3a, 4c

An operational profile of this use case will spell out the relative amount of traffic, so to speak, that we expect each of these scenarios to receive.

Decision Graphs

A common technique for producing an operational profile is a *decision graph*, and it works perfectly for building an operational profile of a use case's scenarios. A decision graph is a means for calculating the probability of an event; in this case, the probability that the user will use one scenario (i.e., path through the use case) over the next.

Calculating Probabilities of Scenarios

As Figure 3.2 illustrates, our use case of Figure 3.1 is easily converted to a decision graph model.

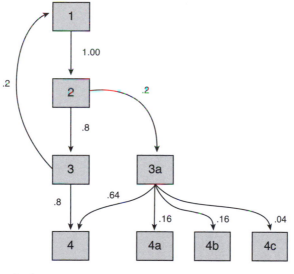

Figure 3.2 *Decision graph of use case.*

In a decision graph model of a use case, each path (or edge as they are called in graph theory) leaving each step in the use case is assigned a probability. It is the probability with which we expect that path to be used relative to alternate paths leaving the same step. The probability of all paths leaving a step must sum to 1. So for example, after a user has executed step 2 in Figure 3.2, we expect that 80% of the time the user will go to step 3 next and 20% of the time they will go to step 3a.

After probabilities are assigned to each path, the probability of each scenario is calculated by taking the product of the probabilities of paths in that scenario. For example, the probability of scenario 1, 2, 3, 4 is

$$1 \times .8 \times .8 = .64$$

What this means is that we expect this scenario to receive 64% of user traffic through the use case. The probability of each scenario of Figure 3.2 is shown in Table 3.1 and displayed as a pie chart in Figure 3.3. A pie chart in particular helps drive home the point that traffic loads through a use case can vary dramatically between scenarios.

Table 3.1   *Probability of each scenario of Figure 3.2 (rounded to two decimal places)*

Scenario	Probability
1, 2, 3, 4	0.64
1, 2, 3, 1	0.16
1, 2, 3a, 4	0.13
1, 2, 3a, 4a	0.03
1, 2, 3a, 4b	0.03
1, 2, 3a, 4c	0.01
TOTAL	1.00

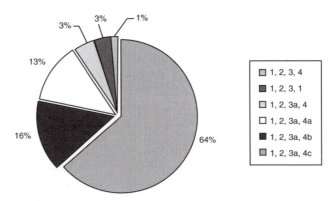

Figure 3.3   *Probability of each scenario of Table 3.1 displayed as pie chart.*

Implementing a Decision Graph as a Spreadsheet Matrix

Calculating probabilities for each scenario can be a chore. One idea to address this is to replace or augment the decision graph with a matrix implemented as a spreadsheet. Figure 3.4 provides a matrix implementation of the decision graph of Figure 3.2.

In the matrix of Figure 3.4, rows and columns are labeled with the steps in the use case. Cells provide the probability of user traffic moving from step X (row) to step Y (column). For example, the circled cell in Figure 3.4 states that from use case step 2 there is an 80% probability that step 3 will be next. A matrix such as this, implemented as a spreadsheet, allows one to then quickly determine the probability of each scenario, as illustrated in Figure 3.5. Broekman and Notenboon (2003) use the matrix approach in lieu of the pictorial decision graph. Which you use is a matter of taste.

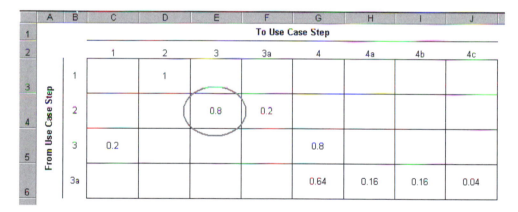

Figure 3.4 *Spreadsheet matrix implementation of decision graph of Figure 3.2. Rows and columns are steps in the use case. Circled cell says that from use case step 2 (row), there is an 80% probability that the user will next go to step 3 (column). All values in a row must sum to 1.0.*

Figure 3.2, Table 3.1, and Figure 3.5 collectively form the operational profile for our use case. You are quite likely to find instances in the literature where the table, the pictorial decision graph, or the matrix, each by itself, is presented as the operational profile. They are essentially different views of the same thing.

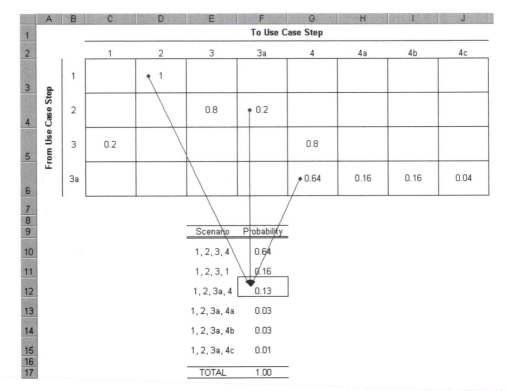

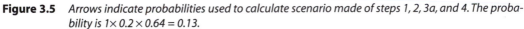

Figure 3.5   *Arrows indicate probabilities used to calculate scenario made of steps 1, 2, 3a, and 4. The probability is 1×0.2×0.64 = 0.13.*

Pareto Principle and Guesstimates

Without empirical results from the field or usability studies, the probabilities you use in your use case decision graph will likely be "guesstimates." Rather than spending a lot of time agonizing over the numbers, there's always the Pareto Principle, which you might find useful to apply to the operational profile.

The term "Pareto Principle" (or Pareto Law, or simply the 80/20 rule) was coined by Joseph Juran in his *Quality Control Handbook*, first released in 1951. He based the term on the work of Italian economist Vilfredo Pareto who observed that in modeling the distribution of wealth and land, 80 percent was held by 20 percent of the population. Juran's original application of this distribution was applied to manufacturing where he observed that 80% of the problems reported stemmed from 20% of all types of defects.

The Pareto Principle has subsequently proved a good model for many phenomena, both in the natural and social world, including software engineering, with rules of thumb such as "20% of the modules contain 80% of the defects" (Juran 1988).

So, when all else fails—you have no empirical data from the field, you don't have time for a usability study, and you are frustrated at guessing—you might find it useful to apply the Pareto Principle to operational profiles: 20% of the paths exiting a use case step will carry 80% of the user traffic. I can't offer you any scientific study that says the Pareto Principle is a proven success on this, but I do think it will help you and your team get over the "analysis paralysis" of agonizing over probabilities of use case step exit paths. Let's see how this works.

Quick, Low-Tech Approach

Here's a really quick, low-tech approach. Take the number of paths exiting a use case step and multiply by 20%; for most use cases this will yield 1 or 2 exit paths (e.g., 20% of 10 exit paths = 2). Distribute 80% of the traffic across these 1 or 2 steps. For the remaining steps, distribute 20% of the traffic across them. It doesn't have to be a uniform distribution. After you've kind of thrown the probabilities out there, step back and let your intuition take over to readjust.

For this to work, you still have to be able to put the exit paths in order from high-traffic to low, but that's a lot easier to do than assigning probabilities. This quick approach to the Pareto Principle will give you a rational approach for guesstimating the probabilities to kind of get you past analysis paralysis. Your intuition can then be used to fine tune things.

Successive Application of Pareto

If you want to get more rigorous in the application of the Pareto Principle, you can do successive applications. For example, after you've split a set of exit paths into two groups, one receiving 80% of the traffic and the other receiving 20%, you can reapply the Pareto Principle to the exit paths within each set. Figures 3.6 and 3.7 illustrate this notion of successive application for the two examples where the initial 80% of traffic is allocated to 1 and 2 exit paths, respectively.

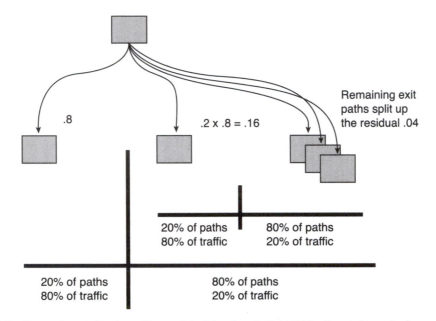

Figure 3.6   *Successive application of Pareto Principle where initial 80% is allocated to a single use case exit path.*

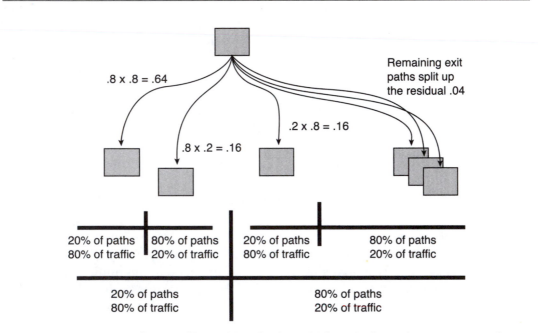

Figure 3.7   *Successive application of Pareto Principle where initial 80% is allocated to two use case exit paths.*

Notice that in both these cases, with just two successive applications of the Pareto Principle, you will have allocated 96% of the traffic. The remaining 4% can then be allocated as you see fit.

So keep these two Pareto patterns in your back pocket; they may be all you need for most use case exit paths:

- .8 for the highest trafficked exit path, .16 for the next, and allocate .04 across the rest

- .64, for the highest trafficked, .16 and .16 for the next two, and then allocate .04 across the rest (for example, see step 3a of Figure 3.2)

Using one of these two patterns is probably as safe a guesstimate as any other.

Working Smarter: Scenarios of a Use Case

To this point, we've been talking about how to build an operational profile of the scenarios that make up a single use case. Now we get to the *working smarter* part of operational profiles: putting them to work.

In this section, we look at examples that illustrate utilizing the use case operational profile in planning. Many of the examples will come from test planning; testing is a key consumer of the operational profile, plays a fundamental role in product reliability, and represents one of the biggest costs in a project. But keep in mind that operational profiles can be used as a way to prioritize and allocate effort and resources for just about every facet of development.

In planning and estimation, two common approaches are time-boxing and bottom-up. Time-boxing is a top-down strategy usually associated with iterative software development in which the duration of task or project (that's the "top") is fixed, forcing hard decisions to be made about what scope can be delivered in the allotted time. The other strategy is bottom-up, in which you start with the scope to be developed and tested (use cases;

that's the "bottom"), then roll-up estimates from that level to determine the time needed for the overall task or project (the "top").

In the next several examples, we look at the operational profile as used in top-down and bottom-up planning.

Time-Boxing an Inspection

Let's say you are planning an inspection of the use case your team has just developed, and the decision graph of Figure 3.2 and operational profile of Table 3.1 are for this new use case. You have a one-time shot at getting key domain experts and customer reps as part of the review team. The inspection is scheduled to last three hours. What is the best use of the review team's time?

First, you determine the order in which to review the materials by using the operational profile for the use case: those with highest relative frequency in the operational profile first. That way, if you run out of time in the review—and chances are, you will—you will have covered the most frequently used scenarios first. Second, the operational profile provides a way to sensibly allocate time in the review in proportion to the relative frequency of the scenarios in the use case.

The spreadsheet of Figure 3.8 illustrates an allocation of review time in hours per scenario based on the operational profile. Scenario **1, 2, 3, 4** accounts for 64% of the traffic we expect through this use case; accordingly, you decide that if the review team is on a roll and finding good issues, you plan to allocate 64% of the review time—1.9 to 2 hours—to just this high-frequency scenario. If the review team finishes in less time, great! Otherwise, it's worth a full two hours. At the end of the two hours, you plan to move on to the next two scenarios—**1, 2, 3, 1** and **1, 2, 3a, 4**—which account for 16% and 13% of the use case traffic, respectively. This works out to about one-half hour of review time each for these two scenarios (3 hours times 16% = .5 hours; 3 hours times 13% = .4 hours).

In the three-hour review, you plan to spend your time on the scenarios that account for 93% of the traffic through the use case. If the review team finishes these scenarios ahead of time, you can move on to the last three, which collectively account for only 7% of the traffic. This, you feel, is a better strategy than having the review team rush to try to get through all six scenarios.

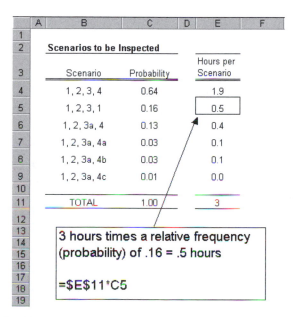

Figure 3.8   *Priority order and breakdown of time (hours) to allocate per use case scenario during inspection.*

As this example illustrates, the idea behind *working smart* with operational profiles is very straightforward: you simply allocate effort, resources, or, in this case, time, based on the relative frequency of each scenario in the use case. Next, you'll see an example of allocation of *resource* via an operational profile; in this case, test cases.

Bottom-Up Estimation of Tests Needed per Scenario

The previous example looked at using an operational profile in a top-down, time-boxing fashion. Another common strategy for planning is bottom-up. In bottom-up planning, you start with the scope to be developed and tested (use cases; that's the "bottom"), make estimates at that level, and then roll them up to determine the time needed for the overall project, event, or phase (the "top"). Here's an example of an operational profile used in bottom-up planning to estimate the number of tests you need for each scenario of a use case. Time estimates, say for test design and or test execution, can be made by multplying the number of tests by an estimate of time needed per test. For a package of use cases, this process would be applied for each use case in the package to get a bottom-up estimate for the package as a whole.

You have been asked to design and run tests on the new **Widget Manager Use Case** and asked for an estimate of how long it might take. The use case has six scenarios, so to get things going you start with the assumption that, at minimum, each scenario will require one test, for a total of six. Using the use case's operational profile—implemented via a spreadsheet—you build the table shown in Figure 3.9 to see how those six tests would be allocated as per the profile.

	A	B	C	D	E	F
1						
2		**Widget Manager Use Case**				
3		Scenario	Probability		Tests (whole & fractions) per Scenario	
4		Main Flow	0.51		3.06	
5		Alternate Flow 1	0.25		1.50	
6		Alternate Flow 2	0.20		1.20	
7		Alternate Flow 3	0.02		0.12	
8		Alternate Flow 4	0.01		0.06	
9		Alternate Flow 5	0.01		0.06	
10						
11		TOTAL	1.00		6	
12						
13						
14		6 tests times a relative frequency				
15		(probability) of .01 = .06 tests				
16						
17						
18		=$E$11*C9				
19						
20						

Figure 3.9   *Allocation of six tests via the operational profile. Formula shown in Excel.*

The operational profile calls for the bulk of tests to be allocated to the first three scenarios, which account for 96% of the use case traffic; this makes sense. You see, however, that the last three scenarios, which only account for 4% of the use case traffic, receive only fractions of a test each. You realize fractions of a test make no sense. But rather than pull tests away from the other scenarios (remember that they are 96% of the use case traffic), you decide to round up all fractions to the next higher whole number of tests (see Figure 3.10).

	B	C	E	G
2	**Widget Manager Use Case**			
3	Scenario	Probability	Tests (whole & fractions) per Scenario	Tests (whole) per Scenario
4	Main Flow	0.51	3.06	4
5	Alternate Flow 1	0.25	1.50	2
6	Alternate Flow 2	0.20	1.20	2
7	Alternate Flow 3	0.02	0.12	1
8	Alternate Flow 4	0.01	0.06	1
9	Alternate Flow 5	0.01	0.06	1
11	TOTAL	1.00	6	11

.06 tests rounded up is 1 test

=ROUNDUP(E9,0)

Figure 3.10 *Fractions of tests as per operational profile are rounded up to the next higher whole number of tests. Formula shown in Excel.*

Eleven tests, as allocated in Figure 3.10, strike a good balance between allocating tests in a way that makes sense as per the operational profile and having at least one test per scenario. Finally, you estimate three staff hours to design and execute a test, for a total of 33 staff hours for the whole use case.

Whether you plan top-down (e.g., time-boxing) or bottom-up, operational profiles are a smart way to allocate time, effort, and resources across the scenarios of a use case.

Operational Profile of a Use Case Package

To this point, we've looked at how to describe and use an operational profile for the scenarios that make up a single use case. Of course, few projects deal with just a single use case, so next we turn to the question of how to describe and use an operational profile for a package of use cases.

Operational profiles are a part of Binder's Extended Use Case Test Design Pattern (2003), and he offers the following simple example of a system with two use cases, **search** and **update**. If you have a product in which, on average, 90,000 searches and 10,000 updates are done daily, the relative frequency of the **search** and **update** use cases are .90 and .10, respectively (see Table 3.2).

Table 3.2　*Simple example of operational profile for two use cases*

Use Case	Times Used per Day	Probability
Update	90,000	0.90
Search	10,000	0.10
TOTAL	100,000	1.00

Notice that this technique does not require a decision graph. It simply estimates the number of times a use case is used per unit time and then calculates the relative frequency, or probability, from that. This is as about as straightforward and simple a way as there is to construct an operational profile for a package of use cases.

Sanity Check Before Proceeding

UML provides for the modeling of generalizations of, and extensions and addition of behavior to, base use cases. In the next section, we are going to look at how to build operational profiles for use cases that utilize these

---

[1] There has been a fair amount of debate in the use case community as to the merit of these relationships—in particular include and extend—in use case modeling. This section describing how to build an operational profile for these relationships is meant neither to encourage nor discourage their use.

relationships.[1] If you don't use these relationships, what was covered in the previous section will be plenty to get you started building operational profiles for a package of use cases. So, if you do not use these relationships, feel free to skip ahead to examples of using the operational profile in planning (see "Working Smarter: Use Case Packages" section).

Use Case Relationships

UML provides simple notation to describe the relationships between use cases. With the release of UML version 1.3, these relationships received major revision, adding a new relationship—generalization—and redefining others.[2] The list that follows includes definitions for the relationships that can be expressed between use cases as they stand in version 2.0 of UML (Rumbaugh, Jacobson, and Booch 2003).

- Generalization—A relationship between a general use case (parent) and a more specific use case (child) that inherits from, and adds to, the features and behavior of the general use case.

- Extend relationship—A relationship between a *base use case* (the use case to be extended) and an *extension use case* (the use case doing the extending). The relationship describes the *conditional* insertion of additional behavior (the extension) into the base use case. The behavior is inserted at the location defined by the extension point in the base use case and referenced by the extend relationship. The base use case does not "see" or "know about" the extension use case, so it cannot access its attributes or operations.

- Include relationship—A relationship between a base use case (the use case to which behavior is to be added) and an inclusion use case (the behavior added). The relationship describes the *mandatory* insertion of additional behavior (the inclusion) into the base use case. The behavior is included at the location defined in the base use case.

---

[2] Armour and Miller (2001) provide a good explanation of these relationships, and in particular changes in the semantics of include and extend from earlier versions (previous to 1.3) of UML.

An example will help illustrate these relationships. For the task at hand I'll focus on those aspects of the relationships that are pertinent to building an operational profile.

Sales Order Example

Figure 3.11 presents a typical sales order use case diagram utilizing relationships *generalization, include*, and *extend*.[3] In this example, we have six *base use cases* (i.e. those that are not inclusions or extensions). First is **Place Order**; this is a generalization that specifies the common behavior of all place order use cases.

The next three use cases—**Place Local Order** (in state)**, National Order** (out of state), and **International Order** (out of the country)—are children of **Place Order** and inherit all its properties and behavior, just like inheritance in objects. Each of the children then specialize these properties and behavior to accommodate their respective situations in terms for example of tax, regulations governing shipping across state and international boundaries, tariffs, and so on.

The last two base use cases are **Cancel Order** and **Check Order Status**, whose functions should be self-evident.

In what follows, we are going to build an operational profile for our sales order example. We'll proceed like this:

1. First, we estimate the frequency of use of *base use cases*, those to which extensions and inclusions will be made.

2. Next, we estimate the frequency of use of include and extend use cases used stand-alone (i.e., by themselves as regular, instantiated use cases, if any).

3. Finally, we estimate the frequency of use of include and extend use cases by the base use cases to which they are related.

At that point, our operational profile will be complete.

---

[3] Example based on Object Modeling Group's spec for UML version 1.5. See the UML Notation Guide at www.uml.org.

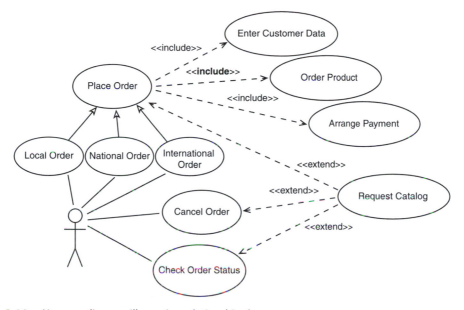

Figure 3.11 *Use case diagram illustrating relationships between use cases.*

Step 1—Start with Base Use Cases

We begin our operational profile with the base use cases—those to which inclusions/extensions are made—and estimate the number of times each is executed in some unit of time; here, daily (see Figure 3.12). This information would come from empirical field data, usability studies, or simply your best educated guess. Notice that in this table **Place Order**, the parent in the generalization relationship of Figure 3.11, is shown with a zero: it turns out to be an *abstract use case* (i.e., it is not fully specified to the point it can be instantiated for standalone use and is used solely for defining the common properties and behavior of its children). For an operational profile, this determination needs to be made for all use case generalizations.

Base Use Cases	Times per Day	Probability
Place Order	⓪	0.00
Place Local Order	50	0.09
Place National Order	350	0.64
Place International Order	25	0.05
Cancel Order	25	0.05
Check Order Status	100	0.18

Figure 3.12 *Base use cases and estimate of times per day each is executed. The zero for Place Order (circled) indicates that it is an abstract use case: not fully specified and never instantiated for use standalone.*

Step 2—Include and Extend Use Cases Used Standalone

Next, we turn our attention to the four include/extend use cases; these are use cases that are used to extend base use cases (**Request Catalog** in Figure 3.11) or be included in base use cases (**Enter Customer Data, Order Product, Arrange Payment** in Figure 3.11).

But a pertinent aspect of these use cases with regards to operational profiles is that per the UML, they may *possibly* be used as standalone use cases. Given they are fully specified (i.e., are not "fragments") they can be instantiated and used as regular use cases (Rumbaugh, Jacobson, and Booch 2005). Another way to look at this, which might make more sense: the UML provides for the use of otherwise "regular" use cases to be used as extensions and inclusions to other "regular" use cases. In such a case, the operational profile needs to take into account such usage.

Figure 3.13 reflects this new information and shows the number of times a day we estimate these use cases will be used standalone: instantiated and executed as regular use cases by themselves, rather than in the role of an extension or inclusion to another base use case.

In Figure 3.13, notice that use cases **Enter Customer Data** and **Order Product** are shown with zeroes (circled). This indicates that these particular use cases are never expected to be used standalone; they are only used as inclusions to base uses cases. Both **Enter Customer Data** and **Order Product**, while necessary, are not sufficient to be standalone in and of themselves (they are use case fragments, i.e., not fully specified, and can't be instantiated). **Arrange Payment** and **Request Catalog**, on the other hand, are fully specified, able to be instantiated, and expected to be used daily at the specified rates. Taking **Request Catalog**, for example, we expect that about forty times a day a customer will phone a salesperson for the sole purpose of requesting a new catalog.

Base Use Cases	Times per Day	Probability
Place Order	0	0.00
Place Local Order	50	0.08
Place Nationall Order	350	0.58
Place International Order	25	0.04
Cancel Order	25	0.04
Check Order Status	100	0.17

Include and Extend Use Cases	Times per Day Standalone	Times per Day with Base Use Case	Times per Day	Probability
Enter Customer Data	0		0	0.00
Order Product	0		0	0.00
Arrange Payment	15		15	0.02
Request Catalog	40		40	0.07
TOTAL			605	1.00

Figure 3.13 *Times per day include and extend use cases are executed standalone. Zeroes (circled) indicate that these use cases are never used standalone.*

Step 3—Include and Extend Use Cases Used with Base Use Cases

The last step in our operational profile is to account for the number of times that include and extend use cases are executed as a result of being inclusions and extensions of base use cases.

In Figure 3.14, notice that the operational profile now includes a matrix titled *Probability of Use by Base Use Case* that describes the include and extend relationships shown in Figure 3.11. Rows of the matrix correspond to base use cases, and columns correspond to include or extend use cases.

A cell in the matrix provides the probability with which we expect the base use case to actually invoke the inclusion or extension.

For example, the cell marked by a circle in Figure 3.14 indicates that with a probability of .20—think 20 times in every 100 times some customer calls a salesperson to check on their order—we expect the customer to additionally request a catalog. Given that we expect the **Check Order Status** use case to execute 100 times a day, we would then expect the **Request Catalog** to be used 20 times a day as an extension to **Check Order Status**.

Base Use Cases	Times per Day	Probability	Probability of Use by Base Use Case			
			Enter Customer Data	Order Product	Arrange Payment	Request Catalog
			Include	Include	Include	Extend
Place Order	0	0.00	0.80	0.80	0.80	0.15
Place Local Order	50	0.03	0.80	0.80	0.80	0.15
Place National Order	350	0.20	0.80	0.80	0.80	0.15
Place International Order	25	0.01	0.80	0.80	0.80	0.15
Cancel Order	25	0.01				0.20
Check Order Status	100	0.06				0.20

Include and Extend Use Cases	Times per Day Standalone	Times per Day with Base Use Case	Times per Day	Probability
Enter Customer Data	0	340	340	0.20
Order Product	0	340	340	0.20
Arrange Payment	15	340	355	0.21
Request Catalog	40	89	129	0.08
TOTAL			1714	1.00

Figure 3.14   *Operational profile with matrix describing probability that a base use case will invoke an inclusion or extension. The circle indicates that Request Catalog extends base use case Check Order Status with probability .20, or 20% of the time.*

This same principle is used for each include and extend use case; the number of times the base use case is executed daily is multiplied times the probability of invocation of the include/extend use case to come up with an estimate of the number of times the include/extend use case is used. In Excel, this is easily done with the **SUMPRODUCT** function; Figure 3.15 shows the formula for calculating the number of times a day **Request Catalog** is used as an extension by the base use cases.

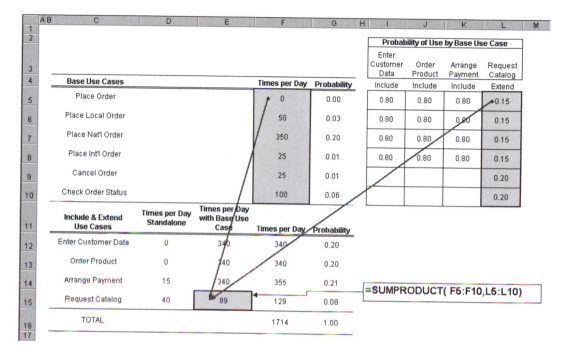

Figure 3.15 *Use of SUMPRODUCT function to calculate estimate of number of times Request Catalog is invoked as an extension daily.*

The grand total number of times an include/extend use case is used daily is the sum of the times it is used standalone plus the number of times it is used as an inclusion or extension.

After the total number of daily executions of both base use cases and include/extend use cases is available, the overall probability of each use case relative to the rest can be calculated; see spreadsheet columns **F** and **G** in Figure 3.15. A pie chart of the operational profile is shown in Figure 3.16.

Remember that a base use case combined with an include/extend use case results in a new use case composed of the two. But keep in mind that the frequency of use information in the operational profile addresses the base use case and include/extend use cases *separately:* any reference to the base use case in the operational profile refers to *just* the base use case, not the use case formed by inclusion/extension.

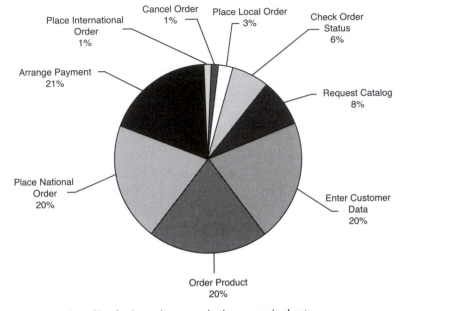

Figure 3.16   *Operational profile of sales order example shown as pie chart.*

With the operational profile in hand, we now have a quantitative way to allocate effort and resources to these use cases in a way that matches their expected frequency of use by the customer. But before we look at examples of how to work smartly with this operational profile, some discussion is in order about establishing the probabilities with which base use cases actually use include/extend use cases.

Probability that Include/Extend Use Cases Are Actually Used

The matrix of Figure 3.14 titled *Probability of Use by Base Use Case* describes the include/extend relationships shown in Figure 3.11. Each cell in the matrix provides the probability with which we expect the base use case (row) to actually invoke the include/extend use case (column). But where do we get those probabilities? How do we know what reasonable values would be?

In what follows, let's look at the detailed way to approach this question and then conclude with a quick, low-tech way. By understanding the detailed way first, you'll have a little better feeling about applying the low-tech way.

The Detailed Approach

Inclusions and extensions in UML both have the property that flow of control returns to the base use case at the same point where the inclusion/extension took place (i.e., the inclusion point or extension point, respectively).[4] Inclusion/extension points are like discrete points on a use case path that are either expanded in-line like a macro (my mental model for include) or act like a subroutine call which leaves and returns to the same point (my mental model for extend).

Given this, let's return to the decision graph of our stylized use case of Figure 3.2 and imagine that it is the decision graph of base use case **Place Order** of the use case diagram of Figure 3.11 and the operational profile of Figure 3.14. Then let's say that steps 3 and 4 of the decision graph of **Place Order** are in fact the inclusion and extension points for **Arrange Payment** and **Request Catalog** use cases, respectively, as illustrated in Figure 3.17.

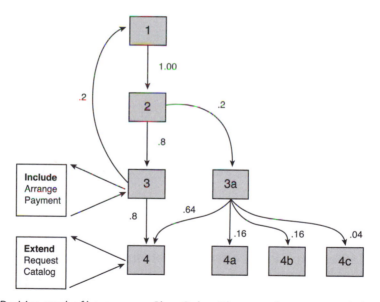

Figure 3.17   *Decision graph of base use case Place Order with arrange Payment as an inclusion point (step 3) and Request Catalog as an extension point (step 4).*

---

[4] Armour and Miller (2001) provide a good discussion on this aspect of inclusion/extension and how it is distinct from alternate flows and exception paths in a use case.

Working from Figure 3.17, let's now ask the question again: What is the probability that **Place Order** will actually invoke the **Arrange Payment** inclusion or the **Request Catalog** extension? Let's start with **Arrange Payment**. Table 3.3 provides the probability of each of the scenarios of Figure 3.17. (This is simply a reprint of Table 3.1, so look there if you are unsure how it was built.)

Table 3.3   *Probability of each scenario of Figure 3.17*

Scenario	Probability
1, 2, 3, 4	0.64
1, 2, 3, 1	0.16
1, 2, 3a, 4	0.13
1, 2, 3a, 4a	0.03
1, 2, 3a, 4b	0.03
1, 2, 3a, 4c	0.01
TOTAL	1.00

In which scenarios do we invoke the inclusion of **Arrange Payment** (remember, it is step 3)? It is invoked in scenarios **1, 2, 3, 4** and **1, 2, 3, 1**. By adding the probability of these two scenarios, we get the probability that **Place Order** will invoke the **Arrange Payment** inclusion:

.64 (probability of 1, 2, 3, 4) + .16 (probability of 1, 2, 3, 1) = .80

OK, now how about the **Request Catalog**? In which scenarios do we invoke the **Request Catalog** extension (remember, it is step 4)? It is invoked in scenarios **1, 2, 3, 4** and **1, 2, 3a, 4**. So the probability of invoking the **Request Catalog** is:

.64 (probability of 1, 2, 3, 4) + .13 (probability of 1, 2, 3a, 4) = .77

Well, that isn't *quite* true for **Request Catalog**; it's an extend use case so it's a tad messier (notice how things never get a tad simpler?). Remember the UML definition of an extend use case: the extension is "subject to specific conditions specified in the extension." If the condition, specified as part of the extend use case, is met, the extension is executed; otherwise, the base use case flow resumes as is (i.e., the extension becomes a "no-op"—nothing happens).

For our particular example, we would likely need field data to indicate the frequency with which a catalog is requested in conjunction with placing an order; otherwise, we make an educated guess. Let's try the educated guess route and use our Pareto Principle heuristic from earlier in the chapter. First, what is the most likely event from high to low, to request a catalog or not? You decide that *no catalog request* is probably the most likely of the two. OK, our Pareto heuristic says that 20% of the exit paths from a use case step will account for 80% of the traffic. Because we've only got two possible choices—they request a catalog or not—we take the probability of no catalog request at .8, which means that the probability for a catalog request is .2.

To summarize, the probability that the **Place Order** use case invokes the **Request Catalog** extension is the probability of the use case flow taking one of the scenarios on which the request catalog extension lies (scenarios **1, 2, 3, 4** and **1, 2, 3a, 4** of Figure 3.17) times the probability that the customer actually wants a new catalog when asked:

$$(.64 + .13) * .2 = .15$$

A Quick, Low-Tech Pareto Principle Approach

To recap what we've just learned, the probability that a base use case will use an include use case is the sum of the probabilities of the scenarios of which it is a part. The probability that a base use case will use an extend use case is the sum of probabilities of scenarios of which it is a part times the probability that the condition for extension is met. Now that we understand how it works, maybe we can take a short cut and make some guesstimates. And, of course, if we don't have operational profiles for the base use cases, we'll have to guesstimate anyway.

Let's take what we've learned about include/extend use cases, re-apply some of the Pareto Principle heuristics from the "Pareto Principle and Guesstimates" section, and see if we can get some ballpark probabilities for include/extend use cases as at least a starting guesstimate.

Figure 3.18 illustrates a quick and dirty Pareto-based heuristic for guesstimating the probability that a base use case will actually use an include/extend use case; a heuristic like this would be used in the absence of empirical data or in the absence of an operational profile of the base use case.

First, we guesstimate the probability that the base use case flow takes one of the scenarios on which the inclusion/extension point lies; this is row 1, 2 and 3 of Figure 3.18. If there is just one scenario in the use case (row 1), the probability is, of course, 1.0. If there is more than one scenario in the use case, we ask which is more likely: that the inclusion/extension point lies on one of the high traffic scenario paths (row 2) or not (row 3)? We assign the probabilities of .8 and .2 for each of these events, respectively.

Second, we guesstimate the probability that if the inclusion/extension point is reached it will actually be utilized. For include use cases, this is easy: UML tells us that if they are encountered they are always utilized, so probability = 1.0 (column 1). For extension points, we ask which is more likely: that when the extension point is reached it will be used (column 2) or not (column 3). We assign the probabilities of .8 and .2 to each of these events, respectively.

That's it. Quick and low tech. But if you don't have any better data, it's probably as safe a guesstimate as you can make. Simply find the cell that matches your need and use that probability as a ballpark starting place; let your instincts take it from there to tweak as you feel is right.

	Include Inclusion is Mandatory (1.0)	Extend where Extension Likely (.8)	Extend where Extension *Not* Likely (.2)
One Scenario in **Base Use Case** Probability of reaching inclusion/extension point is 1.0.	1 x 1 = 1	1 x .8 = .8	1 x .2 = .2
Multiple Scenarios in **Base Use Case** Probability of reaching inclusion/extension point is high (.8).	.8 x 1 = .8	.8 x .8 = .64	.8 x .2 = .16
Multiple Scenarios in **Base Use Case** Probability of reaching inclusion/extension point is low (.2).	.2 x 1 = .2	.2 x .8 = .16	.2 x .2 = .04

Figure 3.18   *Pareto-based heuristic for guesstimating the probability that a base use case will actually use an include/extend use case.*

Concluding Thoughts About Use Case Relationships

As you saw in the previous section, accounting for include and extend relationships can make what started out as a simple approach to operational profiles quite a bit more complicated. It could, however, be worth the effort to identify early in development common parts of the system—represented as include and extend use cases—that are shaping up as hot spots of traffic in the system. The same idea is used in the profiling of code where you are looking for components or subroutines that are utilized heavily by other code. Such hot spots are good candidates for making highly performant, easy to use, and reliable.

Use case generalizations are more straightforward to address in the operational profile: parents and children of a generalization relationship are treated as regular use cases listing their frequency of use separately for each. The only special issue is when the parent use case is an abstract use case (i.e., one that is not fully specified and cannot be instantiated).

Abstract use cases should be excluded from the operational profile or receive a zero for frequency of use as was done in Figure 3.12 for use case **Place Order**.

Working Smarter: Use Case Packages

In the section titled, "Working Smarter: Scenarios of a Use Case," we looked at the use of the operational profile of the scenarios of a single use case as a tool for planning. In this section, we look at examples that illustrate utilizing the operational profile of a package of use cases for planning.

Time-Boxing for a Package of Use Cases

We've already seen time boxing used as a strategy for deciding which scenarios of a use case should be covered in an inspection (see the "Time-Boxing an Inspection" section). To reiterate, time-boxing is a top-down planning strategy in which the duration of the task or project (that's the "top") is fixed, forcing hard decisions to be made about what scope can be delivered or tasks accomplished in the allotted time. One of the most common uses of time-boxing in testing will be to schedule the amount of time spent on test design per use case. Here's a simple example.

Next week, you are to start designing tests for the new sales order component of Figure 3.11. You have one week to spend on the task. To get an idea of how you want to spend your week, you construct the spreadsheet table of Figure 3.19 using the operational profile of the sales order component (refer to Figure 3.14).

To keep it simple, you assume that you have about 40 hours to spend on test design, and then use the operational profile of the sales order component to allocate those hours across the nine use cases of the component. From doing this, you decide to spend a day on each of the four use cases that account for about 81% of the traffic through the component. The last day you'll spend on the other five use cases, which account for 20% of the traffic. Additionally, you decide to approach test design in the order of frequency of use; that way, if time runs out, you have tackled the most critical use cases first.

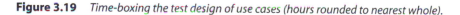

	A	B	C	D	E	F	G
1							
2		Use Case	Probability		Staff Hours per Use Case		
3		Arrange Payment	0.21		8		day 1
4		Place Nat'l Order	0.20		8		day 2
5		Enter Customer Data	0.20		8		day 3
6		Order Product	0.20		8		day 4
7		Request Catalog	0.08		3		
8		Check Order Status	0.06		2		
9		Place Local Order	0.03		1		day 5
10		Place Int'l Order	0.01		1		
11		Cancel Order	0.01		1		
12							
13		TOTAL	1.00		40		

40 hrs times a relative frequency
(probability) of .06 = 2 hrs

=$E$13*C8

Figure 3.19   *Time-boxing the test design of use cases (hours rounded to nearest whole).*

As you can see, applying an operational profile for a package of use cases is really no different from using a profile of the scenarios that make up a single use case. It is used to allocate effort, resources, or time based on the relative frequency of use cases in the package.

Transitioning from High-Level to Low-Level Planning

If it's not obvious yet, the operational profile for a package of use cases and the operational profile of the scenarios of each individual use case are intended to work in concert with one another. The former works at the high level, allocating time, effort, and resources across the use cases of a project or iteration; the latter works at the low level, allocating each use case's allotment across the scenarios. The next example illustrates this transition from high-level to low-level planning.

Your project is setting up an automated regression test bed that will run a smoke test after each build.[5] The smoke test focuses on three key use cases, each with four scenarios. Performance is a big part of your project, so the smoke test simulates a load of 500 users logging on, in different ways, to perform various tasks (the use cases and their scenarios). Login account IDs for 500 "fake" users have been set up on the test bed; you have been asked to decide how to allocate the 500 user login IDs across the use cases and their scenarios.

Starting with the operational profile of the three use cases, you build a spreadsheet table that allocates the total number of login IDs across the three use cases (see Figure 3.20).

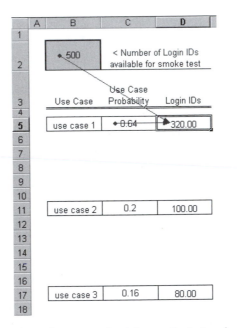

Figure 3.20   *Allocation of login IDs at the use case level. Arrows illustrate calculation of IDs allotted to use case 1 (500 x .64=320).*

Of the 500 login IDs, the profile calls for 320 going to use case 1, 100 to use case 2, and 80 going to use case 3.

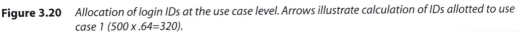

[5] A smoke test is a relatively simple test—typically automated—that runs after each baseline build as a sanity check that the baseline doesn't "smoke" when run and is at least sound enough to warrant further attention (e.g., before going on for more thorough testing). Steve McConnell (1996) provides more details on daily builds and smoke tests as a development best practice.

Next, you extend the spreadsheet table to include the operational profile of scenarios in each of the three use cases; this operational profile takes the number of login IDs allotted to each use case (see Figure 3.20) and further allocates them to the scenario level (see Figure 3.21). The result is a smoke test that loads the system in a manner consistent with how you believe your users will be using the system.

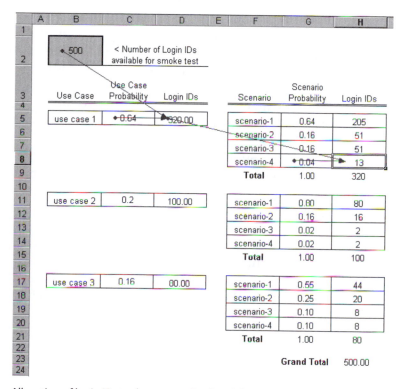

Figure 3.21 *Allocation of login IDs to the use case level and then to the scenario level. Arrows illustrate calculation of IDs allotted to use case 1 (500 x .64=320) and then the subsequent calculation of what part of that allotment is to go to scenario 4 (320 x .04=13).*

Air Bags and Hawaiian Shirts

There are some things you buy in life hoping to never actually use, air bags for example. Use them once and the price paid is well worth the cost. But then there is that Hawaiian shirt you bought while on vacation with the hula-dancer in a grass skirt saying "Mele Kaliki Maka" (that's "Merry Christmas" in

Hawaiian). True, you cut a handsome figure at the office Christmas party in that shirt. But practically speaking, had you paused for a moment and reflected on the number of opportunities in the course of a year that you would actually *wear* that shirt, you probably would not have shelled out the $80 you paid. Sometimes it pays to evaluate the cost of something in terms of how frequently—or *infrequently*—you actually think it will be used.

You are reviewing the operational profile for a package of use cases your project's product manager has been working on with the customer and mentally trying to estimate the effort required to implement each use case. In doing this, it occurs to you that, in general, there is no reason why the cost to implement a use case should go down just because it is infrequently used. A use case that is used once a year can cost just as much to implement as one that is used daily. You decide to try an experiment.

Working with nice round numbers, you do a rough estimate of the staff days to implement each use case; for example, two developers for a month = 40 staff days. Combining these estimates with the operational profile, you build the spreadsheet table of Figure 3.22, which includes a column that calculates the ratio of effort to percentage-point of use for each use case. After some scrutiny of Figures 3.22 and 3.23, which plots a bar chart of this ratio, you decide it's time to talk with the product manager to determine if some of these use cases—for example use case 11—are air bags (used infrequently, but well worth the cost) or Hawaiian shirts (used infrequently and you paid how much?!).

	Use Case	Probability	Est. Effort (Staff Days)	Ratio of Effort to Percentage-point of Use	
3	use case 1	22%	80	3.6	
4	use case 2	22%	100	4.5	
5	use case 3	13%	20	1.5	
6	use case 4	13%	40	3.1	
7	use case 5	11%	10	0.9	
8	use case 6	7%	60	8.6	
9	use case 7	7%	20	2.9	
10	use case 8	2%	20	10.0	
11	use case 9	2%	60	30.0	
12	use case 10	0.5%	20	40.0	
13	use case 11	0.5%	60	120.0	
15	TOTAL	100%			

60 staff days of effort divided by a relative frequency (probability) of .5% = 120 staff days of effort per percentage point of use

=E13/C13/100

Figure 3.22   *Evaluating ratio of effort to percentage point of use. Is use case 11 an "air bag" or "Hawaiian shirt?"*

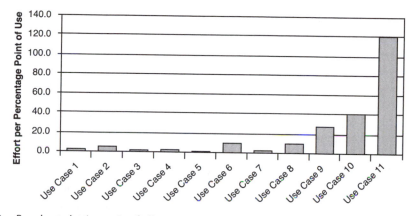

Figure 3.23 *Bar chart plotting ratio of effort to percentage-point of use from Figure 3.22.*

Extending Operational Profiles to Address Critical Use Cases

As noted in the previous section, your car's air bag is one of those items in life you actually hope to never use. If used at all, it's used just once, and you hope it's *reliable*. Air bags are an example of functionality that doesn't fit well into the frequency of use model of reliability: the level of reliability we require from an air bag is not in proportion to its frequency of use.

In the next section, you will see how to extend an operational profile to address critical use cases that, although used infrequently, nevertheless need an appropriate amount of development and test effort and resources dedicated to them to ensure they are reliable.

What Does "Critical" Mean?

Project teams often say things like "That use case is *critical*" or "That's a mission-*critical* use case" or "Do we have a list of *critical* use cases for the next release?". That word—"critical"—has at least two very common meanings. One common meaning of "critical use case" is that the success of a project from a business standpoint is dependent on delivery of that use case. Another meaning of "critical use case" is that severity of use case failure is high. An air bag is a critical feature in a car because the consequence of it failing is high.

Sometimes it's really not clear which—or if maybe both—of these two meanings is intended. Wiegers, in describing scales for prioritizing requirements, uses as an example the scale: *High, Medium,* and *Low,* where *High* is defined as "a mission-critical requirement; required for next release" which can probably be interpreted as being critical in both ways.

Of these two meanings, this section will address "critical" as meaning that the consequence of failure can be severe. But rather than use the word "critical" we'll talk about *severity of failure.* In critical systems—safety-critical, mission-critical, and business-critical—this is a common way to quantify criticality: the higher the severity of failure, the more critical it is.[6]

It's a Calculated Risk

Just as the term "critical" can have different meanings, the term "risk" gets used in a lot of different ways. The type of risk we'll be talking about is quantified and used, for example, in talking about the reliability of safety critical systems. It's also the type of "risk" that the actuarial scientists use in thinking about financial risks: for example, the financial risk an insurance company runs when they issue flood insurance in a given geographical area.

In this type of risk, the *risk of an event* is defined as the *likelihood* that the event will actually happen multiplied by the expected *severity* of the event. Likelihood is expressed in terms of frequency or a probability. If you have an event that is catastrophic in impact, but rarely happens, it could be low risk (dying from shock as a result of winning the lottery for example). This product—likelihood times severity—is called *risk exposure.*

The terms "frequency" and "probability" can be a bit confusing to those of us that are not statisticians. And even the statisticians like to have debates

---

[6] The other type of "critical"—really important from a business perspective—was addressed in Chapter 1, "An Introduction to QFD: Driving Vision Vertically Through the Project," on QFD where critical equates to critical business drivers.

about their meanings and relationship (since about the eighteenth century, in fact). The US Office of Hazardous Materials Safety talks about "frequency" in terms of a measure of the rate at which events occur over time (e.g., "crashes per year") and in the examples we'll see, that's how our likelihood will be expressed. Just be aware that frequency and probability can be, and are, used interchangeably.

So what's all this about "events"…what does that have to do with use cases? Well, each time your customer runs a use case, there is some chance that they will encounter a defect in the product. That's an event. What you'd like to have is a way to quantify the relative risk of such events from use case to use case so you can work smarter, planning to spend time making the riskier use cases more reliable. But before we get to that, let's take an example of calculating the risk of an event.

Hardware Widget Example

A manufacturing plant has a machine with two hardware widgets A and B. When either one fails, production is shut down until they are replaced. Hardware widget A is rated at about 1 failure in 5,000 hours of operation; widget B is more reliable being rated at 1 failure in about 10,000 hours of operation.

Which widget is the bigger *risk* to shutting down production? Your first reaction might well be it's the least reliable of the two, widget A. But, in fact, we can't tell yet because we don't know what the cost of a failure is. Let's say the cost of the widgets themselves is negligible; the bulk of the cost of a failure is in having production shutdown. Widget A can be replaced pretty quickly, and is estimated to affect production by about $6,000. Widget B, on the other hand, requires significantly more time to replace due to its location in the hardware, requiring the manufacturing machine to be partly disassembled. The estimated impact to production when it fails is about four times as long, or about $24,000.

Figure 3.24 illustrates the calculation of the risk of these two widgets failing. The following formula is used to calculate risk exposure:

$$(\text{Failures}/\text{Hours}) \times \text{Cost of Failure} = \text{Risk Exposure}$$

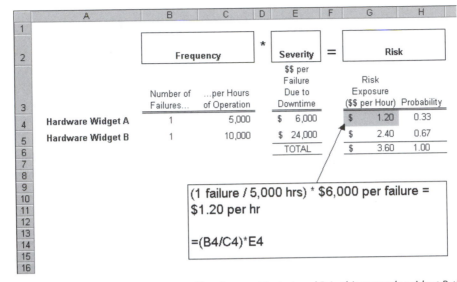

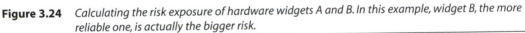

Figure 3.24 *Calculating the risk exposure of hardware widgets A and B. In this example, widget B, the more reliable one, is actually the bigger risk.*

The *risk exposure* in both cases is given in terms of dollars per hour and, as it turns out, *the more reliable component*—hardware widget B—is actually a *bigger risk* than hardware widget A because of the cost of failure. Widget A at one failure in 5,000 hours of operation has a risk exposure of $1.20 per hour compared with a risk exposure of $2.40 per hour for the operation of widget B, based on one failure in 10,000 hours of operation.

Finally, each widget's risk exposure represents some percent of the total risk exposure ($1.2 + $2.4 = $3.60); that percentage is calculated for each widget in the last column of Figure 3.24, labeled *probability*. This is the relative probability of loss from failure that each widget represents.

Profiling Risk in Use Cases

Let's take what we've learned from our hardware widgets and re-apply it to use cases. Using our sales order example of Figure 3.11 and starting with the frequency of use information from its operational profile (see the **Times per Day** column in Figure 3.14), we build an operational profile that takes into account the risk of each use case (see Figure 3.25).

| Frequency | * | Severity | = | Risk |

Use Case	Number of Opportunities for Failure Daily	$$ to Resolve Problem (Order of Magnitude)	Risk Exposure ($$ per Hour)	Probability
Arrange Payment	355	$10	$3,550	0.03
Place National Order	350	$100	$35,000	0.25
Enter Customer Data	340	$100	$34,000	0.24
Order Product	340	$100	$34,000	0.24
Request Catalog	129	$10	$1,290	0.01
Check Order Status	100	$10	$1,000	0.01
Place Local Order	50	$100	$5,000	0.04
Place International Order	25	$1,000	$25,000	0.18
Cancel Order	25	$100	$2,500	0.02
TOTAL	1714	TOTAL	$141,340	1.00

Figure 3.25 *Sales order operational profile extended to cover risk.*

The following sections will walk you through the key points of the operational profile of Figure 3.25, which has been extended to address use case risk.

Frequency of Failure

Recall that in our hardware widget example we specified the frequency of failure in terms of expected failures per hours of operation (e.g., one failure in 10,000 hours of operation) something one would learn, for example, through empirical tests run on batches of widgets. For use cases, we don't have an absolute number like that to work with. We are building a risk profile that can be used very early in the release to help plan activities for development and test. But what we *can* do is talk about the relative frequency of failure from one use case to another.

The first column of Figure 3.25 records the estimated number of times a day that each use case is run; it is the same information as from the operational profile illustrated in Figure 3.14. But rather than saying that use case **Arrange Payment** is run 355 times a day, think of it like this: use case **Arrange Payment** *has 355 opportunities a day to fail.* **Request Catalog** has 129 opportunities a day to fail. So **Arrange Payment** has over twice as many opportunities for failure as **Request Catalog**. In the extreme, a use case that is never run will have no chance to fail.

So while we can't estimate frequency of failure for a use case in absolute terms as we did with the hardware widgets, we can say how many we expect in relation to other use cases, and we do this by simply estimating the times per day we expect each use case to be used. This is essentially the same concept we've seen in the operational profiles previous to this, but restated in such a way as to illustrate how it fits into the overall calculation of risk.

Severity

The severity of a use case failure may be hard to pin down quantitatively. There are three factors that need to be considered. First, there is the matter of the unit of measure for severity. Common units of measure for severity are cost, lost time (e.g., system downtime), and for safety-critical systems, deaths and/or injuries. Given any one of these units of measure—cost, lost time, and so on—you have to also decide what it is that needs to be measured. For example, for cost, is it the cost to repair a failure, the cost of lost revenue due to a failure, or perhaps both? What makes sense for one package of use cases may not make sense for another.

Use caution in arbitrarily adopting a scale of say, 1=low severity, 2=medium severity, 3=high severity. Remember, the resulting profile will be used to allocate time, effort and resources. If you plan on giving one use case three times as much effort as another, make sure that it truly is three times more severe in some absolute sense.

Next, as Musa et al. (1990) point out, the severity of failure depends a lot on whose perspective you choose to measure it from. A defect that is relatively inexpensive to correct from a development standpoint can be catastrophic to a customer, and vice versa.

Finally, there is the issue of actually attributing a number to the severity. Keep in mind that the goal is to get relative values for a profile. So rather than agonizing over whether the severity of the defect represents five versus six hours of down time, consider the suggestion of Musa et al. (1990) to round off severity estimates to the nearest order of magnitude.

Order of magnitude estimates are ones that are given in terms of factors of 10:

$$10^0 = 1$$

$$10^1 = 10$$

$$10^2 = 100$$

$$10^3 = 1000$$

$$10^4 = 10,000$$

and so on

By their nature of separation, it's often easier for a team to categorize things into order of magnitude buckets. For example, what's the *average* life of a person? Rather than getting into debates about the numerous factors that effect people's longevity—health, lifestyle, country, even what century—it's pretty clear that it's on an order of magnitude of 100 years; 10 is way too small and 1000 is way too big.

My inclination is to use orders of magnitude in the same way I use the Pareto Principle, as a heuristic to get a first cut at estimates, and then step back and let gut level intuition tweak things a bit.

Example of Estimating Severity

The third column of Figure 3.25 specifies the severity of failures for each use case of our sales order example. The unit of measure selected is an order of magnitude estimate of dollars to correct problems when discovered. Your reasoning for coming up with estimates of severity for this example might go something like the following.[7]

---

[7] Again, keep in mind that this is an example. The cost to correct a problem may or may not be the right unit of measure for your application.

Use cases, such as **Arrange Payment, Request Catalog**, and **Check Order Status**, can typically be fixed online by a customer representative and are estimated at an order of magnitude of ten dollars to correct. For example, a customer orders a catalog, the system fails to issue request for catalog, and the customer never gets it. The customer phones and complains and the problem is fixed with the re-issue of a catalog.

You decide, however, that use cases that involve the shipment of goods within the country—**Place Local Order** and **Place National Order**—are more on the order of magnitude of one hundred dollars to fix. For example, customer orders widget A, but system issues request for widget B. Customer gets wrong widget and phones to complain. Fixing this involves cost of labor, shipping, and insurance to have wrong widget picked up from customer, shipped back to the warehouse, and re-stocked.

Problems with international orders, you decide, are even more expensive to fix. They incur the same types of costs to fix as local and national orders—only more expensive—plus tariffs going and coming, and so on. You estimate use case **Place International Order** at an order of magnitude of a thousand dollars to fix.

Finally, you note that several of the use cases—**Enter Customer Data** and **Order Product**—are *included* in the generalization use case, **Place Order**, of which the more critical **Place Local, National**, and **International Order** use cases are children. As either of these included use cases could very well play a role in bungling orders, you decide their severity is in line with the place order use cases. Because the predominant use of these included use cases is for local and national orders (400 hundred times daily) versus international orders (25 times daily), you conclude an order of magnitude estimate of their average severity is one hundred dollars.

You reach a similar conclusion about **Cancel Order**, which, while not included in **Place Order**, could, if it failed, result in orders being shipped though actually cancelled. **Cancel Order** is also pegged at average severity on an order of magnitude of one hundred dollars.

Risk Exposure and Probability

The next-to-last column of Figure 3.25 calculates the risk exposure for each use case by taking the frequency of failure, stated in opportunities for failure per day, times severity, stated in dollars per failure. So, risk exposure will be measured in dollars per day. Risk exposure represents the risk in dollars to run a use case for the day. It doesn't mean that is how much money you are necessarily losing; it is the *potential* loss you are exposed to—hence, the term *risk exposure*—from running a use case. It's just a way to compare the risk of one use case to another.

The last column of Figure 3.25 calculates each use case's percent of total risk exposure; in a nutshell, it's the relative probability of loss due to a use case failure. This profile can be used just like the use case package operational profiles we've looked at earlier in the chapter; for example, it can be used for top-down or bottom-up planning. In this case it is based on use case risk rather than just frequency of use.

Plotting the Results

Let's conclude by comparing the operational profile of the sales order example with and without criticality of the use cases being taken into consideration (see Figure 3.26).

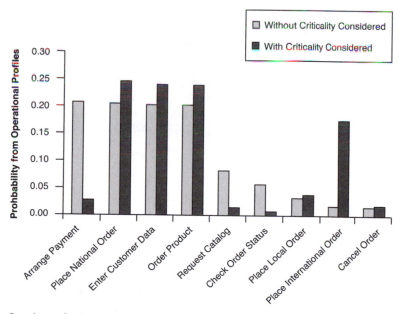

Figure 3.26   *Bar chart of sales order example of Figure 3.11 comparing operational profile of Figure 3.14, without use case criticality, and Figure 3.25, with criticality.*

As Figure 3.26 illustrates, taking criticality of the use cases into consideration in the operational profile can change the lay of the land. Use cases that, while frequently used, are low in criticality, can fall dramatically in relative ranking (e.g., **Arrange Payment**), and use cases that are less frequently used but are critical can rise in ranking (e.g., **Place International Order**).

What Have You Got to Lose?

Adding information about the criticality of use cases to your operational profile will, of course, require more effort. Deciding whether or not it's worth it depends on a number of things.

If your business has elements that are safety-critical, mission-critical, business-critical, and so on, you probably already spend time thinking about how things fail and the cost of failures, so extending the operational profile is probably not that big a jump for you.

On the other hand, even if you deal in critical systems, if the cost of all your failures is astronomical or if the cost of all your failures are on the same order of magnitude, including severity in the profile might not buy you that much; profiling by frequency of use might be all you need.

And, for some businesses, making the connection between things that fail and their associated cost may be hard to establish with much certainty. In the end, it really comes down to asking, "What do I have to lose when a use case fails, can I quantify it and will that help me in planning?"

Chapter Review

In this chapter, we've talked about operational profiles, a quantitative description of frequency of use of use cases and scenario. Let's review:

- Operational profiles allow an engineering team to allocate time, effort, and resources in proportion to the traffic use cases and scenarios are expected to receive. In doing so, the engineering team focuses their efforts on those use cases and scenarios most likely to have defects in operational use by the

customer. The result is a good return on investment in reliability per development and test dollar spent.

- Decision graphs are a common technique for describing operational profiles and are well suited for describing the operational profile of scenarios that make up a use case.

- A simple, straightforward technique for describing the operational profile of a package of use cases is to estimate the number of times each use case is expected to be used in some unit of time, say daily, and then calculate the relative frequency of each. UML generalize, include, and extend use cases can be accommodated in this approach, though include and extend make it a tad more complicated.

- In building an operational profile without empirical results from the field or usability studies, the probabilities you use in your use case decision tree will likely be "guesstimates." The Pareto Principle can often be used to help you get over the "analysis paralysis" of agonizing over probabilities. With an initial guesstimate in place, you can then step back and let your gut instinct help you tweak the numbers.

- Some use cases don't fit well into the frequency of use model of reliability: the level of reliability we require from a use case that controls an air bag is not proportionate to its frequency of use. Use case criticality can be addressed by extending the operational profile to include the risk exposure of each use case: the likelihood of use case failure multiplied by the expected severity.

We have talked about reliability a lot in this chapter, but have not really defined it. In the next chapter, we'll look at a concrete way to talk about reliability allowing us to measure it, set goals in terms of it, and track it in testing.

4

Reliability and Knowing When to Stop Testing

Your product has been in final system test for days; or has it been weeks? Surely it must be time to stop testing and release it? It's the moment of decision, and you realize: *Damned if you do; Damned if you don't.* Release it too early, and you incur the wrath of customers inflicted with a buggy product and the high cost of fixing and testing defects released to production. Hold the product in testing, and you incur the wrath of marketing as they remind you of the revenue that is being lost on top of the cost of too much testing. There is a sweet spot in testing, a point that strikes that perfect balance between releasing the product too early and releasing the product too late.[1] But how do you know you are close to that sweet spot?

The second idea Software Reliability Engineering (SRE) brings to use case development is a quantitative way to talk about reliability, providing a sound basis for determining when a product's reliability goal has been reached, testing can terminate, and the product can be released.

---

[1] Although examples from this chapter are couched in terms of final system test, in the Unified Software Development Process the question of whether to stop or continue testing for and fixing defects is one that is pertinent throughout the construction and transition phase during: Testing of increments of the system at the end of each iteration to determine if moving to the next iteration is warranted; final system test at the end of the construction phase to determine if a product is reliable enough for beta test; beta test during transition phase to determine if the system is ready for full commercial release.

In this chapter, we'll do the following:

- Talk about reliability, how to define it, measure it, set goals in terms of it, and track it in the testing of use case-driven development projects.

- Look at a spreadsheet-based dashboard that lets you track three key factors in knowing whether it's time to stop testing and release a product: failure intensity, open defects, and test coverage as per the operational profile. This dashboard provides at-a-glance monitoring of reliability growth across a large package of use cases.

- Learn how to measure the effectiveness of a use case-driven development process in terms of defect detection and removal, touted by some as the *single* most important metric for improving the capability of a process to produce quality products. And we'll look at how to use this measure to determine if your reliability goals can be raised or lowered for future releases.

Let's begin by defining what we mean by reliability.

What Is "Reliability"?

Use case-driven development and SRE are a natural match, both being usage-driven styles of product development. What SRE brings to the party is a discipline for focusing time, effort, and resources on use cases in proportion to their estimated frequency of use, or criticality, to maximize reliability while minimizing development costs. But what *is* reliability? We spent a lot of time in the last chapter talking about the operational profile as a tool to work smart to achieve reliability, but we have never actually said what reliability is. Software reliability is defined as:

> *The probability of failure-free operation for a specified length of time in a specified environment.*

Though short, this definition has a lot packed into it that doesn't necessarily jump out at you on first read. There are two main themes of which to take notice.

Software Reliability is User-Centric and Dynamic

First, software reliability is defined from the perspective of a user using a system in operation. It is a user-centric, *dynamic* definition of reliability, as opposed to, say, faults per lines of code, which is a developer-centric, static measure.

Consider the phrase "specified environment." This includes the hardware, its configuration, and the user profile (e.g., whether the user is an expert user, novice, and so on). User profile is important because a system designed for use by an expert could well be unreliable in the hands of a novice. The whole "specified environment" idea is only pertinent because you are qualifying expectations of reliability in terms of a system being operated by a user.

How about the phrase "failure-free" operation; what does that imply? A *failure* occurs when a system in operation encounters a defect or fault, causing incorrect results or behavior. A defect or fault is a static concept—it's just there, in the code—but a failure is something that can only happen when the system is in operation. So again, this is a dynamic concept implying a system in operation.

A dynamic, user-centric definition of reliability is more than an academic issue. This part of the definition is at the heart of SRE's ability to deliver high reliability per development and test dollar spent. A use case with lots of defects or faults in its underlying code can seem reliable if the user spends so little time running it that none of the many bugs are found. Conversely, a use case that has few defects or faults in its underlying code can seem unreliable if the user spends so much time running it that they find all those few bugs in operation. This is the concept of *perceived* reliability; it is the reliability the user experiences as opposed to a reliability measure in terms of, say, defect density.

Software Reliability Is Quantifiable

The second key theme in the definition of reliability is that it is quantifiable; the key phrase here is "...*probability of failure-free operation for a specified length of time* ..."

In the last chapter, we saw an example of calculating the risk exposure that two hypothetical hardware widgets posed to a manufacturing machine of which they were a part: when either failed, production was shut down until it was replaced. As part of the calculation of risk, we said that one widget was of a type expected to fail once in 5,000 hours of operation and the other once in 10,000 hours of operation. These were statements about the expected *failure intensity* of the widgets. Failure intensity is the number of failures per some unit time and is probably the most common method of specifying and tracking software reliability.

But technically speaking, to answer the question: "What is the probability of failure-free operation *for a specified length of time*?" we need the formula shown in Equation 4.1 (typically given with Greek letters, which unfortunately makes it "look" more complicated than it actually is) called the *exponential failure law*:

$$R(\tau) = e^{-\lambda\tau}$$

Equation 4.1   *Reliability is the probability of failure-free operation for a specified length of time, which is given by this formula, called the exponential failure law.*

Don't worry about committing this formula to memory: You'll see how to use it as part of a simple spreadsheet formula later in the chapter.

Equation 4.1 reads like: $R(\tau)$ is the probability that a system will run for specified time, τ, given a constant failure intensity of λ, where **e** is the base of the natural logarithm (**e** = 2.7182818284...).

Constant failure rate just means that you aren't fixing bugs or adding new features, both of which would affect the failure rate. A constant failure rate is basically what you have once a system is released for commercial use: the failure rate isn't going to get better or worse; it's constant because you are done working on the system. It is, therefore, a good indicator of what life with the system will be like for your customer.[2]

What does this equation really mean? Well, it is capturing an intuitive aspect of reliability that failure intensity alone doesn't describe. When you read that a hardware widget is expected to fail once in 5,000 hours of operation—that's the failure intensity—a question that may well pop into your mind is "Right, but doesn't the likelihood of failure increase the closer to 5,000 hours of operation you get?" And the answer is yes, and *that* is exactly what the exponential failure law of Equation 4.1 is describing.

Equation 4.2 provides an alternate way to re-write this equation that will help us see this; we simply re-write the equation without a negative exponent:

$$R(\tau) = 1 \: / \: e^{\lambda \tau}$$

Equation 4.2   *Alternate version of Equation 4.1 without a negative exponent.*

Now let's reconsider that question: Given a widget is expected to fail once in 5,000 hours (that's the failure intensity, i.e., $\lambda=1/5000$) isn't it more likely to fail later (say where $\tau = 5000$) than sooner (say where $\tau = 1$)? Looking at Equation 4.2, we see that τ is in the denominator, so the bigger τ is, the smaller the probability $R(\tau)$ that the widget will actually run that long. The smaller τ is, the bigger the probability it will be able to run that long.

So, technically speaking, Equation 4.1 is the "official" definition of reliability per se, as it is what is needed to calculate the probability of failure-free operation for a specified length of time. But the main component of Equation 4.1 is failure intensity, and failure intensity is the bit that is most commonly used in setting and tracking software reliability goals.

---

[2] If you add functionality or fix bugs once a system is released, it is, technically speaking, a new version of the system with a new failure rate.

Reliability: Software Versus Hardware

Finally, if it's not already obvious, it's important to point out there are distinctions between hardware reliability and software reliability. When we talk about hardware widgets with expected lives of 5,000 or 10,000 hours, the source of failure is assumed to be from some part of the widget wearing out from physical use. But software does not wear out per se, leading some to question whether or not it makes sense to apply statistical models, such as the exponential failure law that originated with hardware reliability, to software (Davis 1993).

But the software reliability engineering community counters that though the *source* of failures is different for software—it doesn't wear out—statistical models are nevertheless valid for describing what we *experience* with software: the longer you run software, the higher the probability you'll eventually use it in an untested manner and find a latent defect that results in a failure.

Resolution of these (sometimes theoretical) views notwithstanding, the discipline of software reliability engineering has plenty of ideas I think you will find have practical application to use case development: a user-centric, dynamic, and quantifiable view of reliability. In the next section, you will get a closer look at what is virtually the heart of this view of reliability—failure intensity—and learn how to apply it to your projects.

Failure Intensity

Having a quantifiable definition of reliability, such as *failure intensity*, is the key to being able to measure and track reliability during testing as a means of helping decide if you have reached that sweet spot in testing—not too early, not too late—when it is time to release your product. In this section, you will learn:

- How to "visualize" failure intensity with what is called a *reliability growth curve*.

- About units of measure for failure intensity and what makes sense for your projects.

- How reliability goals are set in terms of failure intensity, called a *failure intensity objective.*

- Ways of determining the right failure intensity objective for your projects.

Visualizing Failure Intensity with a Reliability Growth Curve

A good way to visualize how failure intensity works as a decision aid for when to stop testing is to look at a run chart of failure intensity through time. Figure 4.1 shows a run chart of failure intensity for a large product over a period of about three months from the start of system test to end, at which time the product was released.

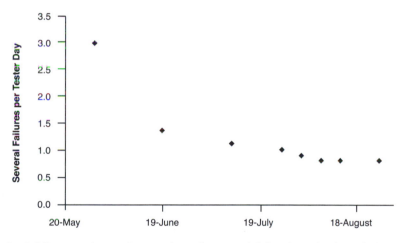

Figure 4.1 *A reliability growth curve is a run chart of a system's failure intensity through time.*

Each point on the run chart in Figure 4.1 calculates the failure intensity to that point in testing (date of measure is provided on X-axis). Failure intensity (Y-axis) is calculated as the number of failures of a *specified severity per unit of time*; in Figure 4.1, it is severe defects per tester day.[3] Sticking with

---

[3] Tester days is a measure of testing effort, like staff days, not calendar time. For example, two testers working for three days = six tester days.

failures of a specified severity is important. As testing proceeds, it is quite possible that the total number of "failures" doesn't necessarily drop significantly; rather, it's the mix of severity types that is changing. Early in testing, the mix will contain a high percentage of severe failures. Toward the end of testing, the percent of severe failures will drop (hopefully) but the number of minor failures reported could very well increase such that the total count is constant.

Run charts of failure intensity, such as that of Figure 4.1, are commonly called *reliability growth curves*. One objection I sometimes get when I show a team a reliability growth curve like that of Figure 4.1, say in a project postmortem, is that it seems counterintuitive for the trend line to go down as an indicator that reliability is increasing. A related measure of reliability that is often used in hardware, Mean Time To Failure (MTTF), is the inverse of failure intensity:

$$MTTF = 1 \text{ / Failure Intensity}$$

$$\text{And Failure Intensity} = 1 \text{ / } MTTF$$

If you would prefer to see a graph trend line that goes up, try plotting MTTF.[4]

Selecting a Unit of Measure for Failure Intensity

Failure intensity is a measure of failures per unit of time. What you use for a unit of time depends on what makes sense for your product and what you can measure in a practical way. Musa et al. (1990) identifies *execution time*—the amount of time the CPU is actually executing instructions—as the preferred unit of measure for best results, but practically speaking, this is difficult for the vast majority of testing organizations to measure. For some applications, it might even make sense to use a non-time-based measure, for example, failures per number of transactions.

---

[4] Another measure used in reliability is Mean Time Between Failure (MTBF). It is defined as MTBF = MTTF + MTTR, where MTTF is mean time to failure and MTTR is the mean time to repair a system once it has failed. The two terms are sometimes used interchangeably where repair time is negligible or not relevant.

For many testing groups, the easiest thing to measure failures against is testing effort because that is something they are already accustomed to tracking for budget accounting. So, for example, three testers running separate testing efforts for a day would be three tester days of effort. Some care, of course, needs to be taken to account for the actual amount of time spent *testing* as opposed to attending staff meetings, setting up of hardware, and so on. As previously noted, the run chart of Figure 4.1 was created using failure intensity based on testing effort (i.e., tester days).

Setting a Failure Intensity Objective

Having a quantifiable definition of reliability, such as failure intensity, allows us to not only measure and track reliability during testing but also set quality goals in terms of that definition. This is done by setting a *failure intensity objective*. In Figure 4.2, the dotted line illustrates a failure intensity objective of one severe defect per tester day as the project's goal for reliability. In this case, the team's goal was to get under this threshold, and the product actually released with a failure intensity of about .80 severe defects per tester day.

Remember, tester day is a measure of work, not elapsed time. Some testing groups prefer to work in terms of tester hours, which has the advantage of not being ambiguous as to how many hours a tester day represents.

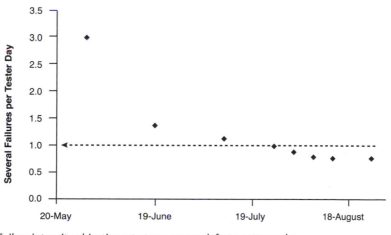

Figure 4.2 *Failure intensity objective set at one severe defect per tester day.*

The reliability growth curve is not always as clean as that shown in Figure 4.2. More often than not, in the messy world of real life development and testing, you will find curves that look more like that of Figure 4.3, where reliability actually gets worse at points (humps in the curve) and seems to stubbornly refuse to converge on your stated failure intensity objective as the scheduled release date looms near. The product whose reliability growth curve is shown in Figure 4.3 was released with failure intensity just under 2.5 severe defects per tester day (failure intensity objective was 1.0 as indicated by arrow), i.e., schedule pressure forced release of the product before the reliability goal was met.

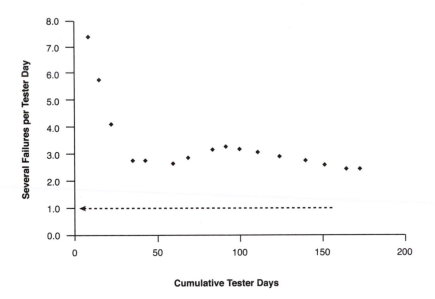

Figure 4.3   *Reliability growth curves are not always neat "curves" converging on your failure intensity objective.*

Figure 4.3 also illustrates the plotting of failure intensity where cumulative time (here tester days) is used for the X-axis rather than calendar time on the X-axis as in Figure 4.2. Which you use is a matter of taste. I like to see calendar time on the X-axis because the spacing between points can sometimes tell a story of their own (e.g., when IT decides to upgrade build servers in the middle of the project shutting down development and testing for two weeks. This will show up on the run chart as a glaring gap between points, a reminder to never let them do that again). The danger of using calendar time on the X-axis is that it can confuse you into thinking failure intensity is in terms of calendar time.

But What's the *Right* Failure Intensity Objective?

In Figure 4.2, we saw an example of a project where the failure intensity objective was set for one severe defect per staff-day of testing, as illustrated by the dotted line. But how do you know what is the right failure rate to use as your objective? There are of course lots of factors that play into this.

For example, who are your customers, and what do they want in terms of reliability? Depending on where your product is in the technology adoption life cycle (Moore 1991) your customer's tolerance for unreliable products—or lack thereof—will change. New products often have customers that are innovators and early adopters and may be more concerned with early availability and new features than having to work around an occasional crash or two. On the other hand, mature products often have customers that demand rock-solid reliability.

In the following sections, we'll look at three ideas for helping you set failure intensity objectives. We'll look at a couple of high-tech approaches for identifying failure intensity objectives for individual use cases and will then conclude with a low-tech approach for setting a failure intensity objective for a whole component or whole product; it may be a good 20/80 approach for you to use delivering 80% of the benefit for 20% of the effort.

Setting Failure Intensity Objectives Based on Severity of Failures

A way to set failure intensity objectives for each individual use case—or all use cases associated with a given component—is to derive them based on an analysis of severity of failures. In this approach, we start with what is bearable in terms of failures—say, cost—then work backwards to determine the corresponding failure intensity.

In the previous chapter, we looked at profiling a package of use cases where the risk exposure of each use case was taken into account. Figure 3.25 illustrated the calculation of the risk exposure for each use case of the sales order component by taking the frequency of failure, stated in opportunities for failure per day, times severity, stated in dollars to resolve per failure. Risk exposure was measured in dollars per day and represents the risk in dollars to run a use case for the day; we calculated risk exposure for the entire use case package at \$141,340 daily. Remember, that doesn't mean that is how much money you are necessarily losing each day; it is the *potential* loss you are exposed to from running the package of use cases. It's the loss you would incur daily if every use case run resulted in a severe failure.

We know that we can't afford to lose \$141,340 a day due to failures in our sales order system; in terms of failure intensity objectives, that just means that a severe failure on 100% of use case runs is not acceptable. But what amount of money *are* we willing to lose to run our sales order system? Musa et al. (1990) provide examples of calculating the financial cost of a given failure intensity objective, but the calculation can also be done the other way (i.e., starting with what is financially a bearable cost for support of failures and then working backwards to determine the corresponding failure intensity).

While this is a difficult way for us to think about our products (no one likes to admit their system is imperfect) it is the approach you need to take in order to set failure intensity objectives based on the severity of failures. Unrealistic answers (e.g., "How about a penny a day?") will result in reliability goals that you will pay for dearly trying to achieve in terms of development and testing.

To keep it simple, let's say that you are willing to lose \$1,000 daily in support of failures in our sales order system. That figure—\$1,000 a day—is about seven tenths of a percent (**.7%**) of the total risk exposure of \$141,340. Translated into failure intensity, it means that you are willing to live with seven tenths of a percent of the use case runs resulting in a severe failure. With this, you are now able to construct the spreadsheet table shown in Figure 4.4; the information on opportunities for failure a day and cost to resolve each failure comes from the profile in Figure 3.25.

Column F—**Failure Intensity Objective**—simply calculates the upper bound on the number of times a day we are willing to have each use case fail in a severe way. Column J—**\$\$ to Resolve (per Day)**—calculates the subsequent daily cost of fixing those failures, with a bottom-line total of \$1,000 daily for the package of use cases.

So, to summarize, in this approach we start with what is financially a bearable cost for support of failures, then work backwards to determine the corresponding failure intensity.

	Use Case		Number of Oppportunities for Failure Daily		Failure Intensity Objective (Failures per Day)		$$ to Resolve (per Failure)		$$ to Resolve (per Day)	
3	Place Nat'l Order		350	x .7% =	2.5		$ 100		$ 248	
4	Enter Customer Data		340	x .7% =	2.4		$ 100		$ 241	
5	Order Product		340	x .7% =	2.4		$ 100		$ 241	
6	Place Int'l Order		25	x .7% =	0.2		$ 1,000		$ 177	
7	Place Local Order		50	x .7% =	0.4		$ 100		$ 35	
8	Arrange Payment		355	x .7% =	2.5		$ 10		$ 25	
9	Cancel Order		25	x .7% =	0.2		$ 100		$ 18	
10	Request Catalog		129	x .7% =	0.9		$ 10		$ 9	
11	Check Order Status		100	x .7% =	0.7		$ 10		$ 7	
13	TOTAL		1714				TOTAL		$ 1,000.00	

Figure 4.4   *Spreadsheet to calculate failure intensity objectives per use case based on failure severity.*

Setting Failure Intensity Objective Using the Exponential Failure Law

Failure intensity and its inverse Mean Time To Failure (MTTF) are measures of the *average* behavior of systems. When we say a widget is expected to fail once in 3 years (i.e., has a MTTF of 3 years) what we are really saying is that widgets of that *type* on average will last for 3 years; some more, some less. The name itself tells us that: *Mean* Time To Failure (i.e., the average time to failure).

Sometimes, statements about average behavior are not good enough and we need to say something stronger about our requirements for reliability. Let's take an example from the world of product warranties. Let's say you manufacture and sell widgets that come with a three-year warranty. You have done an analysis of what it costs to do warranty repairs on failed widgets and have determined that you need to have 75 percent of the widgets outlive the three-year warranty; otherwise, repair costs of failed widgets still under warranty start eating into profits. What MTTF do your widgets need to have to ensure that 75 percent will run longer than the three-year warranty?

For this type of problem, you need to return to the exponential failure law (refer to Equation 4.1) and rewrite the equation so that you can solve for the failure intensity λ (see Equation 4.3).

$$\lambda = \ln (1 / R(\tau)) / \tau$$

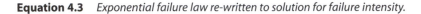

Equation 4.3   *Exponential failure law re-written to solution for failure intensity.*

Interpreting Equation 4.3 in terms of our widget warranty problem, it reads: The failure intensity, λ, of our widgets needs to equal the natural logarithm (**"ln"**) of one over the desired percent of widgets we need to have survive the warranty, **$R(\tau)$**, divided by the length of time of the warranty, **τ.**

You probably aren't going to want to have to remember that formula or calculate it by hand; that's why we have spreadsheets! The spreadsheet in Figure 4.5 shows how to implement Equation 4.3 and computes the target failure intensity and corresponding inverse MTTF for widgets designed such that 75% will outlive a three-year warranty.

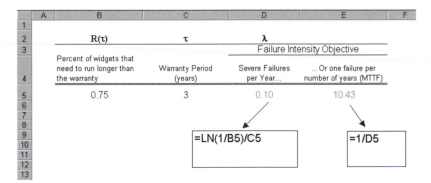

Figure 4.5   *Calculating failure intensity objective for widgets with a three-year warranty based on the need to have 75 percent survive the warranty period. "LN" is the natural logarithm function in Excel.*

What the spreadsheet in Figure 4.5 is telling us is that for a type of widget to reliably (75% of the time) outlast its warranty of three years, it has to be designed with a failure intensity of one failure in 10 years, i.e., a MTTF of 10 years. You can see what is going on here: Because failure intensity and MTTF are *averages*, the exponential failure law tells us we have to boost the "ruggedness" of the widgets such that their average behavior returns our required above-average result of 75% reliability. Simply put, it takes a widget designed for an average life of 10 years to be 75% reliable for three years.

The same principle works with use cases. By their nature, use cases take time to run. Some span seconds, some minutes, and some hours or longer, their duration a function of granularity, but more so of the application domain. In the development of systems to help geologists and geophysicists find oil and gas reservoirs, it is not uncommon to have a use case in which a single step corresponds to behind the scenes processing (which the user does not see) of large amounts of seismic data, or the simulation of the movement of fluids in a reservoir deep in the earth, both quite often measured in hours.

Let's take the widget warranty example and reapply it to use cases. Imagine a use case called Log Call that is part of a police station's 911 PBX system. A typical police station that buys such a system usually runs from 1 to 10 terminals each staffed with an operator. When a call comes in, the operator records the details of the call: name, location, nature of emergency, and so on. Based on analysis of peak call volumes, the reliability goal for the Log Call use case is that at least 80 percent of the deployed PBX terminals should be able to take a 30-minute call without failure. If a failure occurs on a given terminal while running the Log Call use case, the operator can then transfer the call to another terminal (another use case) with minimal wait time resulting for the caller. What then is the failure intensity objective you should use in developing and testing the Log Call use case? The spreadsheet in Figure 4.6 shows the calculation.

	A	B	C	D	E	F
1						
2		$R(\tau)$	τ	λ		
3				Failure Intensity Objective		
4		Percent of PBX terminals on which the use case needs to run to completion without failure	Use Case Runtime (Hours)	Severe Failures per Hour...	...Or one failure per number of hours (MTTF)	
5		0.80	0.5	0.45	2.24	
6						
7				=LN(1/B5)/C5	=1/D5	
8						
9						

Figure 4.6 *Calculating the failure intensity objective for the PBX's Log Call use case.*

The spreadsheet in Figure 4.6 tells you that during development of the Log Call use case you will need to continue testing and fixing defects that result in severe failures until the observed failure rate is at or less than one severe failure per 2.24 hours of use case run time, or .45 severe failures per hour.

One advantage to this approach is that the MTTF number it calculates holds some useful information about how many tests and the test time a use case may require to demonstrate the reliability goal has been met. Assume for a moment that the implemented Log Call use case was defect free; hence, failure free. How many tests would it take to simply demonstrate that Log Call was capable of running 2.24 hours without a failure? You'd need enough tests to stretch out the runtime to 2.24 hours (running one test over and over doesn't count). So looking at the MTTF from a testing standpoint, it provides a minimum amount of time you need to test the use case if you really want to demonstrate the use case's reliability is at the 80% level.

But this also points out a key limitation of testing as a way to demonstrate reliability. Storey (1996) points out in his discussion of reliability assessment that some systems in the safety-critical arena have reliability goals so high (e.g., one failure in 100,000 years) that the use of testing to demonstrate reliability is for practical purposes impossible.

Low-Tech Approach

Many, if not most, software development organizations may not be ready to try to set Failure Intensity Objectives in terms of analysis of severity of failures or by use of the exponential failure law. Here's a simple low-tech approach you might find useful for setting failure intensity objectives for whole components or even whole products; it may be a good 80/20 solution providing a lot of bang for the buck.

Think back to a project that you and your team remember as being successful and that you believe was well received by the customer in terms of reliability. Do a little project archaeology and find out the total number of defects of a specified severity that were found during system test. Divide that number by the amount of time that was expended during testing to find those defects. Use execution time, staff time running tests, or even DB transactions or orders processed; whatever unit of measure works best for your failure intensity. That should give you a ballpark candidate failure intensity objective.

Here's an example. Figure 4.7 shows a spreadsheet constructed from the defect tracking database and test reports of a project as part of its project postmortem. For this project, the cumulative number of severe defects found was 582, with 375 staff days expended on testing, for an overall failure intensity of 582 / 375 = 1.55 severe defects per tester day.

	A	B	C	D	E	F	G	H
1								
2		Test Iteration	From	To	Staff Days of Testing (current iteration)	Staff Days of Testing (cumulative)	Severe Defects (cumulative)	Failure Intensity (cumulative)
3		1	30-Oct	30-Jan	29	29	187	6.56
4		2	31-Jan	7-Mar	90	118	296	2.51
5		3	8-Mar	1-Apr	65	183	370	2.02
6		4	2-Apr	6-May	55	238	458	1.93
7		5	7-May	17-May	22	259	488	1.88
8		6	17-May	6-Jun	57	316	537	1.70
9		7	7-Jun	14-Jun	25	340	564	1.66
10		8	17-Jun	18-Jun	8	348	566	1.63
11		9	18-Jun	24-Jun	27	375	582	1.55
12		Release Party!						
13							=G11/F11	
14								
15								

Figure 4.7 *Spreadsheet calculating failure intensity for project as a whole based on information from defect tracking tool and testing reports. This product released with a cumulative failure intensity of 1.55 severe failures per tester day.*

Besides being simple, this approach has another benefit. One complication that most testing organizations are likely to face is the correlation between testing and customer use (i.e., how does some unit of time spent in testing relate to the same unit of time in the field). Chances are, your product testing is *not* going to be directly equivalent to the use the product will experience in the field; it will either be more rigorous (hopefully) or less rigorous, but probably not exactly the same. In either case—more rigorous or less— there will be a question of how failure intensities in test compare to those that users will experience. This approach of working from some past successful project has the benefit of giving you a failure intensity objective that already correlates well with the use of a happy customer.

In the final analysis, arriving at a failure intensity objective that is right for your line of business, your products, and your customers may involve some trial and error. At the end of this chapter we'll look at a metric to help measure the success of a testing process' defect removal. By tracking failure intensities during testing, followed by analysis of defect removal metrics after release, you should be able to determine whether you can raise, or need to lower, failure intensity objectives. We'll actually revisit the release of Figure 4.7 and determine whether or not a failure intensity of 1.55 severe defects per tester day was indicative of a good release.

The Swamp Report

Deciding it's time to stop testing is one of those things that is easier to get wrong than right. There are ample opportunities to either stop too early or test too long. Finding that sweet spot in final system test that strikes that perfect balance between releasing the product too early and releasing the product too late is by comparison much more difficult.

Having a quantifiable definition of reliability, such as failure intensity, is the key to measuring and tracking reliability during testing as a means of helping decide when to stop testing. There are, however, two other factors that need to be tracked, in conjunction with failure intensity, that play into the decision of when to stop testing. The first is the number of known, open defects. An assumption of software reliability engineering is that known, open (unresolved) defects are fixed at the end of each iteration of testing, and a new version of the software is used for the next testing iteration. In my experience, fixing all known defects before proceeding to the next iteration of test is not a practice that one can always count on. Of the severe defects that will eventually get fixed before release, some portion typically goes unresolved for several iterations of testing, how many actually get fixed being a function of their number and difficulty to resolve. So the capability to measure and track the number of open, unresolved defects becomes a key to making the decision to stop testing.

A second key assumption of software reliability engineering is that testing is being carried out as per the operational profile. For example, if we are testing to the risk profile of Figure 3.25, we would expect **Place National Order** use case to receive 25% of the budgeted test effort and 1% to be for the **Request Catalog** use case. Tracking to see that you are actually meeting this planned test coverage is part of the decision making that goes into knowing when it's time to stop testing.

In this section, we look at a spreadsheet-based dashboard that lets you track these three key factors—failure intensity, open defects, and test coverage as per the operational profile—for a large package of use cases. I have used variations of this dashboard for years as a tool for helping project teams and cross-company, multi-project program teams decide when to release a product. This dashboard was created to provide at-a-glance monitoring of reliability growth across a large number of "pieces" that form a whole (use cases of a component, components of a product, whole products that are part of a program), where the pieces all need to be reliable for the whole to ship. I call this dashboard the "Swamp Report" after the analogy of draining a swamp that is sometimes used to describe the test and fix activities of system test leading up to product release.

Dashboard Layout

Before looking at how to use and read the dashboard, let's review the various parts that make it up. All examples will be given in terms of hours as the unit of measure: planned hours of test as per the operational profile, actual hours of test, and failures per hour.

The dashboard is based on a bar chart with use cases across the bottom. Each use case has a horizontal bar showing the number of staff hours of testing planned for the iteration as spelled out by the operational profile. Each use case also has a vertical bar showing the actual hours expended during the iteration. If actual expenditure of test hours equals plan, the vertical bar touches the horizontal bar (see Figure 4.8).

Both the horizontal and vertical bar use the left-hand scale of the dashboard marked **Hours of Test** (also marked with **# of Must Fix Defects;** we'll get to this soon).

Each use case also has a vertical bar that indicates the failure intensity that was experienced during the test iteration, and a line that indicates the target failure intensity objective (see Figure 4.9). When the vertical bar drops to or below the line, that use case has reached its failure intensity objective. These two indicators share the right-hand scale marked **FI** (Failure Intensity) and **FIO** (Failure Intensity Objective). Each use case can have a different failure intensity objective; however, in Figure 4.9, all use cases are shown with the same failure intensity objective, resulting in a straight, horizontal line spanning the dashboard.

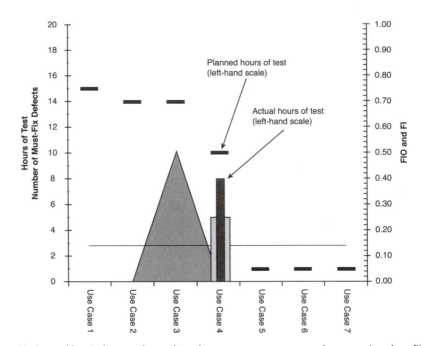

Figure 4.8   *Horizontal bar indicates planned test hours per use case as per the operational profile. Vertical bar shows actual expenditure. Both use left-hand scale.*

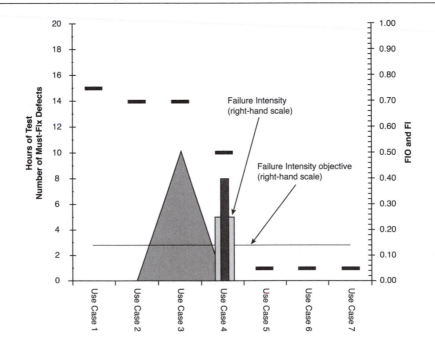

Figure 4.9   *Horizontal line indicates target failure intensity objective. Vertical bar shows actual failure intensity experienced during test iteration. Both use right-hand scale.*

Finally, the dashboard uses an area graph (looks like mountains) to show the number of defects that remain to be fixed before the product can be released; this is "The Swamp," and it looks good color-coded in algae green for effect! The number of defects to be fixed is tracked on the left-hand scale (Figure 4.10).

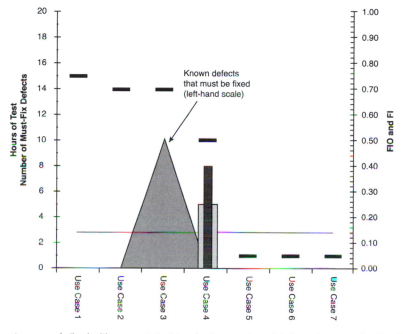

Figure 4.10 *Area graph (looks like mountains) tracks the number of defects that must be fixed before release (uses left-hand scale).*

Now that we've reviewed the parts that make up the dashboard, let's move on to how to actually use and read the dashboard in helping you make the critical decision: *Is it time to stop testing?*

Establish Planned Test Coverage as per Operational Profile

Let's say that the sales order component of Figure 3.11 has finally been completed and is ready to undergo testing as part of system test. Testing of the sales order component will consist of a series of test iterations where two testers will spend about 30 hours each during a week testing the sales order component. After each iteration, development will have several days to fix defects, then rebuild and deliver a new version for the next iteration of testing.

Using the operational profile of Figure 3.25, which includes use case criticality, you build the following spreadsheet shown in Figure 4.11 to allocate each test iteration's 60 staff hours of testing (two testers at 30 hours each) across the nine use cases of the sales order component.

Use Case	Probability (Based on Risk)	Staff Hours per Test Iteration
Place National Order	0.25	15
Enter Customer Data	0.24	14
Order Product	0.24	14
Place International Order	0.18	10
Place Local Order	0.04	2
Arrange Payment	0.03	2
Cancel Order	0.02	1
Request Catalog	0.01	1
Check Order Status	0.01	1
TOTAL	1.00	60

60 staff hours x a probability of .25 = 15 staff hours

Figure 4.11 *Allocation of each test iteration's 60 staff hours of testing across the nine use cases of the sales order component as per the operational profile.*

Initialize Dashboard Before Each Test Iteration

The dashboard is driven from a simple spreadsheet that is initialized before each test iteration and then updated at the end of each test iteration (see Figure 4.12).

For tracking projects with multiple component teams or cross-company multi-project programs, you can implement this as a database to allow concurrent updates from multiple test teams.

Use Case	Planned Hours of Test	Failure Intensity Objective	# Must Fix Defects (cumulative)	Actual Hours of Test (per iteration)	Failures (per iteration)	Failure Intensity
Place Nat'l Order	15	0.15	0			
Enter Customer Data	14	0.15	2			
Order Product	14	0.15	0			
Place Int'l Order	10	0.15	1			
Place Local Order	2	0.15	0			
Arrange Payment	2	0.15	0			
Cancel Order	1	0.15	3			
Request Catalog	1	0.15	0			
Check Order Status	1	0.15	0			

Figure 4.12   *Dashboard spreadsheet table typical of just prior to each test iteration.*

Each row of the spreadsheet in Figure 4.12 is a use case. You start by initializing the spreadsheet portion of the dashboard with the planned staff hours of testing for the iteration, plus the failure intensity objective per use case; see Figure 4.12, columns **Planned Hours of Test** and **Failure Intensity Objective**. For a failure intensity objective, you decide to keep things simple and use a single failure intensity objective for all use cases (i.e., a single failure intensity objective for the sales order component as a whole).[5] From an analysis of a past release similar to that illustrated in Figure 4.7 you arrive at a failure intensity objective of 1.50 severe defects per staff day of testing. But instead of failures per day, you will be working in failures per hour; your sales order department is open ten hours a day, so you divide by ten to arrive at .15 severe defects per hour. Unless there are changes in plan, these two columns will remain unchanged for the duration of testing.

It is quite likely that at the beginning of system testing there are known defects that you know must be fixed before product release but have not yet been fixed. This number is recorded per use case in column **# Must Fix Defects.** This column is cumulative (i.e., it is not cleared at the start of a test

---

[5] Individual failure intensity objectives for each use case could have been set using the results of Figure 4.4.

iteration) but rather reflects the accumulation of defects that must be resolved before product ship. This is *The Swamp!* Until it is drained, the product cannot release. There are two points about this column worth emphasizing:

1. It is common for a product to have a backlog of known defects of varying severity that never get resolved. This column should reflect *just* those defects that are preventing shipment of the product for *this release*.

2. While failure intensity is measured in terms of a *specific* severity level—say, "high"—column **# Must Fix Defects** tracks *all* defects that need to get resolved before release, regardless of severity. When a defect is fixed—regardless of its severity—there is a risk that it will break something else, and/or reveal a new defect that it had previously "hidden." You need to have a count of the fixes that are yet to be made to the product, regardless of the severity of the defects they are resolving.

The next two columns in Figure 4.12, **Actual Hours of Test** and **Failures,** will be filled in at the end of each test iteration. The last column, **Failure Intensity**, is a calculated field for each use case and equals **Failures** divided by **Actual Hours of Test**.

At the start of the first test iteration, and the start of all subsequent test iterations, the dashboard will look something like Figure 4.13, which reflects the settings of the spreadsheet in Figure 4.12.

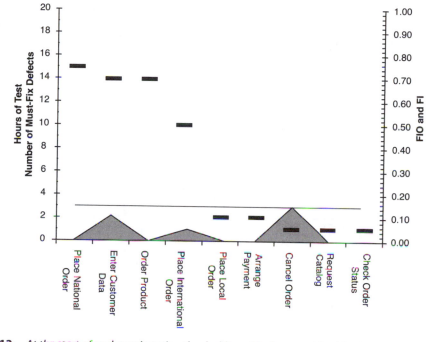

Figure 4.13 *At the start of each test iteration the dashboard looks something like this.*

Update the Dashboard at the End of Each Test Iteration

At the end of each test iteration, the spreadsheet portion of the dashboard is updated to reflect the vital stats of testing. Let's look at some common configurations you are likely to find the dashboard in at the end of a test iteration.

Early Iterations: Low Test Coverage, High Failure Intensity and Open Defects

Figures 4.14 through 4.17 show the dashboard in a state typical of the end of an early test iteration where defects are so prevalent that the testing team is unable to actually expend the total planned amount of test time running tests due to delays from having to re-start failed runs, logging defects in the defect tracking tool, and the inability to run some features of the product.

This is indicated in Figure 4.15 in that the bars showing actual expended test hours do not reach up and touch the target horizontal bars showing planned expenditure via the operational profile. Indeed, some use cases received no testing at all.

	A	B	C	D	E	F	G	H
	Use Case	Planned Hours of Test	Failure Intensity Objective	# Must Fix Defects (cumulative)	Actual Hours of Test (per iteration)	Failures (per iteration)	Failure Intensity
3	Place Nat'l Order	15	0.15	12	10	12	1.20
4	Enter Customer Data	14	0.15	12	9	10	1.11
5	Order Product	14	0.15	7	10	7	0.70
6	Place Int'l Order	10	0.15	9	5	8	1.60
7	Place Local Order	2	0.15	2	1	2	2.00
8	Arrange Payment	2	0.15	1	1	1	1.00
9	Cancel Order	1	0.15	3	0	0	.
10	Request Catalog	1	0.15	0	0	0	.
11	Check Order Status	1	0.15	0	0	0	.

Figure 4.14 *Spreadsheet portion of dashboard indicative of end of an early test iteration.*

It's important to emphasize that if your unit of measure for the operational profile is staff hours or days expended, this needs to reflect time spent actually running tests, not time spent on other activities such as defect tracking, reports, and so on. On the other hand, practically speaking, I think it's more important to be consistent in the reporting than it is to be accurate; after all, it is the relative improvement in reliability we are looking for. And if it came down to tracking reliability with guesstimate data versus not doing it at all, I'd definitely say do it with guesstimate data.

Another key indicator in the dashboard is that the failure intensity experienced in testing is much higher than the target failure intensity objective; this is pointed out in Figure 4.16. For the product to release, the gray bar indicating experienced failure intensity needs to drop down to or below the failure intensity line.

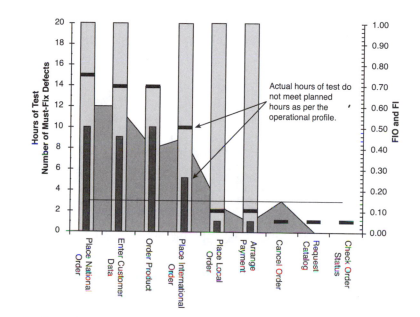

Figure 4.15 *Dashboard showing that actual hours of testing did not meet with planned expenditure. Some use cases (Cancel Order, Request Catalog, and Check Order Status) receive no testing at all.*

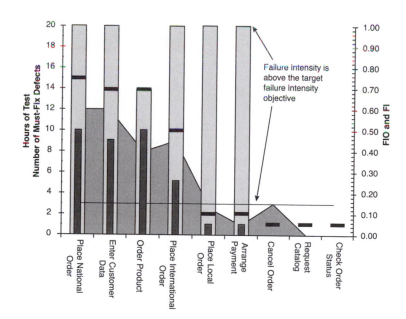

Figure 4.16 *Dashboard showing that experienced failure intensity was much greater than target failure intensity objective.*

And finally, as Figure 4.17 points out, the swamp of defects that need to be fixed before release is on the rise. Remember, open defects are tracked using the left-hand scale.

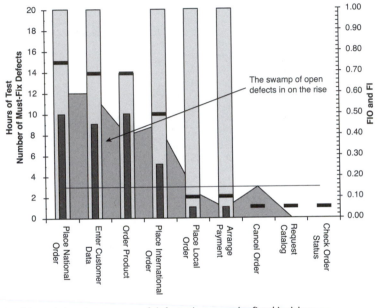

Figure 4.17   *Dashboard showing swamp of defects that must be fixed is rising.*

Good Test Coverage, But...

Let's look at another typical dashboard configuration. Figure 4.18 is typical of the state of the dashboard as you might see it during a middle test iteration. Looking at Figure 4.18, this picture looks rather optimistic—improved coverage of tests, failure intensity dropping—except for the fact that the swamp seems to be rising yet higher. This dashboard display is indicative of a test team that is spinning its wheels until the backlog of defects can be worked off. Yes, the test team is able to spend the planned amount of time on testing each use case, and yes the failure intensity rate is dropping. But it's probably because the test team is running over the same working bits of the system, steering around the known, already reported problems. Unless a significant number of the backlog of defects is fixed, the next test iteration will have a dashboard that looks very much like this one; the test team has found all they can.

After the development group starts fixing the backlog of open defects, two things are going to happen. First, functionality that was previously unusable will finally be tested, revealing yet more defects that had previously been hidden; bugs hidden by other bugs are an effect a colleague of mine calls the "bug shadow." Second, some portion of the fixes will introduce yet more defects. In short, as the swamp of open defects is lowered, the failure intensity will likely rise again.

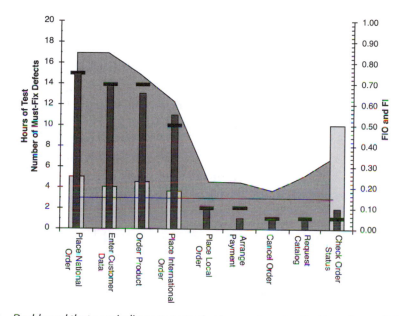

Figure 4.18   *Dashboard that may indicate more testing is a waste unless backlog of open defects is lowered.*

Do We Really Need Another Test Iteration?

This next example requires a bit of explanation as to how such a dashboard could even come to be. Very late in system testing, when the product begins to stabilize and the release date (original or probably revised) looms near, defects that are discovered receive a new type of scrutiny. Not only are they prioritized in terms of their effect on the customer, but they now receive prioritization in terms of their risk to the project. The risk of fixing a defect late in the game, close to the release date, is weighed against three factors:

1. What is the risk that if development fixes this defect, they will break something else? Fixes to some parts of a product can have disastrous

ripple effects. The consequence of fixing one defect could well be the introduction of a host more.

2. How much effort is required to fix this defect? When you are days from a release, fixing a defect that is measured in staff months of effort may simply not be an option.

3. If we fix the defect, how much testing will be needed to verify the fix worked, and to verify it didn't break something else (regression testing)? The simplest of fixes sometimes require huge testing efforts to properly verify.

An easy way to remember this is **R-E-V**: Risk of breaking something else; Effort to make the fix; Verification effort to check the fix and regression test the system. Given this tightened triaging of new defects, a team will sometimes opt to document a severe defect in the release notes rather than fixing it. As the old saying goes, "'Tis better to go with the devil you know than the devil you don't." When this happens, it is quite possible to find yourself staring at a dashboard like that of Figure 4.19.

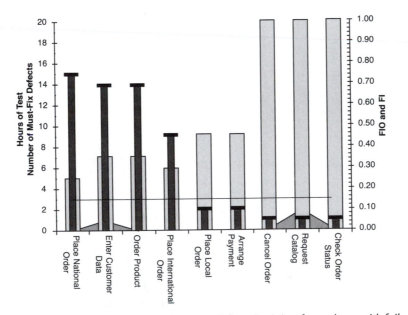

Figure 4.19   *Good test coverage, and virtually no open defects. But is it safe to release with failure intensity levels still so high?*

In this dashboard, test coverage looks good—actual testing was given to use cases in accordance with the plan as per the operational profile—and there are very few defects that are going to be fixed (some were identified as too risky to fix and were removed from the "Swamp"). Why not just fix those few defects that you plan on fixing, do a spot check on the build, and release the product?

The problem, of course, is that you have not met your failure intensity objective. And a high failure intensity is the indicator for a high population of latent defects (i.e., defects that still remain waiting to be discovered). If you were to run another test iteration and vary tests a bit, chances are you would keep finding defects. So the question is, do you go ahead and run another iteration and find a new round of defects or let the customer do it?

Stop Testing!

Figure 4.20 illustrates the dashboard you want to see when it's time to stop testing and ship the product! The testing team is able to run tests on all use cases in proportion to the operational profile; the swamp of defects has been drained and the failure intensity experienced during test is at or under the failure intensity objective.

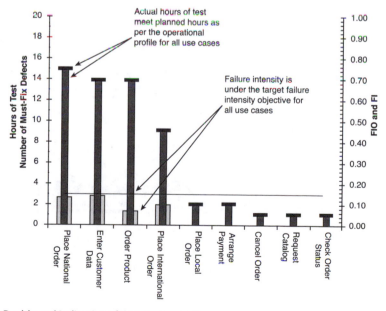

Figure 4.20 *Dashboard indicative of time to stop testing.*

One drawback of the Swamp Report is that it is a look at the system at one instance in time. In the next section, you'll see how to extend that view to provide a look at the system over time, across multiple test iterations, for the entire project length if so desired.

Tracking the Swamp Through Time

A companion report of the Swamp Report that I've found useful is to plot snapshots of the dashboard through time in a format as shown in Figure 4.21, allowing you to gain a perspective on progress through time. Dates of snapshots run across the X-axis; each snapshot plots the key stats from the Swamp Report: failure intensity, open defects, and testing effort expended.

The example in Figure 4.21 shows a large cross-company program consisting of about 35 products and nearly as many project teams that were required to release at the same time as part of a box-set of products. Tools, such as the Swamp Report, were used to track the reliability growth of each of the individual products, with this companion report providing a look at the progress of the whole.

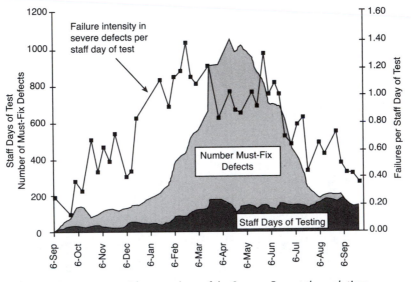

Figure 4.21   *Companion report provides snapshots of the Swamp Report through time.*

To wrap up our look at the "Swamp Report," it is an easy to implement, spreadsheet-based dashboard that provides at-a-glance monitoring of reliability growth across a large number of "pieces" that form a whole (e.g., use cases making up a component, components making up a project, or multiple projects making up a program).

Determining the Effectiveness of Your SRE-Based Test Process

Software reliability engineering promises to help teams work smarter to deliver a reliable product. But how to tell if it is working? This chapter concludes by looking at how to measure the Defect Detection Effectiveness of a testing process, touted by some as the *single* most important quality measure.

Defect Detection Effectiveness (DDE) is a measure of the effectiveness of a testing process to detect defects. The formula for DDE is very simple: it is the number of bugs detected by the testing process before the product release divided by the total population of bugs (see Equation 4.4).

$$DDE = \frac{\text{total defects found in testing}}{\text{total defects found in testing + defects found after testing that were in the product at the time testing was done}}$$

Equation 4.4   *Formula for calculating Defect Detection Effectiveness (DDE).*

A run chart of defects through time is a good way to visualize DDE. Figure 4.22 is a run chart of cumulative severe defects found for a product release; in fact, it is the same release for which we measured the failure intensity earlier in this chapter (see Figure 4.7).

In this case, at the time testing was stopped and the product released, the testing effort had found 582 severe defects. Subsequent to release, an additional 50 severe defects were found; therefore, DDE = 582 / (582+50), or about 92%.

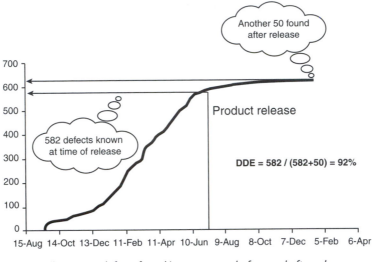

Figure 4.22   *Run chart illustrating defects found in system test before and after release.*

Because product testing is typically not directly equivalent to the use a product experiences in the field from customers—it's usually more rigorous or less rigorous, but not exactly the same—arriving at a failure intensity objective may involve some trial and error. A failure intensity objective that is too low (your reliability goal is too high) keeps a product in testing longer than it needs to be. A failure intensity objective that is too high (your reliability goal is too low) results in unhappy customers inflicted with a buggy product along with the high cost of fixing defects in a deployed product.

In the "But What's the *Right* Failure Intensity Objective?" section, a low-tech approach was described for determining a ballpark failure intensity objective: Think back to a project that you and your team remember as being successful and that you believe was well received by the customer in terms of reliability, then do some project archaeology to determine the failure intensity of that project. DDE provides a quantitative approach allowing you to correlate failure intensity objectives with successful releases measured by DDE. By tracking failure intensities during testing, followed by DDE analysis after the release, you are able to determine whether you can raise or lower failure intensity objectives.

As an example, the project for which we computed the failure intensity at time of release in Figure 4.7 is also the same project for which we have just calculated the DDE in Figure 4.22. So, as it turned out, a failure intensity of 1.55 at the time of release correlated with a DDE of about 92%, which was considered a success. Future projects could therefore use a failure intensity objective of 1.55 with some measure of confidence that they would be releasing a product the customer would perceive as reliable.

Another way to leverage DDE analysis with software reliability engineering is by comparison of defects found soon after release versus much later. This is illustrated in Figure 4.23; arrows show defects found almost immediately after the release compared with defects found up to seven months later. Doing root cause analysis of such defects and asking why some were caught so quickly and others took so long to be found can provide insight into how to improve your system's use cases, operational profile, and test cases.

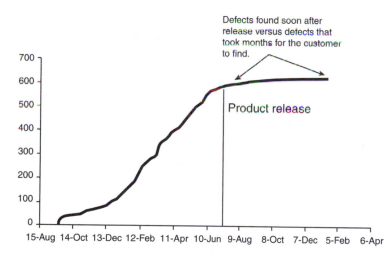

Figure 4.23 *Analysis of defects found sooner rather than later can provide insights into the operational profile of your product as used by the customer.*

Final Notes on DDE

Although DDE is a simple measure, there are caveats of which to be aware. First, DDE is a moving target; because it is impossible to know how many defects there really are in a product, it is computed based on known defects at some point in time, *and that, of course, changes through time*. Looking at the run chart of Figure 4.22, the measured DDE starts at 100% at the time of release (you don't know what you have missed at this point) and then continues to drop through time as defects are discovered after the release. The trick is to identify a period of time after a release that is long enough for the customer base to have adopted the new release and to have had sufficient opportunity to begin finding defects.

There is also some confusion in the literature around this and similar measures. Defect *Removal* Effectiveness is a measure of the effectiveness of a development process to both detect, and then remove, defects. Some literature blurs this distinction (detection versus removal). I prefer detection effectiveness rather than removal effectiveness because many development groups don't necessarily fix every defect they find—even severe ones—for valid business reasons.

Also, some literature blurs the distinction between "efficiency" and "effectiveness" by using the term *defect detection efficiency* as equivalent to defect detection effectiveness. I prefer to keep these two measures distinct—effectiveness versus efficiency, as two organizations can have the same effectiveness to detect/remove defects, with varying efficiency at accomplishing the task. Yet other authors avoid the use of "effectiveness" or "efficiency" altogether, using the term *defect detection percentage*.

So, just be aware that you may come across this measure called out by a different name; your best bet is to simply look at how the measure is calculated.

Chapter Review

In this chapter, we've talked about reliability; how to define it, measure it, set goals in terms of it, and track it in testing. Let's review some key points from this chapter.

- Reliability is the probability of failure-free operation for a specified length of time in a specified environment. This definition is user-centric (defined from the perspective of the user using the system), and dynamic (failures only happen when a product is being used).

- Having a quantifiable definition of reliability is the key to being able to measure and track reliability during testing as a means of helping decide when it's time to stop testing. Two common techniques for quantifying a reliability goal are:

  - Failure intensity, which is the number of failures of a specified severity per unit of time, or number of transactions, and so on.

  - Exponential failure law, which provides the probability for failure-free operation for a specified length of time, when the failure intensity is constant (i.e., you aren't patching the system or adding features, as would generally be the case for a system in use by a customer, in the field).

- A reliability growth curve is a run chart that lets you visualize the failure intensity of a product during development and test. Used in conjunction with a failure intensity objective, the reliability growth curve allows you to tell if your system is getting close to being ready for release.

- The Swamp Report is a spreadsheet-based dashboard that lets you track three key factors to knowing whether it's time to stop testing and release a product: failure intensity, open defects, and test coverage as per the operational profile. It provides at-a-glance monitoring of reliability growth across a large number of "pieces" that form a whole (use cases of a component, components of a product, whole products that are part of a program).

- Defect Detection Effectiveness (DDE) is a measure of the effectiveness of a testing process to detect defects. DDE provides a quantitative approach to correlate failure intensity objectives with successful releases measured by DDE. By tracking failure intensities during testing, followed by DDE analysis after the release, you are able to determine whether you can raise, or need to lower, failure intensity objectives for future releases.

Part 3

Model-Based Specification (Preconditions, Postconditions, and Invariants)

Posing Sharp Questions in Use Case Failure Analysis and Test Design

"The main role of models is not so much to explain and to predict...as to polarize thinking and to pose sharp questions."

—*Marc Kac*, Some Mathematical Models in Science

As the popularity of use cases grows, so grows the need for systematic means of doing failure analysis and test design from use cases. This is particularly true for products—or components of products—that are safety-critical, mission-critical, business-critical, or in general require high assurance. And virtually all products, whether safety-critical or not, have at least a few use cases the project team would like to make sure are rock-solid reliable!

In Chapter 5, "Use Case Preconditions, Postconditions, and Invariants: What They Didn't Tell You, But You Need to Know!" we will look at a time-tested technique for specifying the expected behavior of abstract data types and objects—*model-based specification*—and apply it in a fresh way to pose sharp questions in *use case failure analysis*: the analysis of potential ways a system, specified by a use case, might fail. In doing so, the reader will learn some things about preconditions and postconditions they forgot to mention in "Use Case 101!" This approach—thinking about failures while writing use cases—is a powerful, risk-driven strategy, focusing testing on detection of high impact defects first and providing the requirements needed to design systems that fail in a safe way. The chapter concludes with ideas on how to work smart in applying model-based specification, including the "The Absolute *Least* You Need to Know: One Fundamental Lesson and Three Simple Rules" section, which, if you get nothing else from the chapter, will give you a take away that you can apply to any and all use cases right away.

In Chapter 6, "Triple Threat Test Design for Use Cases," you will learn that not only does model-based specification with its preconditions, postconditions, and invariants provide an integrated basis for use case failure analysis, it also provides just what is needed for test design by using Robert Binder's *Extended Use Case Test Design Pattern*. And because the test cases are designed from the results of our failure analysis, they will target defects that represent high impact failures.

Finally, a brief comment is appropriate about one of the main examples used in both chapters: A tank used to store chemicals needed for a manufacturing process. The storage tank has a pipe through which the chemical flows to fill the tank and a pipe out of which the chemical flows to manufacturing. This example is a variation of the classic "bathtub" problem that is used in teaching systems thinking or system dynamics (Weinberg and Weinberg 1998).[1] The problem, though easy to state and initially understand, turns out to have many nuances that tend to elude intuition, requiring some systematic method—such as modeling—which *leads* us to pose the sharp questions that need to be asked in use case failure analysis.

---

[1] A similar example is used by Storey (1996) as part of the discussion on fault-tolerant architectures.

5

Use Case Preconditions, Postconditions, and Invariants: What They Didn't Tell You, But You Need to Know!

With the growth in popularity of use case-driven development, in some cases being applied to product components requiring high assurance—e.g., safety-critical[1] or mission-critical systems—there is an increased need for a systematic means of doing failure analysis and test design from use cases.

From a black-box testing perspective, preconditions and postconditions are the quintessential elements of a use case, saying what it does without saying how. They are the ideal basis for black-box testing; what more could one need for specifying tests? And in failure analysis, preconditions play the role of specifying those conditions under which the use case is intended to work correctly, and conversely the conditions under which the system might fail. A system can then be implemented by using techniques such as *design by contract* or *defensive programming*, where routines check their preconditions—called assertions because they assert what the routine assumes to be true—before running. If the precondition is false, the routine can handle the exception safely (i.e., *fail safe*).[2]

---

[1] See, for example, the role of use cases in "drive by wire" cars in Johannessen et al. (2001).

[2] Storey (1996) discusses the role of assertions in safety-critical systems and Binder (2000) looks at their use in automated testing.

In reality, however, few use cases are produced with preconditions and postconditions of substance enough to test from. If you look at your favorite book on use cases, you are likely to find use cases with preconditions but no postconditions (the significance of which will make sense later) and postconditions with no preconditions. And even when both are present, you would likely be hard pressed to tell *what a use case did based solely on the pre- and postconditions*. While developers may be willing to keep use cases informal (Cockburn, 2002)[3] when it comes to failure analysis and test design, something a bit more concrete is needed; hence, a number of proposals for making use cases more test-ready have appeared.[4]

In this chapter, we look briefly at the history of preconditions and postconditions and learn what they forgot to tell you in "Use Case 101": *preconditions can be calculated from postconditions*, and often with little more than simple algebra! The usefulness of this fact should be obvious from a black-box testing and failure analysis standpoint: given a black-box's outputs (the postcondition), you can calculate the set of inputs and starting states which produce it (the precondition) and conversely the inputs and starting states, which are excluded, could spell system failure, and might warrant error handling tests. In this chapter, we also discuss invariants, which are to use cases what safety requirements are to safety-critical systems. This chapter concludes with some suggestions on working smart to apply the techniques presented, including a section that gives you *the very least you need to know* to apply the lessons of model-based specification *today*.

Sanity Check Before Proceeding

Unlike the other parts of this book where the ideas presented are fairly new to use case development, the use case community already has existing definitions of "precondition" and "postcondition" and how they relate to use cases. This makes for potential confusion when this chapter presents alternate perspectives and even an idea or two that conflict with the views often put forth by the use case community. One such difference I will mention now to hopefully prevent confusion as you start to read.

---

[3] See Alistair Cockburn's "Use Cases, Ten Years Later" (2002) for a discussion of this topic.

[4] See, for example, (Binder 2000) and David Gelperin's "Precise Use Cases."

In this chapter, you will be looking at preconditions and postconditions of *individual operations* or steps that make up a use case.[5] This is a different perspective from that of most use case literature that talks about pre- and postconditions of the use case "as a whole." One consequence of the latter perspective is that the use case community has focused primarily on preconditions that must be satisfied before the use case can *start*. But from a failure analysis and test design standpoint this is not sufficient: there are usually operations (for instance, later in the use case) whose preconditions are to be satisfied by the postcondition of another operation earlier in the same use case. While such preconditions do not prevent the use case from *starting*, their violation can translate into system failure nevertheless.

While the presentation of pre- and postconditions in this chapter is, I believe, consistent with UML in general (*The UML Reference Manual* defines preconditions and postconditions in terms of operations [Rumbaugh, Jacobson, and Booch 2005]), the chapter could be a little confusing if you read it with the mindset that the only type of use case precondition is one that must be satisfied before the use case starts.

This issue and others are discussed in more detail near the end of this chapter; if you care to read ahead, see the "Further Thoughts: Preconditions, Postconditions, and Invariants in Use Cases" section. Remember, the goal of this chapter is *not* to rehash what has already been said about preconditions and postconditions in the use case literature. The goal of this chapter is to think outside the box a bit and present to you a look at preconditions and postconditions and how they relate to use cases from a whole new perspective, that of model-based specification.

A Brief History of Preconditions and Postconditions

Preconditions and postconditions were a relatively recent addition to what Alistair Cockburn, in his article "Use Cases, Ten Years Later," calls the fully dressed use case. They weren't a part of Jacobson's original use cases, or

---

[5] As a classifier in UML, use cases have attributes and operations. A use case operation represents "a piece of work the use case can perform." For additional details on the structure of use cases, refer to Rumbaugh, Jacobson, and Booch (2005).

OMT's scenarios. But though a newcomer to use cases, the history of pre- and postconditions goes back to at least the late 1960s with the work of researchers like Floyd, Hoare, and Dijkstra.[6]

Preconditions and postconditions played a key role in reasoning about programs (Does this program meet its specification?) and later with formal specification languages like **VDM** (Vienna Development Method) and **Z** (pronounced "Zed") as a way to specify the behavior of Abstract Data Types. Much of what we today ascribe to being "object-oriented" is rooted in the concept of Abstract Data Types (ADT). This is particularly true of the matter of specifying the *expected behavior* of an object, which is an issue of *great* interest to testing. In 1971, David Parnas introduced "Information Hiding," which wrapped each "design decision" in a module with a defined interface *eliminating the need for details of how the module was programmed.* But if you are going to hide the details of the implementation of your new widget from your fellow programmers, you need some way of communicating to them what the widget *does.* By the mid-to-late 1970s, two approaches to tackling the problem were underway: the algebraic specification approach and the model-based specification approach. **VDM** and **Z** were outgrowths of the work on the latter.[7] These formal specification languages and techniques in turn influenced the object-oriented community e.g., Bertrand Meyer's Eiffel (1998) with its Design by Contract, pre-UML "unified" object-oriented methodologies such as Fusion (Coleman et al. 1994), and more recently UML's Object Constraint Language (OCL) (Warmer and Kleppe 1994).

Fast forwarding to today, though preconditions and postconditions are now a part of the fully dressed use case, a key facet in their history, one central to their use in reasoning about programs and specifications, has been overlooked a tad. *Preconditions can be calculated from postconditions.* In fact, that was pretty much the point originally. You can calculate preconditions from postconditions as opposed to intuitively making them up. And in the early days, there was even discussion as to whether it was better to generate the precondition from the postcondition, or vice versa; the former eventually won out and has been the norm since.

---

[6] A paper by Cliff Jones (2003) even traces roots going back to work by pioneers such as Von Neuman and Turing in the late 1940s.

[7] For an overview of algebraic and model-based specification, see Sommerville (2000).

This technique is usually described in terms of *Hoare triples* or *predicate transformer* for calculating the *weakest precondition* (i.e., a technique that transforms one predicate, the postcondition, into another, the precondition). The version of the technique we'll see in this book is basically that used by **Z**, and in that literature it is often just called "calculating the precondition."

The intent here is not to say that calculating the precondition is the *only*, or even the *right* way you get preconditions for use cases; even in writing specifications in formal languages like **Z**, one usually comes up with preconditions in an intuitive sort of way. But that connection between precondition and postcondition is always there to leverage (e.g., as a way to demonstrate the validity of an intuitively derived precondition or to tell if there are additional preconditions that have been overlooked). And it turns out to be a handy tool for failure analysis of and test design from use cases.

Calculating Preconditions from Postconditions

The best way to illustrate this technique is through examples, so let's dive in and work through an example, and then step back and evaluate the process.

Use Case Overview

A new on-line merchant has just introduced gift cards. You can buy a gift card online and have it mailed to a friend. Each card has a unique ID; to buy something you go to the Web site, log in using the ID, and then buy something. If you have change coming, a check for the difference is mailed to you; this is seen as marketing differentiation from competitors that force the customer to spend the full gift card price or more or lose the difference. Figure 5.1 shows the main scenario for the **Buy Something With Gift Card** use case.

Use Case Steps
1. Customer goes to Web site and logs in with gift card ID
2. Customer selects item of interest
3. Customer enters address, confirms, and checks out
4. System signals inventory to mail item to address
5. System signals accounts payable to mail check for difference between gift card value and price of item

Figure 5.1   *Buy Something With Gift Card use case, main scenario.*

With a typical use case description in hand, we are ready to think about how the system, as described by this use case, could fail and identify preconditions that would guard against such failure.

Step 1. Find a "Risky" Postcondition: Model as an Equation

First, we identify an operation or step of the use case, the postcondition for which we wish to calculate the precondition. In general, it's not safe to assume that the postconditions provided (if any) are the only postconditions. You'll need to read the body of the use case and look for operations where outputs are produced or state is changed, paying particular attention to ones doing "risky things." Looking at our example, this operation certainly fits the bill, so we'll focus on it:

"System signals accounts payable to mail check for difference between gift card value and price of item"

Next, we write the operation's postcondition in the form of a simple equation:

$$CheckAmount = GiftCardValue - PriceOfItem$$

That was pretty easy. It's important to note that the "=" is *not assignment*; it is *equality*, and the equation describes a relationship between the three variables. Use of equality is what allows us to leverage the power of algebra that makes this technique work.[8]

---

[8] Gries and Schneider (1993) provide in-depth coverage of equality, equational logic and leveraging simple algebra-style thinking applied to reasoning about programs.

Step 2. Identify a Potential Failure: State an Invariant

This next step is at the heart of this technique, so a bit of discussion is in order. In a use case, postconditions are where the action is. They describe the output produced and state changed by the use case. And it is precisely when you are generating outputs and changing state that the opportunity for really "screwing things up" occurs; as the old saying goes: "To err is human. To really screw up you need a computer." So how does one judge if the computation described by a postcondition is valid (i.e., isn't going to screw something up)? To do so, we need some statement of what a valid output or valid system state is. These statements of validity are typically called *invariants*. In the formal methods community, they are variously called data invariants or state invariants: statements that should always be true about the data and system state being described. In the object-oriented community, they are called class invariants: something that should always be true about a class and any object instantiated from it (class invariants were inherited—no pun intended—from the formal methods community, so they are quite similar). In the study of program algorithms, there are loop invariants: something that should always be true about the loop being programmed (loop as in "While X do Y"). The word "invariant" simply means something that does not vary; is always true. The common denominator in all these invariants is that they set constraints that post-conditions should not "violate."

So as a sanity check for the postconditions of our use case, we introduce the use of invariants. Given these invariants, we can then ask if the computation described by the postcondition preserves them. As it turns out, the answer is usually something like, "Yes, assuming that such and such is true when the computation happens." *And that is a precondition: the "such and such" that must be true in order that the postcondition preserves the invariant (i.e., nothing gets "screwed up").*

Explanation aside, let's look at the next step. Looking at our postcondition, we ask what bad things could happen with respect to the computation the postcondition is describing? One that comes immediately to mind is cutting a check for more than the gift card was worth; that is literally a money-losing proposition. So an invariant for this postcondition—remember, something we always want to be true—is that the refund check amount should *never* be more than the value of the gift card:

Invariant: CheckAmount < GiftCardValue

In the field of safety-critical systems—systems where failures pose risk of injury or death—this process of asking what bad things can happen is called *Hazard Identification and Analysis*. One identifies the hazards of a system (controller overfills storage tank with toxic chemicals), then analyzes the conditions and failures that would need to occur to cause the hazard to occur (e.g., using techniques such as fault tree analysis). One then formulates safety requirements for the system designed to prevent that combination of conditions and failures. This is a powerful risk-based testing strategy, helping testing to focus on high-impact defects first, and is essentially what we've done in this step.

Step 3. Compute the Precondition

All that remains now is to "turn the crank" to produce a precondition from the postcondition and invariant (see Figure 5.2).

CheckAmount < GiftCardValue   Start with the invariant.

GiftCardValue − PriceOfItem < GiftCardValue   In the expression above, sustitute **CheckAmount** with its value from the postcondition.

−PriceOfItem < 0   Simplify the expression above by substracting **GiftCardValue** from both sides.

PriceOfItem > 0   Flip the sign of **Price.**

This is our precondition!

Figure 5.2   *Calculating the precondition for invariant CheckAmount < GiftCardValue.*

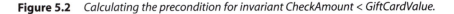

Let's put all the pieces together and see what we have. This postcondition:

$$CheckAmount = GiftCardValue - PriceOfItem$$

…meets this invariant (a property we want to always be true):

$$CheckAmount < GiftCardValue$$

…as long as this precondition holds:

$$PriceOfItem > 0$$

The postcondition, precondition, and invariant work together as a unit, as a team. They are like parts of a complete sentence; take away one, and the full meaning is not known.

Your first reaction to the precondition we've just calculated may be something like: "But of course! Everyone *assumes* that prices are greater than zero!" Right you are. And because everyone *assumes* it, it's *just* the type of precondition easily overlooked for error testing. But, in fact, it *is* a precondition for the successful computation of the refund check, and things do go awry: sign errors in coding, typing mistakes while entering prices in a database, sabotage, and so on.

Why Does This Work?!

If you are completely happy to use this technique for calculating preconditions without having to know why it works, feel free to skip this next bit. Trying to explain why the precondition results from the postcondition and invariant is probably harder to do than actually doing it. For an intuitive explanation, let's think back to some things you may remember learning in algebra. Let's take this equation:

$$y=3x-4$$

You'll recall that given a single equation such as this, there are an infinite number of solutions (values of **x** and **y**), and you may remember having to graph equations like this one to visualize all the possible values of **x** and **y** that satisfy this equation. Figure 5.3 is a graph for this equation; the line stretches to infinity in both directions.

If we now add a second equation to the first and consider the two *simultaneously* as a pair, the second equation constrains the values of **x** and **y** to be those that not only satisfy the first equation, but also the second:

$$y=3x-4$$

$$y=2x$$

This is visualized by graphing these two equations together; the two lines intersect at **x=4** and **y=8**, the one solution that simultaneously satisfies both equations (see Figure 5.4).

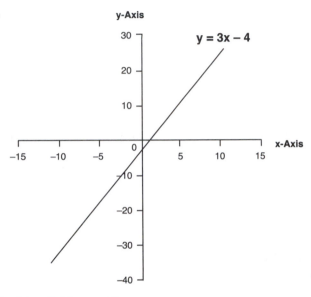

Figure 5.3   *Graph of points satisfying equation.*

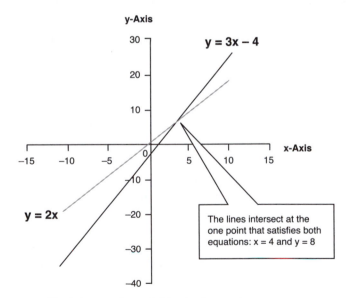

Figure 5.4   *Intersection of lines shows value satisfying both equations.*

While graphing simultaneous equations is one way to solve them—and it certainly helps to visualize what is going on (i.e., you are looking for the set of values where the two equations overlap)—the preferred method is the "algebraic solution." You start with the original equations:

$$y=3x-4$$

$$y=2x$$

Now take the value of **y** from the first equation, and substitute it in the second equation:

$$3x-4 = 2x$$

Then simplify:

$$x-4=0$$

$$x=4$$

You could then substitute the value for **x** (i.e., 4) into either of the original equations to give you the value of **y**:

$$y=2x$$

$$y=2*4 = 8$$

Now let's apply this idea to calculating preconditions. Previously we said the postcondition, precondition, and invariant work together as a unit. We can use our lesson from simultaneous equations to get a feel for the role each plays. Let's start with this postcondition from our example:

$$CheckAmount = GiftCardValue - PriceOfItem$$

For what values of **CheckAmount**, **GiftCardValue**, and **PriceOfItem** is this equation valid? We know from our previous algebra example that it is valid for an infinite number of values, *some of which might result in undesired behavior* (e.g., when **PriceOfItem** is *negative*). So, we decide to constrain the values by adding a second equation, actually an inequality:

$$CheckAmount < GiftCardValue$$

This inequality—our *invariant*—was selected to constrain the values to ones that we felt were safe (i.e., we should never be writing checks for greater than the original gift card's value). *So the postcondition and invariant are like simultaneous equations from algebra.* And solving simultaneous equations—either graphically or algebraically—involves looking for the set of values that simultaneously satisfy both equations, and that… you guessed it…is what the precondition is: *the set of values that simultaneously satisfy both the postcondition and invariant* (see Figure 5.5).

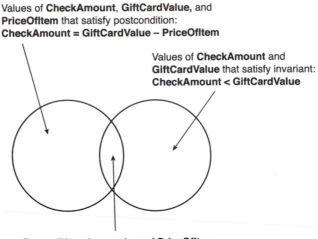

Values of **CheckAmount, GiftCardValue,** and **PriceOfItem** that satisfy postcondition:
CheckAmount = GiftCardValue − PriceOfItem

Values of **CheckAmount** and **GiftCardValue** that satisfy invariant:
CheckAmount < GiftCardValue

Precondition: those values of **PriceOfItem** where both postcondition and invariant are satisfied

Figure 5.5   *Venn diagram illustration of precondition as those values which simultaneously satisfy the post-condition and invariant.*

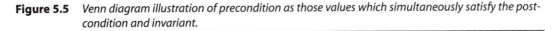

So, at least in principle, you learned everything you need to know about computing preconditions from postconditions and invariants in algebra class!

Modeling State Change

Frequently, a use case involves change to the state of a system. In such instances, in order to calculate preconditions, we need a way to model the system's *before* and *after* state. Again, a simple example is the best way to illustrate. In the following example, **WidgetsInStock** is a state variable; a set of state variables such as **WidgetsInStock** are what define the state of, say, an inventory control system. We can represent the after version of a state variable with the postfix prime ('). This equation describes the expected results of one step in a use case, that of shipping widgets. It describes the relationship between the number of widgets that were in stock when the use case started (no prime) versus the number of widgets in stock *after* some number were shipped (primed):

$$WidgetsInStock' = WidgetsInStock - WidgetsShipped$$

Again, keep in mind that "=" is equality, not assignment: the equation describes a *relationship* between the variables.[9]

Having *before* and *after* versions of state variables allows us to talk about invariants that involve both. The state variable **WidgetsInStock** is subject to the invariant that it should *always* be greater than or equal to zero, and this should be true *before* and *after* the postcondition completes. Here is this invariant stated for the *after* version of the state variable, i.e., this use case should *never* ship more widgets than are in stock (that's the failure to be avoided):

$$Invariant: WidgetsInStock' \geq 0$$

Turning the crank, we get the precondition that ensures the postcondition meets this invariant (see Figure 5.6).

WidgetsInStock' ≥ 0	Start with the invariant.
WidgetsInStock − WidgetsShipped ≥ 0	In the expression above, substitute **WidgetsInStock'** with its value from the postcondition.
WidgetsInStock ≥ WidgetsShipped	Simplify the expression above by adding **WidgetsShipped** to both sides. This is our precondition.

Figure 5.6   *Calculating precondition for invariant WidgetsInStock' ≥ 0.*

[9] The convention used here of decorating state variables with prime follows that of the model-based specification languages Z and VDM. In Eiffel, the prefix *old* is used.

WidgetsInStock = *old* WidgetsInStock − WidgetsShipped. See Meyer (1988). In UML's Object Constraint Language (OCL) the postfix @pre is used:

WidgetsInStock = WidgetsInStock@pre − WidgetsShipped. See Warmer and Kleppe (1999).

Working through simple examples such as this allows you to gain confidence that the technique yields results you intuitively know are true.

Model-Based Specification

Models—explicit or mental—play a big role in failure analysis and in test design. This technique is a style of modeling aptly named *model-based specification*: it relies on building a simple model of the data and/or state of the thing being specified, then operations (e.g., steps in a use case) are defined in terms of how they modify that model.

There is a subtle but very important point that needs to be made about the state variables used in model-based specification, especially if you are accustomed to "instance variables" or "member variables" in object-oriented programming languages. The variables **WidgetsInStock** and **WidgetsInStock'** *are two separate variables in the model we are building.* They do refer to the same single instance/member variable in the application (assuming that is how the application was implemented), but it requires multiple, separate variables in the model-based specification itself in order to be able to talk about the different states the application instance/member variable might be in.

Reasoning About State Through Time

Working with *before* and *after* versions of state variables, unprimed and primed respectively (and remember they are separate variables in the model) can take some getting accustomed to, but it is a *powerful* technique for reasoning about use cases. It's basically the same technique physicists use when they talk about, say, the velocity of an object at *time-zero* with a variable like V^0 versus the velocity at *time-n* with a variable like V^n. Let's work through another example using this technique.

Use Case Overview

A manufacturing plant uses a storage tank to hold chemicals needed for its widget production; see Figure 5.7. The storage tank has a pipe through which the chemical flows to fill the tank and a pipe out of which the chemical flows to the machine that manufactures widgets. Rate of production by manufacturing determines the rate at which the chemical is needed and, hence, the rate of flow out of the tank. A new computer-based controller is being built to monitor levels in the tank, increasing or decreasing flow into the tank as needed. Sensors provide the controller with the current level in the tank, and the controller is programmed with a set target at which levels are ideally maintained in order to achieve a desired fluid pressure in the tank.

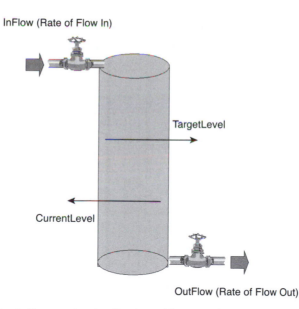

Figure 5.7   *Chemical tank diagram showing flow in and flow out of the tank.*

Figure 5.8 is the main scenario of the use case for maintaining the level of the chemical in the tank at the target level. The actor in this use case is the controller.

Use Case Steps
1. Controller notices that chemical has dropped below target level
2. Controller increases the flow into the tank
3. Controller monitors rise of level in tank
4. When chemical reaches target level, controller reduces flow into the tank so as not to overfill the tank. Chemical is restored to target level

Figure 5.8   *Main scenario, controller's use case for maintaining level of chemical in tank.*

Use case description in hand, we are ready to think about how the controller might fail while executing this use case and identify preconditions that would guard against it.

Step 1. Find "Risky" Postconditions: Model as Equations

Clearly, controlling the rate of flow into the tank is the heart of this use case and a source of risk. Focusing on the control of this, we build a simple model of the postconditions of this facet of the use case (see Figure 5.9).

Step 2. Identify a Potential Failure: State an Invariant

There are two obvious failures this use case presents: failure to properly control the level resulting in the level dropping too low for manufacturing purposes or overfilling the tank resulting in a chemical spill.

0 ≤ InFlow ≤ MaxFlow
0 ≤ OutFlow ≤ MaxFlow

A good place to start any model is to define the *domain*—the set of all possible valid values—for the variables. Domain definitions act like invariants: they are assumed to always be true (for example, InFlow should never drop below zero, or be greater than MaxFlow)

Lower Boundary: In this case, simply asking if **InFlow** and **OutFlow** could be negative leads to the question of direction of flow of fluid in the pipes. A negative flow would indicate backward movement through the pipes, known as backwash. We decide this is a real possibility, but one to be covered by another use case. This use case will deal only with forward movement through the pipe.

Upper Boundary: MaxFlow is some upper bound that specifies the maximum safe rate of flow into, or out of, the tank (safe in terms of design limits on flow valves, tank construction, and so on.)

InFlow' = OutFlow + Delta

The first step in the use case is that the controller notices that levels are too low and acts to increase flow into the tank to start refilling.

This postcondition describes the results of that operation: It says the flow into the tank is changed by amount Delta,[1] causing the level to rise. Note the use of prime to distinguish the new rate of flow (primed) from the initial (unprimed).

InFlow'' = OutFlow'

At some point, the level of the chemical reaches the target level. To prevent the level from continuing to rise, the rate of flow into the tank is changed, once again, this time to match the rate of flow out. This will hold the level at a steady state until such time as the flow rate out of the tank changes again. Notice the use of primes to distinguish the final rate of flow in (double primed) from the initial rate (unprimed) and the intermediate rate (one prime).

Notice also the use of primes to distinguish the rate of flow out of the tank subsequent to the start of refilling, through to the end of use case (primed) versus the initial rate (unprimed); because filling the tank will take time, the rate of flow out of the tank may have changed from its initial value by the time the use case completes.

---

[1] "Delta," the Greek letter, is often used to denote change. Here it represents the incremental increase in rate of flow into the tank used for refilling. It is a constant whose actual value the model does not specify.

Figure 5.9 *Model of main scenario for refilling chemical tank.*

From these potential failures, let's identify invariants, something that should always be true about the rates of flow into, and out of, the tank for this use case. In this use case, we have identified these state variables representing the rate of flow into and out of the tank at different points in time:

InFlow—initial rate of flow into the tank when the use case starts

InFlow'—the flow rate to increase the level in the tank

InFlow"—the flow rate at the end of the use case to stabilize the level

OutFlow—initial rate of flow out of the tank when the use case starts

OutFlow'—the rate of flow out of the tank subsequent to the start of refilling through to end of use case

For this use case, the invariants of Figure 5.10 should always be true about these state variables; if postconditions of the use case violate them, the failures identified previously are possible outcomes.

Invariant: InFlow' > OutFlow	If this were not true, the level would not rise.
Invariant: InFlow" < InFlow'	If the rate of flow is high enough to cause the level to rise (**InFlow'**), it will have to be reduced at the end of the use case scenario to prevent overfilling (**InFlow"**). Hence, **InFlow"** must be lower than **InFlow'** or overfilling will occur. In relational database lingo, this is similar to what C.J. Date calls a transition constraint; it constrains the legal transitions of a variable from one value to another.

Figure 5.10   *Invariants that should always be true when refilling the tank.*

We now have a model of the postconditions and invariants they should not violate (i.e., cause to fail). We are ready to calculate preconditions needed to guard the invariants.

Step 3. Calculate Preconditions

We now calculate the precondition for each of these invariants one at a time. Remember a precondition guards a specific invariant from one or more specific postconditions. They work as a unit. We start with **InFlow' > OutFlow** (see Figure 5.11).

InFlow' > OutFlow	Start with the invariant.
OutFlow + Delta > OutFlow	In the expression above, substitute **InFlow'** with its value from the postcondition (that is, **InFlow' = OutFlow + Delta**).
Delta > 0	Solve the expression above for **Delta.** This is our precondition.

Figure 5.11 *Calculating the precondition to guard invariant InFlow' > OutFlow.*

A precondition of **Delta > 0** is intuitive and probably assumed. But, as noted previously, assumptions are often overlooked; from a testing perspective, one would want to ensure that the system checks for this case as ignoring it could eventually lead to depletion of chemicals in the tank.

Now we calculate the precondition for the next invariant, **InFlow" < InFlow'** (see Figure 5.12).

InFlow" < InFlow'	Start with the invariant.
OutFlow < OutFlow + Delta	In the expression above, substitute **InFlow'** and **InFlow"** with their values from these postconditions: **InFlow" = OutFlow'** **InFlow' = OutFlow + Delta**
	The result can't be simplified anymore; This is our precondition.

Figure 5.12 *Calculate precondition to guard invariant InFlow" < InFlow'.*

What does **OutFlow' < OutFlow + Delta** as a precondition mean? This precondition has identified a potentially hazardous race condition in our use case. Because filling the tank takes time, the rate of flow out of the tank may change before the target level is reached. If, during the filling of the tank, **OutFlow'** increased to be *equal* to **OutFlow + Delta**, the level in the tank would stop rising, stabilize, and the use case would not terminate until the flow out changed again. If, during the filling of the tank, **OutFlow'** increased to be *greater* than **OutFlow + Delta**, the level in the tank would fall, potentially depleting chemicals in the tank. This precondition has identified that for the invariant to be met, **OutFlow'** can fluctuate up or down but *only* if it stays strictly less than **OutFlow + Delta.** Clearly such a race condition cannot be allowed and something will need to be done to prevent this (e.g., some semaphore or constraint mechanism to prevent variance in the flow out of the tank caused by manufacturing while the use case is in progress).

In short, this precondition has found the holy grail of test cases: a defect found before it reaches code!

Exploring Boundary Condition Failures

Many system failures don't show up until the system is operated at or near its boundary conditions; this is the motivation behind testing techniques such as boundary-value analysis and domain analysis for example. Let's see how we can apply model-based specification to our chemical tank use case, identifying the preconditions that specify when a system can be operated safely at its boundaries and conversely when we can expect failures to occur.

Step 1. Identify Postconditions Associated with Boundaries of Operation

In the previous section, boundaries were identified on the rate of flow in and out of the chemical tank:

$$0 \leq InFlow \leq MaxFlow$$

$$0 \leq OutFlow \leq MaxFlow$$

Now we need to identify those postconditions that modify these variables and therefore have the potential of pushing the system beyond its specified bounds; in our chemical tank example, we have identified these two:

$$InFlow' = OutFlow + Delta$$

$$InFlow'' = OutFlow'$$

Step 2. State an Invariant the Postconditions Should Not Violate

In a model-based specification, when you define the boundaries on an initial state variable (unprimed)—in testing this is called the *domain* of the variable—it applies not only to the initial form of the variable (i.e., **InFlow and OutFlow**) but also to the *primed* versions as well, **InFlow'**, **InFlow"** and **OutFlow'**. The domain definition of a variable is an invariant in its own right, one that is said to be true for all versions of the variable, primed and unprimed, in any scenario of the use case. What this means is that these boundary definitions:

$$0 \leq \text{InFlow} \leq \text{MaxFlow}$$

$$0 \leq \text{OutFlow} \leq \text{MaxFlow}$$

also imply these, which we take as invariants that we want to assure never fail:

$$0 \leq \text{InFlow'} \leq \text{MaxFlow}$$

$$0 \leq \text{InFlow"} \leq \text{MaxFlow}$$

$$0 \leq \text{OutFlow'} \leq \text{MaxFlow}$$

Step 3. Calculate Preconditions

We want to determine what additional preconditions—if any—are needed to prevent the postconditions of Step 1 from causing the invariants of Step 2 to fail. But what did I mean by *if any*? When calculating preconditions, there are four possible outcomes:

1. The precondition is such that it is *always* true or, said another way, *there is no precondition*, meaning the postcondition should work in all circumstances.

2. The calculated precondition is already *implied* by another existing precondition; in this event, no additional precondition is needed.

3. The calculated precondition is *identical* to one already noted; again, no new precondition is needed.

4. Or—bingo! We identify a missing precondition that is needed to avert failure.

The boundary statements stated earlier work out to be six separate precondition calculations: three boundary statements (**InFlow'**, **InFlow"**, and **OutFlow'**) with each requiring one calculation for the lower bound, and one for the upper bound. As it turns out, of the six calculated preconditions, five are either implied or equal to existing preconditions. For brevity's sake, we won't do those calculations here. But one boundary does, in fact, identify a failure scenario, and we calculate the precondition needed to guard against it in Figure 5.13.

InFlow' ≤ MaxFlow	Start with the invariant.
OutFlow + Delta ≤ MaxFlow	In the expression above, substitute **InFlow'** with its value from the postcondition, (that is, **InFlow' = OutFlow + Delta**).
OutFlow ≤ MaxFlow – Delta	Solve for **OutFlow.** This is our precondition.

Figure 5.13 *Calculating precondition to guard invariant InFlow' ≤ MaxFlow.*

The failure scenario we have identified is this: If at the start of the use case, the flow *out* of the tank is running at maximum (i.e., **OutFlow = MaxFlow**), it will not be possible to increase the flow into the tank high enough to start refilling the tank without setting **InFlow'** to a value *higher* than **MaxFlow**, the upper bound on safe rate of flow in and out of the tank. The precondition states the use case can only be expected to work if **OutFlow** is *less than maximum* when the use case starts. As we have already established **Delta > 0**, we know **OutFlow** *will* be less than the maximum in the precondition.

Notice also that this precondition is a stronger constraint than the original domain definition (i.e., the new precondition **OutFlow ≤ MaxFlow – Delta** *implies* the domain definition condition of **OutFlow ≤ MaxFlow**, but not vice versa) so the former is said to be the *stronger* condition and the latter the *weaker*. In effect, the stronger overrides the weaker.

Further Thoughts: Preconditions, Postconditions, and Invariants in Use Cases

This is a good time to step back and look at some issues associated with preconditions, postconditions, and invariants as they apply to use cases. If you are already familiar with preconditions and postconditions through the use case literature, you have likely already noticed a few differences between that perspective and the model-based perspective presented here; we'll explore these and other issues here.

Preconditions and Postconditions of Individual Operations Versus the Use Case as a Whole

In this chapter, you have been looking at preconditions and postconditions of *individual operations* or steps that make up a use case. This is a different perspective from that of the use case literature, which generally talks about pre- and postconditions of the *use case as a whole*. How do these two perspectives relate to one another?

Let's start with postconditions: What is the relationship between postconditions of individual operations and the postconditions of the use case as a whole? The change made by a *use case as a whole* is the collective change made by the operations that make up the use case, so the postconditions specifying the change of the *use case as a whole* are the collective postconditions of the operations that make up the use case. If we choose to collect them together into a postcondition section of the use case, that is a matter of style rather than substance. Of course, working at the level of individual operations you'll probably be able to identify more postconditions than you might have had you worked at the use case level only, but that's a matter of thoroughness, not a substantive difference.

A similar argument can be made for preconditions, but with one key difference. The use case literature typically defines preconditions as those conditions that are necessary for *the use case to start*. But when working at the level of individual operations, the preconditions define those conditions that are necessary for *the individual operation to start*.[10] The collection of

---

[10] This is consistent with the definition used by Rumbaugh et al. (2005).

all preconditions for all operations that form the use case can be divided into two groups:

1. Those preconditions that are satisfied external to the use case and therefore must be satisfied *before* the use case starts.

2. Those preconditions that will be satisfied *after* the use case starts by a postcondition of some operation within the same use case.

While the use case community has focused primarily on the first group— labeling these "use case [as a whole] preconditions"—from a failure analysis and test design standpoint this is not sufficient: the second group of preconditions can just as easily be a source of system failure. The failure to satisfy an operation's precondition—whether it be the fault of something totally outside of the use case or some previous step in the same use case— spells potential system failure either way.

Scope of Preconditions and Postconditions: Scenario Versus Whole Use Case

Another difference you may have noticed between the model-based perspective and the "standard" use case perspective is that of scope. In some use case literature, you will read that preconditions and postconditions should apply to all scenarios of a use case (i.e., to all possible paths through a use case). From a model-based perspective, this is usually *not* true. Because the model-based perspective views preconditions and postconditions as tied to operations performed by the steps of the use case, and because the steps of a use case vary from scenario to scenario, we should expect that their preconditions and postconditions will vary as well.

If this were simply an academic issue, it probably would not matter, but at least from a black-box specification, testing, and failure analysis standpoint, the model-based perspective of preconditions and postconditions is preferred. Preconditions and postconditions are the quintessential tools for black-box specification: saying what a thing does without saying how. If the postconditions of a use case are—by definition—so general as to be valid for all possible use case scenarios, they are likely not to be useful as a basis for specifying expected behavior in test design or failure analysis. For example, the outputs and final state of a failed attempt to withdraw cash from an ATM are not the same as a successful withdrawal: if your postconditions reflect this, they too will differ; if your postconditions *don't* reflect this, you can't use them to specify the expected behavior of tests.

So, in this respect, the model-based perspective of preconditions and postconditions does indeed differ from that commonly presented in the use case literature.

Postconditions Can Have More than One Precondition

It may have been obvious from our chemical tank example, but it's good to be clear; a postcondition can be associated with more than one precondition. Given that a postcondition can potentially wreak havoc on more than one invariant in the use case, it only makes sense that we need separate preconditions for each of the invariants that are to be guarded. We saw just such an example of this in our chemical tank use case. The postcondition

$$InFlow' = OutFlow + Delta$$

requires this precondition **Delta > 0** to guard this invariant **InFlow' > OutFlow.** But it also requires this precondition **OutFlow ≤ MaxFlow – Delta,** to guard this invariant, **InFlow' ≤ MaxFlow**.

This further reinforces the concept that a specific precondition, postcondition, and invariant are a "team." And the team members can play on more than one team!

Weak and Strong Preconditions

The preconditions calculated with the techniques described in this chapter are often called the *weakest* preconditions needed to prevent failure of the invariant. These two examples from our chemical tank use case illustrate what this means. In that use case, we computed two preconditions for the chemical tank. First, we found that:

This precondition: Delta > 0

…was needed to prevent failure of invariant: InFlow' > OutFlow

Delta > 0 is the weakest precondition needed to ensure that the invariant does not fail. "Weakest" simply means *at the very least* **Delta** must be greater than zero; though, practically speaking, the use case probably requires **Delta** have some value considerably bigger than zero to refill the tank in a timely manner, for example, **Delta = 50** (gallons per minute).

The other example from the chemical tank use case was this:

This precondition: OutFlow' < OutFlow + Delta

…was needed to prevent failure of invariant: InFlow" < InFlow'

OutFlow' < OutFlow + Delta is the weakest precondition needed to ensure the invariant does not fail. But again, practically speaking, the use case probably needs something stronger to ensure the rate of refill stays constant, for instance, the precondition that **OutFlow'** remains less than or equal to **OutFlow** throughout the refilling process, to the end of the use case (i.e., **OutFlow' ≤ Outflow**).

These preconditions, **Delta = 50** and **OutFlow' ≤ OutFlow**, are said to be *stronger* preconditions because they *imply* the weaker forms, but not vice versa. What does imply mean? Well, if **Delta = 50**, then certainly **Delta > 0**, right? But if **Delta > 0**, it is not necessarily the case that **Delta = 50**!

And if **OutFlow' ≤ OutFlow,** then certainly **OutFlow' < OutFlow + Delta** (given that **Delta** is greater than zero, which we have said is the case). But if **OutFlow' < OutFlow + Delta**, it is not necessarily the case that **OutFlow' ≤ OutFlow**.

That's what we mean by weak and strong preconditions. Strong preconditions imply weak ones, but not vice versa. So, in a use case where we derive a precondition to prevent an invariant from failing, we may decide to strengthen the precondition, and that's perfectly OK; the stronger precondition will still guard the invariant. But we can't weaken the precondition. The one that is calculated is already the weakest form.

As we continue with our chemical tank example in the next chapter, we will keep our calculated, weakest preconditions (i.e., **Delta > 0** and **OutFlow' < OutFlow + Delta**) but know that in "real life" one would probably replace them with stronger, more practical ones.

Types of Invariants in Use Cases

The one thing that all invariants have in common is their role[11]. The role of an invariant in a model-based specification of a use case is to:

1. State a property, as a predicate (is either true or false), whose violation (the predicate is false) may result in system failure.

2. Provide the basis for computing a precondition, in conjunction with some postcondition.

As has already been noted, the role of invariants is very much like *safety requirements* in safety critical systems. In safety critical systems, *hazard identification and analysis* involves the identification of hazardous system failures followed by analysis of the combinations of conditions that could cause such failures. The final step is to then formulate safety requirements designed to prevent the identified combination of conditions. These safety requirements, not coincidentally, are often stated as invariant properties of the system, called *safety invariants* (Storey 1996).

But, though all invariants have the same role, there are different types. As already noted, "invariant" simply means something that is said to be always true. But the scope of what "always" means bears some discussion. The de facto standard is that when the term "invariant" is used, it is generally assumed you mean *global* invariant. But, in fact, not all invariants are global; some are *local* invariants. The scope of what "always" means differs between global and local invariants. A common example of a local invariant is a loop invariant (loop as in "While X do Y"). The scope of "always" for a loop invariant is local to a specific loop; it is a statement of truth about that one loop. It is *not* a statement of truth about, say, all loops. Let's look at examples of these two types of invariants using the examples we've seen thus far.

---

[11] Gluch et al. (2002) make a distinction between invariants, assertions (which they define as local invariants whose scope is confined to a single point of execution) and constraints (i.e., what is called here a transition constraint). These distinctions are not made here; if it plays the role of an invariant as defined, it will be called an invariant.

Global Invariants: Preconditions on Steroids

Global invariants are ones that are true for all states of a system, and as they apply to use cases, they are true for all scenarios of the use case and probably for all use cases of the system.[12] The most common type of global invariant is the *data invariant*, which expresses some property that is true about data: inputs, outputs or state variables. They are variously called *state invariants* when used with state variables and *class invariants* when used in the context of classes. This type of invariant may be stated in terms of a single variable or a relationship over several variables. These are global data invariants from our examples:

$$WidgetsInStock \geq 0$$

$$CheckAmount < GiftCardValue$$

Another common type of data invariant is the *domain definition*, a statement about the set of all possible values a variable can take on; here are two from the chemical tank example:

$$0 \leq InFlow \leq MaxFlow$$

$$0 \leq OutFlow \leq MaxFlow$$

Domain definitions are essentially also global data invariants: they make claims about the values of the variables that should always be true.[13]

---

[12] Because use cases are used in so many ways—at various levels of abstraction and granularity, from classes, to sub-systems, to whole products, and for all types of applications, from object-oriented, to relational databases, to hardware—giving a general rule about the scope of invariants across use cases is tricky. Look at where the invariant is coming from and determine what the scope is there. So, for example, if the invariant is a class invariant, it will be true for any use cases written about that class. If the invariant is an integrity constraint on data in a relational database, it will apply for all use cases that create, read, update or delete that data. If the invariant is some safety requirement associated with a piece of hardware, the invariant will be true for all use cases written about that hardware.

[13] The application of domain definitions as global invariants was illustrated in the "Exploring Boundary Condition Failures" section.

In a model-based specification, global invariants are stated in terms of *unprimed* state variables: their initial state *before* they are modified by a postcondition (i.e., the state they are in when the use case begins). It is then understood that the invariant applies to *all* subsequent *primed* versions of the state variable as well: their state *after* they are modified by postconditions. For example:

Given this invariant: WidgetsInStock ≥ 0

...this would be true: WidgetsInStock' ≥ 0

...as well as this: WidgetsInStock" ≥ 0

...and so on

As this applies to use cases, the invariant—both unprimed and primed forms—applies to all scenarios of the use case; if **WidgetsInStock**, **WidgetsInStock'**, **WidgetsInStock"**, or **WidgetsInStock'"** appeared in other scenarios of the use case, it is assumed that they would each be equal to or greater than zero.

This is also true if multiple variables are involved in the invariant:

Given this invariant: CheckAmount < GiftCardValue

...this would be true: CheckAmount < GiftCardValue'

...as well as this: CheckAmount' < GiftCardValue"

...and this: CheckAmount" < GiftCardValue'"

...and so on

Global invariants are, in a sense, *preconditions on steroids*. Whereas a "regular" precondition may only guard one specific postcondition, global invariants act as guards to *all* postconditions that use the state variables covered in the global invariant. From a failure analysis and testing perspective, it is useful to keep this point in mind because they provide additional ways to validate the correct functioning of the system. *A global invariant is a mini test case that can be repeated over and over to reaffirm that property of the system is still holding.*

Local Invariants

Local invariants are ones that are not necessarily true for all states of the system, and so may only be true for the scope of a specific scenario. Local invariants are a postcondition-like statement that strengthens another existing postcondition in order to constrain the values that satisfy that postcondition. Here's an example from the chemical tank use case:

This invariant: InFlow' > OutFlow

...strengthens this postcondition: InFlow' = OutFlow + Delta

The easiest way to spot a local invariant in a model-based spec is that it involves the use of one or more *primed* variables. A local invariant stated about a primed variable cannot be assumed to apply to all unprimed and primed versions of the invariant. For example:

From this invariant: InFlow' > OutFlow

...we *cannot* conclude that: InFlow > OutFlow

...or that: InFlow" > OutFlow

...or: InFlow" > OutFlow'

...and so on

Transition Constraints: A Special Kind of Local Invariant

There is a particular kind of local invariant that you've seen in the chemical tank example that is used to express properties about state transitions. These are what C.J. Date (2000) calls a *transition constraint*: they constrain the legal transition of a state variable from one value to another. This is not the same thing as a state invariant. A state invariant describes a valid state or states; a transition constraint describes the allowed transition *between* states. The easiest way to spot a transition constraint is that it involves the primed and/or unprimed versions of a single state variable. This is a transition constraint from our chemical tank example:

InFlow" < InFlow'

Transition constraints, though local invariants, may sometimes be describing global properties, but just at a local level. Let's say that we have an application that tracks the number of persons that enter a secured area in the morning, and then counts the number that leave that night, allowing for a check that no one has remained in the secure area unauthorized overnight. The normal flow for the use case that tracks entry might be modeled with a postcondition like:

$$Entered' = Entered + 1$$

This flow of the use case is executed each time a person enters one of several turnstiles. If we had an alternate flow to the use case that tracked, say, persons entering the area via elevator, we might model it with a postcondition, such as:

$$Entered' = Entered + NumberOnElevator$$

The following invariant, though stated locally in terms of primed variables, expresses a property that is true across both use case scenarios, which is to say that the state variable **Entered** should never decrease but should always advance:

$$Entered' > Entered$$

So, though stated as a local invariant, they may in fact be describing a global, cross-scenario property.

Working Smart in How You Apply What You've Learned

Mathematically based techniques, such as model-based specification, are called formal methods. As with any rigorous technique, you might not want to apply it to *every* use case. And you might not even want to apply the full technique. So, let's see if we can put things in perspective and look at ways to apply what you've learned in a sensible manner, namely:

- Prioritize where you apply model-based specification

- Stick to numeric problems

- Or, forget everything else and just use three simple rules!

Prioritize Where You Apply Model-Based Specification

The first suggestion is to prioritize where you apply model-based specification. A good approach to applying this technique would be to triage use cases based on risk—a function of frequency of use and criticality of the use case—and apply it to high-risk use cases. A low-tech, visual approach to the triage of use cases is a "Boston Matrix" with the horizontal axis representing frequency of use and vertical axis representing use case criticality (see Figure 5.14).[14] Each use case is assigned to one of four quadrants as shown below, with high-risk use cases receiving the most attention. The upper-right quadrant represents those use cases that are both frequently used and critical in nature, and where the biggest bang for the buck from applying failure analysis via model-based specification will come from.

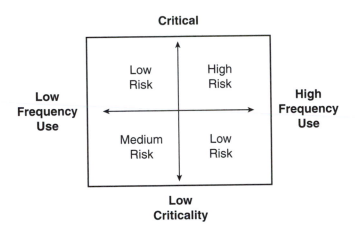

Critical

| Low Risk | High Risk |
| Medium Risk | Low Risk |

Low Frequency Use   **High Frequency Use**

Low Criticality

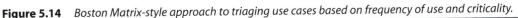

Figure 5.14   *Boston Matrix-style approach to triaging use cases based on frequency of use and criticality.*

---

[14] Additional techniques for helping to triage use cases based on frequency of use and criticality are provided in Part 2, "Software Reliability Engineering." Part 1, "Quality Function Deployment (QFD)," provides help in the use of QFD to prioritize use cases by business drivers in general.

Stick to Numeric Problems

All the examples in this chapter have been ones where the model was numeric in nature (e.g., models of money, widgets in stock, and rates of flow). Numeric problems probably provide the biggest "bang for the buck" application of model-based specification. First, there are many, many problems that can be stated numerically; after all, numerical computation is the birthplace of computing. Most applications, even if not predominantly numerically oriented, are likely to have some component that *is* numeric in nature. And second, applying this technique to numeric models is as easy as it gets, requiring little more than simple algebra.[15] So the combination of the wide range of problems to which it can be applied, coupled with ease of learning and ease of use, makes the application of model-based specification to the numerical component of use cases a high ROI proposition, *especially* when the cost of failure is high.

The Absolute *Least* You Need to Know: One Fundamental Lesson and Three Simple Rules

If, prior to reading this book, your only exposure to preconditions and postconditions has been via the use case literature, this chapter may be a bit like as they say—"drinking from a fire hose." So if you are thinking this is way too complicated, let me leave you with *one fundamental lesson and three simple rules* that anyone can use on absolutely any use case anytime. Period.

As I noted previously, mathematically based techniques like this are called formal methods. I coined the term *Blue Collar Formal Methods* to capture the idea that for many formal methods—e.g., model-based specification—there is often a less rigorous application of the method that provides benefit without necessarily getting into all the math. It's like there is a *fundamental lesson* to be learned from the formal method, but when learned you can use that lesson without the math itself.

---

[15] Model-based specification of non-numeric problems requires models using sets and relations; fairly simple ideas from set theory but they are more difficult.

What would a Blue Collar version of this technique look like? Do you remember that at the start of this chapter I made the comment "*If you look at your favorite book on use cases you are likely to find use cases with preconditions but no postconditions (the significance of which will make sense later)...*". Do you see the significance now? If preconditions are calculated from a postcondition to preserve an invariant, what sense does it make to have a precondition *without* a postcondition or an invariant?

Here then is the fundamental lesson that model-based specification teaches:

> *Preconditions, postconditions and invariants work as a team. They travel as a trio. If you see one without the others, something is missing! Remember, the team that plays together stays together.*

Here are three simple rules for applying that fundamental lesson:

1. When you write or see a lone precondition for a use case, your first thought should be, "Hmm...I wonder what happens if it fails?". Ask yourself what postcondition it is associated with and what hazard (violated invariant) it prevents the postcondition from causing. Yes, you intuitively know that precondition is needed, but take some time to try and identify *why* it's needed and the *consequence* of its failure. Remember: the precondition is part of a trio; find the rest of the team.

2. Postconditions are where the action is at in the use case, describing the output produced and state changed. And it is precisely when you are generating outputs and changing state that bad things can happen. When you write or see a lone postcondition, ask yourself, "I wonder what hazard this postcondition poses (violated invariant) and what precondition could prevent it?" Think *team*. Think *trio*.

3. Start thinking in terms of *what must always be true about a use case* (i.e., its invariants). A good way to identify invariants is to think about what can go wrong—*hazard identification*—then work backwards from the hazard to identify what needs to stay right to prevent it. And once you have identified an invariant look for operations whose postconditions could violate it, then apply rule #2.

Finally, for failure analysis and test design these rules need to be applied at the operation level (i.e., to the individual steps that make up the use case).

That's it. Math aside, that is the heart of model-based specification condensed into one fundamental lesson and three simple rules that reflect the tight coupling between preconditions, postconditions, and invariants: something not readily evident from the use case literature, but something you need to know!

Chapter Review

Let's review the key points from this chapter:

- Model-based specification is a technique for crisply specifying the expected behavior of use cases. Its components—a simplified model of inputs, outputs and state; preconditions; postconditions *and invariants*—provide an integrated basis for use case failure analysis and test design.

- Preconditions, postconditions, and invariants *work as a team.* The precondition identifies the conditions under which a postcondition—which describes the results of a use case operation—will work correctly and not cause the invariant to fail.

- Invariants are to use cases what safety requirements are to safety critical systems. They are a statement of properties about the use case that we expect to be true. A good way to identify invariants is to identify potential hazards of the use case, then work backwards to identify what must be true to prevent the hazard.

- A technique exists for the calculation of preconditions from a postcondition and an invariant. For numeric applications, the technique requires little more than simple algebra.

- Each operation or step that makes up a use case can have preconditions that describe the conditions under which that operation will work and postconditions that describe outputs and state change of the operation. These operation preconditions and postconditions are the source of preconditions and postconditions that the use case literature associates with the use case as a whole.

In the next chapter, we apply what we have learned to test case design to catch system failures before they get to the customer. We'll learn that when it comes to testing, preconditions, postconditions, and invariants, *taken as a unit*, are a veritable *triple threat* test case. And we'll learn to do test design by leveraging the best of model-based specification and Robert Binder's Extended Use Case Test Design Pattern.

6

Triple Threat Test Design for Use Cases

Testing plays a critical role in failure prevention, finding defects in the product that could potentially lead to costly failure after the product is released. In this chapter, you'll learn that not only does the model-based specification with its preconditions, postconditions, and invariants provide an integrated basis for use case failure analysis, it also provides just what is needed for test design.

In the first section of this chapter, you'll see why preconditions, postconditions, and invariants are ideal for design of test cases.

In the second section, you'll learn how to take the preconditions, postconditions, and invariants generated from failure analysis and design test cases using Robert Binder's Extended Use Case Test Design Pattern. And because the test cases are designed from the results of failure analysis, they will target defects that represent high-impact failures in the use case.

"Triple Threat" Test Cases?

In software testing, the terms "precondition" and "postcondition" are used, by some, almost synonymously with "test case." It should be no surprise, then, that when it comes to testing, the preconditions, postconditions, and invariants of the model-based specification, *taken as a unit*, are a veritable *triple threat* test case. Let's look at why this is so.

Threat #1—The Precondition

When it comes to testing, a key question is always what test points to select. A *test point* is a specific value selected for an input or state variable to make a test case. Preconditions are an ideal source for test point selection both in terms of valid test cases and failure scenario testing (i.e., tests of the software's error-handling capabilities). Why is this?

Remember that a precondition is that set of values for an input or state variable that satisfies *both* the postcondition and the invariant so that it forms a type of "boundary" between valid test points (those that satisfy the postcondition *and* invariant) and failure scenario test points (those that satisfy one or the other *but not both*). Hence, preconditions often provide just the detail needed to apply testing techniques that involve boundary value analysis where you pick test points on, off, or inside "boundaries."

Threat #2—The Postcondition

The postcondition is that part of a model-based specification that describes what a use case step does, in terms of how it modifies the model. In that sense, it is the very heart of model-based specification. For testing, the postcondition is the primary means of stating what the expected result of a test case should be. As Boris Beizer (1990) has said, test cases without expected results are like a game of billiards where you don't call the pocket until after the ball goes in.

Threat # 3—The Invariant

And finally, rounding out the triple threat is the invariant. One might think that the role of the invariant is pretty much done after the precondition has been calculated. But invariants play several supporting roles in test cases. First, the invariant can be used in a test case to *cross-check* the results of the postcondition.

Recall that the postcondition and invariant act like simultaneous equations: any actual result produced by the software must pass the check of not only the postcondition (primary expected result), but also a cross-check against the invariant. This provides an extra boost to the expected result of the test case. This is particularly true in situations where you have not derived a precondition. The invariant can essentially act as a fallback precondition "after the fact"; i.e., a precondition is a check to see if conditions are good *before* execution of an operation. An invariant can be used to perform the same check *after* the operation executes; as the saying goes, "Better late than never!"

Second, you will recall that global invariants are in a sense, preconditions on steroids.[1] Whereas a regular precondition guards one specific postcondition, global invariants act as guards to *all* postconditions that use the state variables covered in the global invariant. From a failure analysis and testing perspective, global invariants are system properties that can be tested for repeatedly. For example, in our widget shipping example from the first chapter, the global invariant **WidgetsInStock** $\geq$ **0** is a mini test case that can be performed repeatedly throughout all scenarios of the use case, and even across all use cases (given that the scope of "global" is determined to be application wide, e.g., it's a business rule of the underlying database). If at any time it is found that **WidgetsInStock < 0**, something has gone wrong and the potential for failure is there.

In summary, preconditions, postconditions, and invariants are ideal for test design for the following reasons:

- Preconditions identify conditions for operation success and failure and provide a sound basis for test point selection

- Postconditions provide the expected results

- Invariants serve to cross-check expected results and, if global, provide a mini-test case for checking system properties anytime, anywhere

---

[1] See the "Global Invariants: Preconditions on Steroids" section in Chapter 5, "Preconditions, Postconditions, and Invariants: What They Didn't Tell You, But You Need to Know!"

The next section looks at applying this testing trio to the design of test cases for the chemical tank example from Chapter 5.

Applying the Extended Use Case Test Design Pattern

Robert Binder (2000) has laid out a process for defining a suite of test cases for use cases as part of his Extended Use Case Test Design Pattern. There are four steps in the process:

1. Identify the operational variables of the use case

2. Define the domain of each variable

3. Develop an operational relation for the use case

4. Build test cases

Not to put too fine a line on it, the approach identifies a set of *operational variables* and an *operational relation*, which are to use cases what instance/member variables and class invariant are to a class, respectively. The combinations of different operational variable values and relationships between the variables define the various states of the use case, each state corresponding roughly to a different scenario or "variant" of the use case.

In this section, you will see this four-step procedure applied to the chemical tank example from the previous chapter. The description will deviate slightly from Binder's to better fit the model-based specification approach, which includes preconditions, postconditions, invariants, and unprimed/primed state variables.

A key point to gain from this section is that by building a model-based specification, as was done in the previous chapter, you have essentially done all the hard work of test design: a model-based specification is what Binder calls a *test-ready model*, and all that is left is to essentially "fill in the blanks" of the Extended Use Case Test Design Pattern.

Step 1. Identify Operational Variables

Binder's procedure begins by identifying the *operational variables*: those factors that vary from scenario to scenario and which determine different results from one use case scenario to the next.[2] Operational variables include inputs, outputs, and abstractions of the state of the system as examples; all items that our model-based specification of the use case supplies. The operational variables for the chemical tank use case are the initial state variables (unprimed), outputs, and changed state variables (primed) utilized in the model-based specification of the use case:

- **InFlow**—Initial rate of flow into the tank when the use case starts.

- **OutFlow**—Initial rate of flow out of the tank when the use case starts.

- **Delta**—The incremental increase in rate of flow into the tank used for refilling: A constant whose actual value the model does not specify.

- **InFlow'**—The flow rate to increase the level in the tank.

- **InFlow"**—The flow rate at the end of the use case to stabilize the level.

- **OutFlow'**—The rate of flow out of tank subsequent to the start of refilling through to the end of the use case.

This is a good opportunity to re-emphasize that primed and unprimed versions of a variable are actually *separate* variables in the model. **InFlow**, **InFlow'**, and **InFlow"** are separate variables representing three separate states of one aspect of the chemical tank, that is to say the rate of flow into the tank. If they were not separate variables in the model, one would not be able to specify relationships between them (e.g., **InFlow" < InFlow'**).

---

[2] Binder actually says different "variants" and makes a distinction between variants and scenarios; for simplicity, the focus here will be scenarios.

Independent Operational Variables

Having identified the set of operational variables, it remains to identify which are independent: an *independent variable* is one that is not defined in terms of another variable and therefore can be varied for testing purposes. In a model-based specification, these are *generally* inputs (parameters passed into the use case, which we do not have in our chemical tank example) and the initial, unprimed state variables. For our example, the independent variables are:

> InFlow—initial rate of flow into the tank when the use case starts

> OutFlow—initial rate of flow out of the tank when the use case starts

> OutFlow'—the rate of flow out of tank subsequent to the start of refilling through to the end of the use case

It is not common to have a primed variable, such as **OutFlow'**, as an independent variable in a model-based specification, but in this case, this variable is not defined in terms of other variables, is controlled external to the use case by the rate of production of manufacturing, and so can be manipulated for testing purposes.

Step 2. Define Domains of the Operational Variables

The second step of the Extended Use Case Test Design Pattern is to define the *domain* of each operational variable: the set of all possible values. As part of the model developed in the last chapter, these domain definitions have already been defined:

> $0 \leq \text{InFlow} \leq \text{MaxFlow}$

> $0 \leq \text{OutFlow} \leq \text{MaxFlow}$

Recall that **MaxFlow** is some upper bound that specifies the maximum safe rate of flow into, or out of, the chemical tank. It is a positive constant whose specific value is not addressed in the model.

Because domain definitions are essentially global data invariants, the following are also true:[3]

$0 \leq \text{InFlow}' \leq \text{MaxFlow}$

$0 \leq \text{InFlow}'' \leq \text{MaxFlow}$

$0 \leq \text{OutFlow}' \leq \text{MaxFlow}$

Step 3. Develop the Operational Relation

Relations are a common way to specify the expected behavior—and hence test cases—of all manner of "black boxes," be they software or hardware. They allow us to specify what something should do without having to say how it is to be done. The Extended Use Case Test Design pattern applies this idea to use cases in the form of what is called an operational relation, implemented via a decision table.[4] In this step, we'll take the preconditions, postconditions, and invariants of our model-based specification and put them into the decision table format of Binder's Extended Use Case Test Design Pattern.

Tables as Relations

A common way to think of a relation is as a table. Figure 6.1 is part of a table for computing personal income tax in the United States.

The tax table in Figure 6.1 defines a relationship between an input—your annual *taxable income* (line 40 on the tax form)—and various outputs, *taxes due*, for various filing status: *single, married filed jointly, married*

---

[3] This concept was discussed in Chapter 5, "Preconditions, Postconditions, and Invariants: What They Didn't Tell You, But You Need to Know!" Refer to the "Global Invariants: Preconditions on Steroids" section.

[4] Leffingwell and Widrig (2003) use a similar approach to specify test cases but call it a matrix.

filing separately, and *head of household.* Each row provides a different scenario in your own personal "paying taxes" use case; if your income meets the conditions predicated on the inputs (your income is "At least" X "But less than" Y), that row outputs the tax rates that apply to you for the various filing statuses. If you were testing a software program for doing personal income taxes, you might use a table such as this to specify the expected outputs of the program.

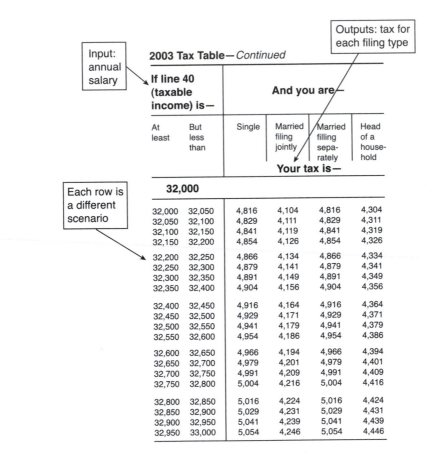

Figure 6.1   *Table for computing personal income tax in the United States.*

Operational Relation Table for Chemical Tank Use Case

Binder's operational relation applies this use of relations, implemented via a decision table, to specify the expected behavior of use cases. To implement the operational relation, one needs to specify the relationships that exist between each of the operational variables. We begin by listing the operational variables as columns in a table, as shown in Figure 6.2.

Independent Variables			Expected Results			
InFlow	OutFlow	OutFlow'	Delta	InFlow'	InFlow"	Status/Action
Initial rate of flow into the tank	Initial rate of flow out of tank	Rate of flow out of tank subsequent to start of refilling to end of use case	Amount flow is increased to fill tank	Adjusted rate of flow to fill tank	Final rate of flow set to stabilize level	Status message and action taken

Figure 6.2 *Operational variables form the columns of the operational relation of the chemical tank use case.*

The first three columns are the independent variables that can be controlled for testing. The next four columns provide the expected results: outputs and state change that we expect to see. An extra column (last) has been added to the model to output status messages.

Next, we populate the first row with the use case main scenario, using the domain definitions, preconditions, postconditions, and invariants from our model-based specification to specify the range of values of each operational variable, constraints on, and relationships between, the operational variables (see Figure 6.3).

	Independent Variables			Expected Results			
	InFlow	OutFlow	OutFlow'	Delta	InFlow'	InFlow"	Status/Action
	Initial rate of flow into the tank	Initial rate of flow out of tank	Rate of flow out of tank subsequent to start of refilling to end of use case	Amount flow is increased to fill tank	Adjusted rate of flow to fill tank	Final rate of flow set to stabilize level	Status message and action taken
Use Case Main Scenario	0 ≤ Inflow ≤ Maxflow	0 ≤ OutFlow ≤ Maxflow OutFlow ≤ MaxFlow − Delta	0 ≤ OutFlow' ≤ MaxFlow OutFlow' < OutFlow + Delta	Delta > 0	0 ≤ InFlow' ≤ MaxFlow InFlow' = OutFlow + Delta InFlow' > OutFlow InFlow' ≤ MaxFlow	0 ≤ InFlow" ≤ Maxflow InFlow" = OutFlow' InFlow" < InFlow'	OK

Figure 6.3 *Operational relation for main scenario of the chemical tank use case.*

In Binder's operational relation, one scenario of the use case is allocated one row of the table. Because our use case for refilling the chemical tank only has a main scenario, the table has just one row. Keep in mind, however, that this one row is like a database query: it uses variables to describe all possible instances of the main scenario.[5]

That's it; the operational relation is defined. As this example illustrates, a model-based specification with its preconditions, postconditions, and invariants is itself a description of a relation,[6] so it is just a matter of rearranging the information to put it into the format of the Extended Use Case Test Design Pattern's operational relation.

An Alternate Format for the Operational Relation Table

As just noted, in Binder's operational relation, one scenario of the use case is allocated one row of the table. While this results in a compact table, there are drawbacks. First, use cases are by their nature workflow oriented, often describing step-by-step procedures. This workflow information can be useful for testers during testing. Placing a scenario in one column tends to compress out this workflow aspect of the use case; information that might be useful to testers is lost. Second, restricting a scenario to a single row also makes it difficult to see which preconditions, postconditions, and invariants are working together as a team.

To address these two issues, you may find this alternate, expanded format useful in which each use case scenario gets its own table (see Figures 6.4 and 6.5).

---

[5] In set theory, relations—which are sets of "records," to use a database analogy—can be described in two ways: by extension, like the tax table in Figure 6.1, where every record of the relation is enumerated one by one; or by intension, like the operational relation in Figure 6.3, where variables are used to describe the properties of all records of the relation, just like a database query. They are both relations, just described in different ways. This distinction is also called set enumeration versus set comprehension.

[6] Model-based specification is rooted in set theory, of which relations are a part.

Use Case Step	Test Case Footnotes		Independent Variables			Expected Results			
			InFlow	OutFlow	OutFlow'	Delta	InFlow'	InFlow"	Status/Action
			Initial rate of flow into the tank	Initial rate of flow out of tank	Rate of flow out of tank subsequent to start of refilling to end of use case	Amount flow is increased to fill tank	Adjusted rate of flow to fill tank	Final rate of flow set to stabilize level	Status message and action taken
Domain definition for InFlow	1		$0 \leq Inflow \leq Maxflow$				$0 \leq InFlow' \leq MaxFlow$	$0 \leq InFlow" \leq Maxflow$	
Domain definition for OutFlow	1			$0 \leq OutFlow \leq Maxflow$	$0 \leq OutFlow' \leq MaxFlow$				
Level drops below target level; controller increases flow into the tank to start refilling	2	Preconditions		$OutFlow \leq MaxFlow - Delta$		$Delta > 0$			
	3	Postcondition					$InFlow' = OutFlow + Delta$		
	4a	Check Invariant					$InFlow' > OutFlow$		
	4b	Check Invariant					$InFlow' \leq MaxFlow$		
Level rises to target level; controller re-adjusts flow into tank to stabilize level	5	Precondition			$OutFlow' < OutFlow + Delta$				
	6	Postcondition						$InFlow" = OutFlow'$	
	7	Check Invariant						$InFlow" < InFlow'$	
Use completed successfully; return status OK	8	Postcondition							OK

Figure 6.4   *Operational relation with main scenario in expanded format (each scenario gets its own table). Gray shows preconditions, postconditions, and invariants that are working together to describe a use case step.*

This expanded format has a number of advantages. First, the workflow nature of the use case is preserved: use case steps—stated in natural language—are listed in the first column. The second column allows references to footnotes that are pertinent to testing; footnotes are listed at the bottom of the table (refer to Figure 6.5).

Second, this overall combination of natural language augmented with a model provides a test case that is both understandable while also being rigorous. Al Davis' (1995) philosophy on requirements—"Augment, Never Replace, Natural Language"—is, I believe, as appropriate for test cases as it is for requirements.[7]

---

[7] See (Davis 1995), particularly Principle 54: Augment, Never Replace, Natural Language.

Test Case Footnotes

1. Domain definitions are global invariants and apply to unprimed and primed state variables alike.

2. Preconditions for refilling the tank: For this operation to work as per the invariant, the value used to increase the flow into the tank must be greater than zero.

   Also, if the flow out of the tank is too high, e.g. OutFlow = MaxFlow, it will not be possible to increase the flow into the tank high enough to start refilling the tank. For this operation to work as per the invariant, OutFlow must be less than or equal to MaxFlow – Delta in order to allow refilling to proceed.

3. Post Condition describing expected change once refilling starts.

4a. As an additional check on the expected result, if this invariant is not true once refilling begins, the level will not rise and there is a problem.

4b. As an additional check on the expected result, this invariant should still be true after refilling begins.

5. Precondition for stabilize level operation. Because filling the tank will take time, the rate of flow out of the tank may change before the target level is reached. If during the filling of the tank, OutFlow' increases to be equal to OutFlow + Delta, the level in the tank would stop rising, stabilize, and the use case would not terminate until the flow out changed again. If during the filling of the tank OutFlow' were to increase to be greater than OutFlow + Delta, the level in the tank would fall, potentially depleting chemicals in the tank.

   For the stabilization operation to work as per the invariant, OutFlow', the rate of flow out of the tank subsequent to refilling through to the end of the use case, must be less than specified rate of flow.

6. Postcondition describing expected change once stabilization operation occurs.

7. As an additional check on the expected result, InFlow" must be lower than InFlow' or overfilling will occur. If the rate of flow is high enough to cause the level to rise (InFlow'), it will have to be reduced to stabilize the level and prevent overfilling (InFlow").

8. Postcondition: output "OK" message to signal successful completion of use case.

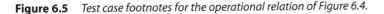

Figure 6.5   *Test case footnotes for the operational relation of Figure 6.4.*

And finally, the *team* of preconditions, postconditions, and invariants that models and describes a use case step is directly associated *with* the step, and each item receives a row in the matrix.[8] The team that plays together stays together!

It's worth re-emphasizing that the content of Figure 6.4 is the same as that of Figure 6.3: if the former were collapsed into a single row it would result in the latter.

---

[8] An alternate approach is to allocate each use case step one row and combine all its associated preconditions, postconditions, and invariants on that one row.

Step 4. Build Test Cases

The final step of the Extended Use Case Test Design Pattern actually involves two tasks:

1. The selection of *test points*: values to be used for inputs and state variables in test cases. The Extended Use Case Test Design Pattern calls for two types of test points:

    a. *Valid* test points: for a model-based specification, this involves test points where all preconditions and invariants are satisfied.

    b. Test points that should cause a *failure*: for a model-based specification, this involves test points where at least one precondition/invariant fails. This is essentially a test of the software's error-handling capability.

2. The creation of test cases using the selected test points.

The next two sections look at these tasks in more detail.

Select Test Points

In our operational relation of Figure 6.4, we have three independent variables for which we need to select test points: **InFlow**, **OutFlow**, and **OutFlow'**. Remember, the independent operational variables are the ones not defined in terms of other operational variables, so they are the source of variation for testing purposes.

As noted previously, preconditions are a good source from which to select test points for an independent variable. *But* a variable may be constrained by *several preconditions* in a use case scenario: the valid test points we identify must simultaneously satisfy *all* preconditions that constrain a variable as well as its domain definition.[9] Figure 6.6 illustrates a straightforward, low-tech approach you can use to identify such test points.

---

[9] In software testing, the process of selecting test points from an input's or state variable's domain by analyzing constraints on the variable is called domain analysis (Binder 2000).

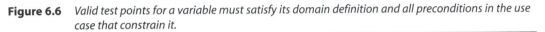

	Independent Variables		
	InFlow	OutFlow	OutFlow'
Domain definition	0 ≤ InFlow ≤ MaxFlow	0 ≤ OutFlow ≤ MaxFlow	0 ≤ OutFlow' ≤ MaxFlow
Precondition-1	n/a	OutFlow ≤ MaxFlow − Delta	OutFlow' < OutFlow + Delta
Precondition-2	n/a	n/a	n/a
Subdomain satisfying all preconditions	0 ≤ InFlow ≤ MaxFlow	0 ≤ OutFlow ≤ MaxFlow − Delta	0 ≤ OutFlow' < OutFlow + Delta

Figure 6.6   *Valid test points for a variable must satisfy its domain definition and all preconditions in the use case that constrain it.*

In the table in Figure 6.6, the independent operational variables for the use case are listed across the top as columns. The domain definition (the set of all possible values) for each variable is listed in the first row of the table (refer to section "Step 2. Define Domains of the Operational Variables"). In subsequent rows, any preconditions that further constrain the values of each variable are listed. Finally, for each variable the final row shows the subset of the domain—called a *subdomain*—that meets all the preconditions in a column. This is arrived at by simple visual inspection looking for the "lowest common denominator" for each column, so to speak. That subset, or subdomain, is then entered in the last row of the column.[10]

It is the last row of the table in Figure 6.6 from which test points for **InFlow**, **OutFlow**, and **OutFlow'** should be selected. The table in Figure 6.7 shows test points (rows) to be used for valid and failure scenario test cases selected from each variable's subdomain (columns).

The test points of the table in Figure 6.7 were selected using the "1×1" or "one-by-one" domain testing strategy.[11] For the variables of Figure 6.7, each subdomain has two boundaries: a lower bound and upper bound. The one-by-one strategy calls for *two test points per boundary*: one that is valid and one that should cause failure. For the example here this results in a total of four test points per variable.

---

[10] Rather than building a separate table, in "real life" you might do this directly from inspection of the operational relation itself as it is the source of domain definition and preconditions for the table. The table in Figure 6.6 is constructed here primarily as an aid to the reader, helping to focus on just the parts of the operational relation that are pertinent.

[11] The Extended Use Case Test Design Pattern does not suggest a particular test point selection strategy other than that test points should include valid test points and test points that should cause failure. The one-by-one strategy certainly meets this criterion. See Binder (2000), particularly the "The One-By-One Selection Criteria" section.

Test points having been selected, they now need to be incorporated into test cases.

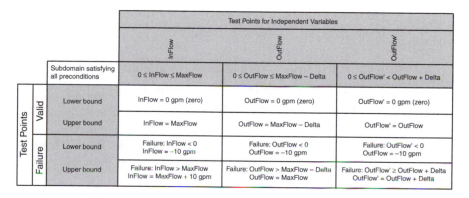

			Test Points for Independent Variables		
			InFlow	OutFlow	OutFlow'
		Subdomain satisfying all preconditions	0 ≤ InFlow ≤ MaxFlow	0 ≤ OutFlow ≤ MaxFlow − Delta	0 ≤ OutFlow' < OutFlow + Delta
Test Points	Valid	Lower bound	InFlow = 0 gpm (zero)	OutFlow = 0 gpm (zero)	OutFlow' = 0 gpm (zero)
		Upper bound	InFlow = MaxFlow	OutFlow = MaxFlow − Delta	OutFlow' = OutFlow
	Failure	Lower bound	Failure: InFlow < 0 InFlow = −10 gpm	Failure: OutFlow < 0 OutFlow = −10 gpm	Failure: OutFlow' < 0 OutFlow = −10 gpm
		Upper bound	Failure: InFlow > MaxFlow InFlow = MaxFlow + 10 gpm	Failure: OutFlow > MaxFlow − Delta OutFlow = MaxFlow	Failure: OutFlow' ≥ OutFlow + Delta OutFlow' = OutFlow + Delta

Figure 6.7   *For the upper and lower boundary of each variable's subdomain, two test points are selected: one that is valid and one that should cause a failure. Flow rates are stated in Gallons Per Minute (gpm).*

Use Test Points in Test Cases

The final task of the Extended Use Case Test Design Pattern is to use the test points of Figure 6.7 in actual test cases, including expected results. Expected results for valid test points can be determined using the operational relation of Figure 6.3 or Figure 6.4.

For test points intended to cause failure, the operational relation would need to be extended to cover each failure scenario. For the sake of brevity, such an extension is not shown here, although it is assumed such an extension is available as a basis for determining the expected results of the failure test points.

While valid test points can be combined into the same test case, test points intended to cause failure typically require a test case of their own. Hence, as is clear from the table in Figure 6.7, the chemical tank use case requires six different test cases to cover each of the six failure scenarios identified. Briefly, the failure scenarios are as follows:

- Failure Scenario 1—Backwash in the InFlow valve when use case starts (i.e., InFlow is negative)

- Failure Scenario 2—Initial InFlow is too high at start of use case

- Failure Scenario 3—Backwash in the OutFlow valve when use case starts (i.e., OutFlow is negative)

- Failure Scenario 4—Initial OutFlow at start of use case is so high that tank can't be refilled at rate Delta without raising InFlow' past the MaxFlow rate

- Failure Scenario 5—OutFlow' is set to be negative (backwash) after refilling begins but before target level is reached

- Failure Scenario 6—OutFlow' is increased to be ≥ OutFlow + Delta after refilling begins but before target level is reached

Figure 6.8 shows a table of test cases in the style of the Extended Use Case Test Design Pattern with one test case per row. Shown are two valid tests of the main scenario and six failure scenario tests. Blank cells indicate that the value of the corresponding variable is irrelevant; Binder uses "DC" (Don't Care) for this purpose. Footnotes (none shown) would provide additional explanation to the tester on test setup, execution, and expected results, including preconditions and invariants to be aware of and/or monitored.

With test cases in place, the Extended Use Case Test Design Pattern is complete.

		Test Case Footnotes	Independent Variables			Expected Results			
			InFlow	OutFlow	OutFlow'	Delta	InFlow'	InFlow"	Status/Action
Valid Tests	Main Scenario Valid Test 1	—	Inflow = 0	OutFlow = MaxFlow – Delta	OutFlow' = OutFlow = MaxFlow – Delta	Delta > 0	Inflow' = Maxflow	InFlow" = OutFlow = MaxFlow – Delta	OK
	Main Scenario Valid Test 2	—	Inflow = Maxflow	OutFlow = 0	OutFlow' = 0	Delta > 0	Inflow' = Delta	InFlow" = 0	OK
Failure Scenarios	Test Failure Scenario 1	—	Failure: InFlow < 0 Set InFlow = –10 gpm		OutFlow' = 0	Delta > 0	Inflow' = 0	InFlow" = 0	Raise alert. Seal InFlow & OutFlow valves to stop backwash. Signal manufacturing to stop.
	Test Failure Scenario 2	—	Failure: InFlow > MaxFlow Set InFlow = MaxFlow + 10 gpm		OutFlow' = 0	Delta > 0	Inflow' = 0	InFlow" = 0	Raise alert. Stop flow into tank. Signal manufacting to stop (which controls flow out of tank).
	Test Failure Scenario 3	—		Failure: OutFlow < 0 Set OutFlow = –10 gpm	OutFlow' = 0	Delta > 0	Inflow' = 0	InFlow" = 0	Raise alert. Seal InFlow & OutFlow valves to stop backwash. Signal manufacturing to stop.
	Test Failure Scenario 4	—		Failure: OutFlow > MaxFlow – Delta Set OutFlow – MaxFlow	OutFlow' = 0	Delta > 0	Set Inflow' = 0	InFlow" = 0	Raise alert. Stop flow into tank. Signal manufacting to stop (which controls flow out of tank).
	Test Failure Scenario 5	—			Failure: OutFlow' < 0 Set OutFlow' = –10 gpm	Delta > 0	Inflow' = OutFlow + Delta	InFlow" = 0	Raise alert. Stop flow into tank. Signal manufacting to stop (which controls flow out of tank).
	Test Failure Scenario 6	—			Failure: OutFlow' ≥ OutFlow + Delta Set OutFlow' = OutFlow + Delta	Delta > 0	Inflow' = OutFlow + Delta	Set InFlow" = 0	Raise alert. Stop flow into tank. Signal manufacting to stop (which controls flow out of tank).

Figure 6.8   *Table of test cases in the style of the Extended Use Case Test Design Pattern.*

Closing Thoughts

Remember that in the last chapter I talked about *Blue Collar Formal Methods,* my concept of scaling down a formal method to something easier to learn and use that still affords a little rigor, but with little or none of the math.[12] With just a few simple extensions to Binder's operational relation

---

[12] See Chapter 5, the "The Absolute Least You Need to Know: One Fundamental Lesson and Three Simple Rules" section.

decision table concept, you have what makes for a decent *Blue Collar Model-based Specification* of a use case, namely:

- Use of unprimed and primed state variables for operational variables in the style of Figure 6.4 to raise visibility to state change in the use case and allow you to talk about the *before* and *after* versions of state variables when describing preconditions, postconditions, and invariants.

- Expansion of the table format in the style of Figure 6.4 to allow a row per use case step's precondition, postcondition, and invariant.

- Dispense with the math and instead describing your preconditions, postconditions and invariants in natural language while following the "one fundamental lesson and three simple rules" from Chapter 5.[13]

The operational relation extended with a few tricks from model-based specification is a winning combination not only for test design, but use case analysis in general.

Chapter Review

The overall lesson of this chapter is that model-based specification, in addition to being a good tool for use case failure analysis, is a good tool for test design: any work done modeling the use case for failure analysis is easily translated into test cases. Here's a review of the two major sections of this chapter.

In the first section, you learned why preconditions, postconditions, and invariants, taken as a unit, are a veritable triple threat test case for black-box testing:

---

[13] Again, see Chapter 5, the "The Absolute Least You Need to Know: One Fundamental Lesson and Three Simple Rules" section.

- Preconditions are an ideal source for test point selection both in terms of valid and failure scenario test cases.

- Postconditions provide the all important primary expected result.

- Invariants provide a crosscheck on the expected result of the postcondition or can act as a "better late than never" precondition if a precondition is not available. Plus, global invariants have the added benefit of being both a precondition on steroids and a mini test case that can be executed anytime, anywhere in the use case.

The second section reviewed Binder's Extended Use Case Test Design Pattern, a method of specifying test cases from a use case by modeling the use case as a relation described via a decision table, called an *operational relation*. You also learned that model-based specification can be used as a relational description of a use case and is easily translated into the decision table format of an operational relation. This approach—a model-based specification-style operational relation—coupled with an expanded table format, has a number of benefits:

- The workflow nature of a use case is preserved, which is handy for testing.

- The overall combination of a test case described in natural language augmented with a model stated in terms of preconditions, postconditions, and invariants provides a test case that is both understandable and rigorous.

- Use of unprimed and primed state variables allows you to talk about the *before* and *after* versions of state variables when describing preconditions, postconditions, and invariants.

- Preconditions, postconditions, and invariants are grouped in such a way to make evident their "team" structure and the use case operation or step they are describing.

Part 4

Use Case Configuration Management

Calculating ROI and Leveraging in Project Portfolio Management

"If by…negligence, one withdraw from them their ordinary food, he shall be penny wise, and pound foolish."

—*Edward Topsell,* The History of Four-Footed Beasts, *1607*

The role of Configuration Management (CM) in quality is so fundamental that it's easy to overlook. But it's pretty easy to imagine—or as the case may be, *remember*—scenarios in which CM failures directly affect the quality of products. CM is important enough that it is in the foundational layer—a Level 2 Key Process Area (KPA)—of the Capability Maturity Model.

Briefly put, the role of CM in quality management is

- Building a product with the *right parts*, assembled in the *right way*.

- When correctly assembled, controlling change to prevent, or at least minimize, introduction of defects.

In addition to its importance in the Capability Maturity Model, configuration management also plays an important role in many of the newer development methodologies. McCarthy's (1995) philosophy of software development includes development rules, such as *Rule #32: If you build it, it will ship* and *Rule #33: Get to a known state, and stay there*, which put CM center stage in development. And Alistair Cockburn remarks that software configuration management tools are one of the tools most critical to the success of the agile project (Hass 2003).

While we naturally associate CM with source code, its scope includes many other work products and deliverables of the project (e.g. release notes, user manuals, installation instructions, and even the tracking of defects, both resolved and unresolved). And lest we forget, *CM most definitely applies to use cases*! Leffingwell and Widrig (2003) discuss the benefits of requirements management based on a CM approach, what they call "requirements configuration management," or as it applies specifically to use cases, *use case configuration management.*

Although CM does not necessarily imply tool support, if your projects and products are of any significant size, manual CM is typically not practical. But while there is no shortage of available commercial CM systems, using these tools to support the CM of requirements, and specifically use cases, is a newer concept for many companies. As Leffingwell and Widrig (2003) have noted, even organizations that have rigorous CM of source code are often lacking in CM of requirements such as use cases. Given the importance of requirements and the high cost of fixing defects in them, are such companies "*penny wise but pound foolish*" in avoiding the IT expense, training, and process needed for more rigorous use case configuration management?

In this part of the book, we are going to look at tool support for CM of use cases, ask whether it makes sense for your company, and see a powerful way to leverage it if you have it.

In Chapter 7, "Calculating Your Company's ROI in Use Case Configuration Management," you will learn about some of the benefits of tool support for use case CM, couched in terms of a Return on Investment (ROI) model. You will learn about:

- A common method for calculating the Return On Investment (ROI) for IT investments.

- A model you can use as a starting basis to evaluate your company's ROI in tool support of use case CM.

- Typical sources of cost associated with the introduction and use of a tool for use case CM.

- How to estimate the savings for your company due to reduction in operating expenses (e.g., daily time savings and eliminated rework) due to the introduction of a tool for use case CM.

In Chapter 8, "Leveraging Your Investment in Use Case CM in Project Portfolio Management," you'll learn more ways that tool support of use case CM can benefit your company. You will:

- Learn how to leverage your company's investment in use case CM to provide metrics and reports for what could well be *the most far-reaching, single process improvement* possible in your company: Project Portfolio Management.

- See how to leverage some *simple* use case-based metrics to evaluate whether or not your portfolio of projects is reasonable given your company's limited development resources, evaluate the mix of strategic project types in the project portfolio, and track the status of large numbers of projects in the portfolio.

7

Calculating Your Company's ROI in Use Case Configuration Management

There is no question that a commercial requirements management tool is useful for use case management, but can it pay for itself at your company? This chapter looks at a model to help you calculate the return on investment (ROI) on requirements management tools for use case management. Not only will it help you decide if such tools make sense for your company, it also helps illustrate some of the problems CM of use cases is meant to address.[1]

Overview of ROI

ROI is a popular method of measuring the success of process improvements and IT investments. It is a measure of the dollars returned on dollars invested. And as Payne (1999) points out, ROI is an effective approach for arguing the need for, or demonstrating the success of, process improvements and IT investments.

---

[1] See Hass (2003), particularly the "Calculation of Profitability" section of Chapter 5, "Scoping the Configuration Management Task," for an overview of configuration management ROI in general.

Though there are a number of methods of calculating ROI, one straightforward, simple to understand method is the Benefit to Cost Ratio, which simply divides the benefits in dollars of process improvement or IT investment by the costs.

$$\text{Benefit to Cost Ratio} = \text{Benefits} / \text{Cost}$$

So, a Benefit to Cost Ratio of 3 would mean that for each dollar spent on the cost of process change and IT, three dollars in benefits were realized.

In doing an ROI assessment, typical sources of cost include:

- Initial IT investments

- Training staff in new processes and IT tools

- Consulting needed to assist process change and IT installation

- Recurring cost associated with new process and IT, for example maintenance

Typical benefits that are considered in an ROI assessment include:

- Increased revenue (e.g., increased sales or sales margins)

- Retention of sales that would otherwise have been lost

- Reduction in operating expense (e.g., daily time savings and eliminated rework)

In this chapter, we'll look at how to do a Benefit to Cost model for process change and IT investment of putting a requirements management tool in place in your company. Although this model was developed with the rollout of a commercial tool in mind, it should be readily adaptable to development and rollout of "home grown" tools.

Requirements Management Tools

Requirements management tools are to use cases what defect tracking tools are to defects. They provide an environment for, and database approach to, managing large numbers of use cases related in potentially complex ways (traceability), over time, across projects, through staff changes and company reorganizations. They are a corporate memory for requirements.

In a project setting, a requirements management tool is used in a number of contexts:

- Planning the scope of a release or a series of releases (key in iterative, incremental projects)

- Managing plan execution: who is responsible for what, when

- Tracking project status

- Change control of scope, particularly in evaluating the impact of proposed changes (this is where traceability of requirements is critical)

For a large company, dealing with thousands of use cases (in support of, for example, enterprise-wide project portfolio management; see Chapter 8, "Leveraging Your Investment in Use Case CM in Project Portfolio Management") moving to a database approach to requirements management allows a metrics-based style of managing use cases that is simply not practical with paper document-oriented approaches.

Calculating the ROI

Again, there is no question that a requirements management tool is very useful; but can it pay for itself at your company? The ROI model presented here provides specific improvements you might expect from installing a requirements management tool, and then tries to quantify the benefits from that perspective. The model is loosely based on one originally developed for a company of about 500 R&D staff rolling out a commercially available product; the ROI assessment was done about 1.5 years into the rollout.

Keep in mind that the costs and savings presented here are just examples and not meant as an indication of what such an effort would cost or save your company. *The main point of this chapter is to describe how to go about building an ROI model for your company, not to analyze the results of a particular case study.*

Conventions and Starting Assumptions

I'll begin by making a number of starting assumptions and noting some conventions that will be used throughout the ROI model. The model is implemented as a spreadsheet. Formulas will not be shown: most are straightforward and it is hopefully obvious how the calculations are being done; showing them would add clutter and confusion.

There are a number of parts of the model which are highly subjective and/or will vary by company, industry, and so on. These parts of the model are marked with gray cells. The end of this chapter includes suggestions for dealing with this uncertainty.

Assumptions About Cost of a Fully Burdened Employee

We need to begin the ROI model by calculating the cost of a fully burdened employee per work day, per hour, and per minute as shown in Figure 7.1.[2] By "fully burdened" we simply mean the total cost to the company: salary + total benefits. As a rule of thumb, the fully burdened cost of an employee (i.e., salary plus health insurance, vacation, holidays, sick leave, taxes paid by employer, and so on) is usually about 1.5 times salary.

---

[2] All dollar amounts in this model, both for costs and savings, are shown in US currency.

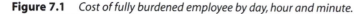

$ 120,000	Average fully burdened cost per employee per year
230	Work days per year
$ 522	Employee cost per work day
$ 65	per hour
$ 1.1	per minute

Figure 7.1   *Cost of fully burdened employee by day, hour and minute.*

Initial Actual Data about Use Cases

Next we capture some actuals in terms of numbers of use cases that were entered into the requirements management tool as of the date of the ROI assessment; in this case, about 1.5 years after initial rollout (see Figure 7.2). Of the approximately 5,000 use cases entered, about 1,000 had already been implemented and shipped as part of some project and some 200 had been rejected, meaning that a decision had been made that these use cases would never be addressed in any future release.

5000	Use Cases entered to date
1000	Use Cases implemented thus far
200	Use Cases rejected
3800	Use Cases remaining open for future projects

Figure 7.2   *Use cases entered, implemented, rejected, and remaining open.*

The Cost

An ROI assessment must be done for some fixed period of time; both the cost and the benefits must be calculated for the same fixed period. The costs presented here reflect those about 1.5 years into the rollout of a new requirements management process and tool.

Cost of Tools, Training, Consulting, and Rollout Team

The most obvious cost of any IT rollout such as this is the cost of the software, hardware, cost of outside consultants, plus the impact to your staff in terms of training classes, staff dedicated to the rollout, and so on.

Figure 7.3 shows the calculation of the cost of the tool and process rollout.[3]

Software	$ 45,000	Server and Client licenses, plus maintenance to date
Training	7	Number of training classes
	$ 8,100	Cost per class including instructor airfaire, hotel, meals, car, etc.
	15	Number of students per class
	2	Duration of class in days
	522	Fully burdened cost per day per employee
	23,752	Total per Class
	$ 166,265	Total for all classes
Consulting	$ 25,000	On-site support beyond training classes
Rollout Team Time	1.50	Elapsed years of rollout to date
	1.00	Number of staff working at 25% time on the rollout
	3.00	Number of staff working at 10% time on the rollout
	0.83	Staff years of effort
	$ 99,000	Total cost for rollout team

Figure 7.3   *Cost of software, training, consulting, and rollout team.*

Item *Consulting* refers to on-site support beyond classes: additional support needed to aid in the rollout of the tool and process. Item *Rollout Team Time* refers to a core set of staff that spends a portion of its working time in support of the process and tool rollout.

Cost of Tool Use Overhead

Another cost accounted for in the model is tool use overhead (see Figure 7.4). Just as the proper entry of a defect into a defect-tracking tool requires

---

[3] This is not meant to be an exhaustive list, but rather an example of the types of things you need to account for.

some time, the proper entry of use cases into a requirements management tool requires more time than, say, a capture on the back of a napkin or Excel spreadsheet. As noted above, gray cells are ones where the values entered are highly subjective, tool use overhead certainly being one.

An objective approach for determining a number such as this is to perform usability studies. This was *not* done in this case, however, and I suspect that most software development organizations don't have the staff, facilities, or inclination to do such a study.

In this particular case—as with many of the subjective parts of the model— I found that a straightforward approach was to poll staff that were using the tool and *ask them* how much additional time they felt they spent due to tool use overhead. After talking with a number of people, a good average number will hopefully emerge.[4]

Tool Use Overhead	15	Overhead (staff minutes) per use case to use the tool beyond what would be done in say Excel, Word, and so on.
	5000	Use cases entered to date
	75000	Staff minutes
	$ 81,522	Total

Figure 7.4 *Cost of tool use overhead.*

Cost of Added Review and Rigor

Finally, we account for the added review and "rigor" in use case management that we are asking teams to effect (see Figure 7.5). For example, use cases that would otherwise be recorded on a white board in an office or someone's laptop are now entered into a public repository. This increase in easy-to-access use cases leads to additional review, discussion, test planning, change control, and so on.[5] The cost of doing the job right is, nevertheless, a cost, and is captured in the ROI model here.

---

[4] Additional suggestions on dealing with these subjective values are given at the end of this chapter.

[5] Note that the model assumes that use cases are being written somewhere one way or another, so the cost being estimated here is not that of writing a use case, but rather the cost of the increased activity that surrounds a use case because it is now publicly available.

Added Review and Rigor	1000	Use cases implemented
	5000	Number of pages based on five pages per use case
	7	Pages reviewed per hour per person
	5	Number of persons on a team that use a use case for direction in their work to plan, develop, test, develop user documentation, and training materials, and so on.
	3571	Staff hours
	$ 232,919	Cost
	4000	Use cases entered, but not implemented
	8000	Number of pages based on two pages per use case
	70	Pages reviewed per hour per peron. Use cases not currently being implemented receive less scrutiny, so go faster
	5	Number of people on a team that use a use case for direction in their work to plan, develop, test, develop user documentaion and training material, and so on.
	571	Staff hours
	$ 37,267	Cost
	$ 270,186	Total for added review and rigor

Figure 7.5   *Cost of added review and rigor.*

Again, this is a very subjective value. How can we hope to get a ballpark number for the additional time that is being spent by staff because use cases are now publicly accessible?

In Ed Weller's "Calculating the Economics of Inspections," he states that the recommended rate for preparation for and actual inspection of a requirements specification is about seven pages an hour.[6] This seems a reasonable heuristic for estimating the *average* cost of additional review and rigor on use cases that were actually implemented.

The model divides the use cases into those that were implemented and those not yet implemented. For those implemented, let's assume that one use case is, on average, equivalent to about five pages of text.[7] Of the use

---

[6] This is not the writing of the document. "Preparation" here refers to the time spent by the team before the actual inspection begins (e.g., reading the document and recording questions and issues).

[7] IBM Rational's RUP Director Per Kroll as "Dr. Process" fields various questions put to him on the IBM Rational Web site. In response to the question "How long should a use case description be?" Dr. Process responds, "…a use case description that covers all the alternative flows of events typically ends up being two to five pages long…". My personal experience backs this up as a good average, but ultimately for this model you need to use a number that works for your company.

cases not yet implemented, many are likely to be much shorter, some similar in length to Extreme Programming (XP) stories (an XP story is supposed to fit on an index card). For these, we'll assume that a use case is on average about two pages. Additionally, the use cases that were entered, but not implemented, receive much less scrutiny (they are on the backburner, so to speak). We'll model these as receiving one-tenth of the effort, or a factor of 10 increase in speed at which they are reviewed.

The Benefits

Now we'll move to calculating the benefits of managing use cases with a requirements management tool. Of the categories of benefits discussed previously, increased or retained sales and reduced operating costs, the model will focus solely on reduced operating costs for the company. This is fairly common for most IT investment ROI models. In the case of a requirements management tool, one could probably make an argument that increased sales, or at least retention of sales, are realized due to increased customer satisfaction resulting from better requirements management.

Savings from Staff Working more Efficiently

We begin by calculating the savings realized from staff on projects having a readily available, always up-to-date, common source of use cases upon which they can base their work. It is a cost reduction from staff working more efficiently to plan, develop, test, document, and develop training materials for a product (see Figure 7.6).

1000	Use cases implemented
5	Number of people on a team that use a use case for direction in their work
1.5	Time saved in hours, per person, per use case, because they have a documented use case, readily available in a company-wide repository upon which they can base their work
7,500	Total hours of saving for all staff
$ 489,130	Total $ savings

Figure 7.6   *Savings from staff working more efficiently.*

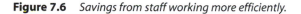

Scenarios where inefficiencies occur when use cases are not readily available to staff include:

- Use cases exist only in Joan's head, so each and every staff member that needs that information to plan tests or write a user manual makes a trip to Joan's office

- Use cases are recorded on Joe's laptop, but Joe is at the client site for the next two weeks

- Bob writes the user manual based on the woefully outdated hardcopy of use cases he has on his desk, requiring significant rework later

Note that this part of the model is not about doing a better job; *it's about doing the same job more efficiently.*

This is, again, a highly subjective number, objective numbers being difficult to come by. In talking with staff members that were using the tool, all agreed there was a savings in time, but how much varied. One way to use a model such as this one is to pick a number that is so low that everyone automatically is willing to buy into it, and then use the model to show how even that little savings translates into big dollars accrued over large numbers of use cases and staff. As illustrated here, just a savings of 1.5 hours (representative of responses I got from staff) per team member adds up to large savings.

Savings from Avoiding the Cost of Lost Use Cases from Staff Churn

Staff churn is a common problem for maintaining project consistency over time. Staff members quit the company; staff members move to other projects or are promoted; whole projects get re-staffed through company reorganization. When use cases are not recorded and managed in a company-wide system, they are subject to loss due to staff churn. The loss means that the use case must be "rediscovered" and re-engineered again and again. Figure 7.7 models the savings in avoiding the cost of lost use cases due to staff churn based on 12% staff churn per year reported by some HR groups.

5000	Use cases
1000	Already implemented so loss is not a problem
4000	Pending implementation and subject to being lost
12%	Percent staff churn…assume X% churn of staff causes X% churn of requirements
480	Estimate number of use cases that fall through the cracks and are lost due to staff churn and other causes
3	Staff days to re-engineering lost use cases…this could be a huge effort for some
1440	Total staff days of work re-engineering lost use cases
$ 751, 304	Total $ savings

Figure 7.7 *Savings from avoiding lost requirements.*

And of course, staff churn is only *one* way in which use cases can be lost over time if not under some formal means of configuration management. Use cases recorded on white boards are erased; use cases recorded on laptops are lost when the laptop is stolen; use cases, like socks in a dryer, can just disappear!

Savings from Avoiding Cost of Unnecessary Development

One of the benefits of a company-wide requirements management tool is the increased visibility that use cases receive. The people on various projects are able to see what others are doing; redundancy, conflicts and misunderstandings are spotted; and priorities are better managed. The result: use cases get rejected! This leads to a cost savings in avoiding work on use cases that are rejected due to increased visibility in the company (see Figure 7.8).

200	Use cases that were rejected
25%	Percent of these, which, had they not been recorded and subsequently rejected, may have gone forward
50	Use cases that may have gotten implemented
20	Total staff days spent implementing the use case: Coding, testing, documentation, and so on
1000	Total staff days for all unstopped use cases
$ 521,739	Total $ savings

Figure 7.8 *Savings from avoiding cost of unnecessary development.*
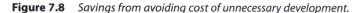

Savings from Reducing the Cost of Requirements-Related Defects

Finally, let's look at the cost savings in terms of fixing requirements related defects. For this part of the model, we'll use a few concepts also used in doing inspection ROI assessments (Weller 2002). We'll do this by:

1. Building a baseline model of what we believe was the cost of defect detection and removal *before* we added the new process and requirements management tool

2. Recalibrating the baseline model with improved defect detection and removal, the cost of which we paid for as **Added Review & Rigor** mentioned previously (refer to Figure 7.5)

3. Calculating our cost saving by subtracting the cost of baseline-2 from baseline-1

In the following, a "requirements defect" is a defect in the use case itself, either of commission (e.g., the use case said "X" but should have said "Y") or omission (e.g., the use case didn't say anything about "X" but very well should have).

It's almost an industry cliché that the later a defect is found in the development life-cycle, the higher the cost to fix. The relative amount of the increase varies from industry to industry. Here I use a simple three-phase defect-removal model:

- Removal of requirements defects anytime before coding (peer review, analysis)

- Removal of defects after they are committed to code (unit test, system test)

- Removal of defects after they are released to the customer

The relative cost of fixing defects will be 1 staff day, 5 staff days, and 25 staff days, respectively, an increase of a factor of 5 from phase to phase, well below averages that are cited in the literature.[8]

Baseline Estimate: Cost of Requirements Defects without Tool Support

Now let's look at the model. We start by estimating the number of requirements-related defects (see Figure 7.9). Unless we are willing to acknowledge the possibility of a perfect use case, it's safe to assume that all the use cases have *at least one defect*, on average. If you are not comfortable with that assumption, adjust the percent as needed.

1000	Use cases implemented
100%	Percentage of use cases that initially have at least one defect
1000	Initial number or requirements defects

Figure 7.9   *Estimating number of requirements-based defects.*

Next, we estimate the number of requirements-related defects removed prior to commitment to code and the associated cost (see Figure 7.10). A removal effectiveness of 50% means that of the total population of defects, 50% were caught and fixed. We'll assume that, on average, a defect at this stage can be found and fixed in one staff day; changes that don't involve code are simply cheaper to make.

50%	Removal effectiveness for this stage based on ballpark industry average
500	Requirements related defects removed
1	Staff days expended to find and fix one defect at this stage
$ 260,870	Cost defect removal before defects are committed to code

Figure 7.10   *Cost of requirement defects removal prior to being committed to code.*

---

[8] The larger the factor increase, the better the ROI in this model. A factor 10 increase in cost from phase to phase is commonly cited in the literature, but a factor of 5 is closer to the case study this model was built from. You will need to use numbers that make sense for your company and industry.

In Figure 7.11, we estimate the number of requirements-related defects removed from the code itself (e.g., unit, integration, and system test) and the associated cost. The calculation starts with the number of defects that remain undetected and unfixed from the previous stage. Because we are now dealing with code, the cost of finding and fixing a defect rises from one staff day per defect to five staff days per defect. Note that this is the total cost in staff effort incurred, including testers, developers, and configuration management.

500	Defects remaining that slip through to code
80%	Removal effectiveness for this stage based on ballpark industry average
400	Requirements related defects removed
5	Staff days expended to find and fix one defect at this stage
$ 1,043,478	Cost of defect removal from code, prior to commercial release

Figure 7.11   *Cost of requirement defect removal from code.*

At this point, let's review the total defect removal effectiveness of the first two stages (see Figure 7.12).

1000	Total number of requirements defects initially
900	Total number defects removed by previous two phases before release
90%	Combined defect removal effectiveness of previous stages

Figure 7.12   *Defect removal effectiveness.*

Defect removal effectiveness (DRE) is a measure of the effectiveness of a development process to detect and remove defects.[9] DRE = total defects found and fixed, divided by total number of defects. In this case, we have 900 found and fixed (500 from Figure 7.10 + 400 from Figure 7.11) over a total of 1000 to start with (Figure 7.9) for a DRE of 90%; an acceptable value for the industry. The point of computing this is to make sure that our model isn't skewed with a low DRE, thereby resulting in an unusually high number of the defects being caught in the last, most expensive phase of detection (i.e., after release).

---

[9] Refer also to the "Defect Detection Effectiveness" section in Chapter 4, "Reliability and Knowing When to Stop Testing."

Finally, we calculate the cost of defects shipped with the product to the customer (see Figure 7.13). At this stage, "finding" the bug is not so much a factor in the cost; the customer does that for you! Now the cost of defects is determined by factors such as customer support calls, loss of sales from unhappy customers, and the increased cost to patch software in the field. The cost of defects at this point varies greatly depending on the industry; safety-critical products are an example of where the cost can be very high.

100	Defects remaining that slip through to the customer
25	Staff days expended to support and fix one defect at this stage
$ 1,304,348	Cost to support and fix remaining defects in the field

Figure 7.13 *Cost of requirement defect removal after product ships.*

Our baseline cost—the cost before introducing a requirements management tool and process—for finding, supporting, and fixing requirements-based defects in use cases is $260,870 (Figure 7.10) + $1,043,478 (Figure 7.11) + $1,304,348 (Figure 7.13) = $2,608,696.

New Estimate: Cost of Requirements Defects after Tool Support

Now we rerun the baseline, but with a 10% increase in defect removal effectiveness at each of the first two stages (the third stage, where your customer finds the requirements defects for you, will not benefit from improvements due to a requirements management tool and process).[10]

So if our first phase of defect removal involved removing 500 defects (refer to Figure 7.10), we would expect to find 10% more defects now (i.e., 550 defects removed). This works out to a new DRE of 55%: 550 found / 1000 total.[11] The improvement in defect removal effectiveness is due to the added review and rigor we paid for previously in Figure 7.5.

---

[10] At least a 10% improvement is probably a reasonable expectation. Leffingwell (2003) uses a range of 10% to 40%.

[11] Notice that a 10% improvement in the DRE doesn't translate into a jump from 50% to 60%. It's calculated as new-DRE = old-DRE + old-DRE×10%.

Figure 7.14 shows the new figures. The new cost of defect removal is now calculated at $2,024,348; a cost savings of $584,348 over the old cost of $2,608,696.

	1000	Requirements implemented
	100%	Percentage of requirements that initially have at least one defect
	1000	Initial number of requirements defects
	55%	Removal effectiveness for this stage based on ballpark industry average
10% increase	550	Requirements related defects removed
	1	Staff days expende to find and fix one defect at this stage
	$ 286,957	Cost of defect removal before defects are committed to code
10% increase		
	450	Defects remaining that slip through to code
	88%	Removal effectiveness for this stage based on ballpark industry average
	396	Requirements related defects removed
	5	Staff days expended to find and fix one defect at this stage
	$ 1,033,043	Cost of defect removal from code, prior to commercial release
	1000	Tota number of requirements defects initially
	946	Total number defects removed by previous two phases before release
	95%	Combined defect removal effectiveness of previous stages
	54	Defects remaining that slip through to the customer
	25	Staff days expended to support and fix one defect at this stage
	$ 704,348	Cost to support and fix remaining defects in the field
	$ 2,024,348	New cost

Figure 7.14   *Cost of defect removal after 10% improvement in defect removal effectiveness due to improved requirements management tool and process.*

Bottom Line: Benefit to Cost Ratio

All that is left is to tally the benefit to cost ratio. As shown in Figure 7.15, the benefit to cost ratio for this particular case study—1.5 years into the tool and process rollout—is 3.4 to 1, meaning that for every dollar spent you estimate that 3.4 dollars were saved.

Recall that cost at this point includes one-time expenses, such as initial software purchase and initial on-site consulting and training, so the benefit to cost ratio should improve over time with those one-time expenses out of the way. On the other side of the equation, any future ROI models would need to take into account costs of ongoing maintenance of the tool and process (e.g., IT staff to support the tool, training for new employees, and so on).

I'll re-emphasize what I mentioned earlier: the main point of this chapter is to describe how to build an ROI model for tool support of use case CM, *not the results of this particular case study*. I suggest taking this model only as a starting point, extending what it covers in terms of costs and benefits and calibrating the model with data from your company and industry.

As they say, "Your mileage may vary."

Cost	$ 686,973	Estimated total cost at 1.5 years into process an IT rollout
Savings	$ 489,130	Savings from staff working more efficiently
	$ 751,304	Savings from avoiding lost requirements
	$ 521,739	Savings from avoiding cost of unnecessary development
	$ 584,348	Saving from improved defect removal effectiveness
	$ 2,346,522	Total savings
	3.4	Benefit to Cost Ratio

Figure 7.15   *Benefit to cost ratio.*

Dealing with Uncertainty in the Model

As noted previously, cells that are gray filled are ones where the values entered are highly subjective and vary depending on your company, industry, and so on. Here are some ideas for dealing with these uncertainties in the model.

When originally building this model, I found that a useful approach to using it was to talk with people who had been using the tool and have them provide values for these areas of uncertainty. In that way, they could see if the values they are willing to buy into resulted in a good benefit to cost ratio. This may not result in a definitive benefit to cost study, but it certainly is useful for getting grassroots acceptance of the tool (assuming that their values result in benefits greater than cost, which has always been the case when I've tried this).

A variation on this idea is to assemble a group in your company and apply a technique like Wideband Delphi to determine reasonable values for areas of uncertainty in the model. Wideband Delphi is a group problem-solving technique that is often applied to project schedule and effort estimation that allows a group to converge on an answer that is better than any individual would have come up with alone.[12]

Another common technique for dealing with uncertainties in numeric-based models is to build a Min and Max version of the model. These values could come, for example, from your interviews with the staff members who are using the tool. If you want to get a bit more sophisticated, you can even run the model through a tool like @Risk, a Monte Carlo simulation add-in tool for Excel. This provides a probability distribution function of the benefit to cost ratio: a report that tells you the likelihood of a range of possible benefit to cost ratios based on the uncertainties in your model. It may sound complicated, but it's actually very straightforward, and add-ins for Excel are relatively inexpensive.

Finally, it's always a good idea to run up estimates based on different models. Leffingwell (2003) provides an alternate model based on project cost and benefits due to reduction in requirements errors. It would be a good cross-check on the results of this model after both are calibrated to the values that make sense for your company and industry.

---

[12] Wideband Delphi is explained in more detail in Chapter 1, "An Introduction to QFD: Driving Vision Vertically Through the Project."

Chapter Review

To review, this chapter has presented a model you can use as a *starting point* for evaluating your company's ROI in the use of a requirements management tool for configuration management of use cases. Key points from the chapter include the following:

- ROI is a popular method of measuring the need for, or success of, process improvements and IT investments. The model presented calculates ROI based on the ratio of benefit to cost.

- Sources of cost used in the model include:

  - Cost of software, training, consulting and rollout team

  - Cost of tool use overhead

  - Cost of added review and rigor as a result of new tool and process

- Benefits considered in the model are only those related to reduction in operating expense (e.g., daily time savings and eliminated rework). Benefits accrued from tool support of use case CM include:

  - Savings from staff working more efficiently because they have a common, readily available, source of use cases to work from.

  - Savings from avoiding rework due to lost use cases over time (e.g., from staff churn).

  - Savings from avoiding cost of unnecessary development due to lack of visibility of use cases within projects and across projects.

- Savings from reduced rework costs due to improved requirements defect removal from use cases.

- ROI from this model, with values provided, shows a 3.4 to 1 benefit to cost ratio. Your mileage will no doubt vary. The model is intended *only* as a starting place for you to run your own ROI evaluation.

8

Leveraging Your Investment in Use Case CM in Project Portfolio Management

Project portfolio management is the measured allocation of development resources according to some strategic plan.[1,2] Think of it as basically the same thing as portfolio management of your stocks, bonds, cash, and so on applied to projects your company is undertaking, or is thinking about undertaking. Project portfolio management can be viewed as the top-level management of business requirements for a company. It seeks to understand the business requirements of the company and what portfolio of projects should be undertaken to achieve them.

It is through portfolio management that each individual project should receive its allotted business requirements, which in turn drive the specific use cases that are planned for delivery by each project. It is *without* portfolio management that a company can find itself squandering precious time, staff, and resources on the wrong projects, while burning out staff in the process of trying to complete more projects than is reasonable for available resources.

---

[1] For a Unified Software Development Process slant, refer to Scott Ambler's Enterprise Unified Process, an extension to the Unified Software Development Process that includes project portfolio management as a core discipline.

[2] Project Management Institute's PMBOK Guide 2000 edition defines project portfolio management as the "selection and support of projects or program investments. These investments in project and programs are guided by the organization's strategic plan and available resources."

Without some formal project portfolio management process in place, it becomes difficult to tell if the suite of projects underway is really balanced resource-wise to the corporate strategy as the company grows. Additionally, the industry trend is that most companies have more projects going and planned than they can actually accomplish. The result is similar to operating systems where running too many processes for a given amount of memory leads to *thrashing*: the CPU seems to be working really hard, but not a lot seems to be getting completed. This is why I say that balancing your portfolio of projects (i.e., sorting the vital few projects from the trivial many) could well be the single most far-reaching process improvement possible in your company, removing the pressure that prevents staff from doing the right job, the right way.[3] As Peter Drucker has said, there is nothing so inefficient as making more efficient that which shouldn't be done at all!

What this Chapter Is (and Isn't) About

In very simple terms, portfolio management is concerned with two problems:

1. Determining the right mix of project types in a company to meet a corporate goal.

2. Determining whether (and how) a set of projects in the portfolio can be executed by a company in a specified time, given finite development resources in the company. This is called *pipeline management*.[4]

Because of the breadth of the topic, I'll clarify what we'll be tackling in this chapter, especially because it is just one small, albeit critical, piece.

---

[3] (Demarco 2001) is a good read if you are interested in how "too much work, too little time" affects software development projects and the quality of what they produce (see, for example, his chapter 7, "The Cost of Pressure").

[4] Pipeline management is sometimes treated as a separate topic from portfolio management. But where you see one discussed, you usually see the other as well. It is treated here as part of the larger portfolio management problem.

In this chapter, you will learn how to leverage your company's investment in use case CM to provide the measurements and reports you need to manage these two key problems of portfolio management: *mix of project types* and *pipeline management*.[5]

Both the project portfolio management process and use case CM process are assumed to involve databases (if your company is small enough to do either by "hand" you probably don't need project portfolio management anyway!). You will be shown a minimal set of data that each database needs to track in order to allow you to measure and report the mix of project types and measure and report whether the projects in the portfolio are executable given the finite set of development resources in the company.

If you already have a project portfolio in place, the framework described in this chapter is an excellent sanity check, comparing what you *think* your allocation of resource by strategic project type is to what your use case CM database reveals. If you don't already have a project portfolio database, you will learn what you need to get started on a bare-bones project portfolio.

In conjunction with textual descriptions of data and reports, the appendices referred to in this chapter include Microsoft Access examples of tables and queries to better illustrate the implementation details of what is being discussed without getting in the way of the discussion here in this chapter. I use Access not because I feel that it is the ideal tool for implementing a project portfolio database, but because it presents database tables and queries in a relatively non-technical format. Having said that, I *have* used Access as a tool to prototype a functional project portfolio database, including a hookup to a commercial requirements management tool in which use cases and other requirements were stored. The Access prototype was used for well over a year by the company and allowed the portfolio management team to get the ball rolling, do some real portfolio management, and learn from the experience in preparation for selection of a replacement for Access.

What you will *not* learn in this chapter is various theories of project portfolio management or what mix is right for your company. On the other hand, in the spirit of 20/80 that runs through this book —i.e., showing the 20% of

---

[5] See (Hass 2003) for a general discussion of the use of configuration management as a source of metrics to facilitate project management and process improvement.

a discipline that may well deliver 80% of the value—what you are present-ed in this chapter may be all the portfolio management you need, or at least all you'll realistically ever get around to using. For many companies, simply putting into place a simple framework for measurement is all that is need-ed for the "lights to go on" ("We're planning how much new product devel-opment?! That will require three times the number of staff we have!"). And to progress into more sophisticated project portfolio management, you will have to take this first step anyway. As Cooper et al. (1998) suggest, perhaps the place to start in answering *What mix is right?* is to simply begin by ask-ing *What mix do you already have?* a question they state many companies are unable to answer.[6]

The Good Thing About Use Cases...

Fundamental to portfolio management is the ability to *measure* the current and planned allocation of development resources according to some strategic plan. To do this, we need to be able to estimate the effort planned for each project in the portfolio, and then roll the results up by one or more strategic project types (e.g., effort planned for research projects). It is in the estimation of the planned effort for each project that the use case comes into play. For use case-driven projects, use cases provide a good basis for bottom-up estimation of the effort planned for the project.[7]

First, the early availability of use cases in projects means they are, well…available. This is an important requisite as a basis for bottom-up esti-mation; use cases are likely to be available when few other work products are available as a basis for estimation.

Use cases have a level of abstraction that is just about right. True, the level of abstraction of use cases fluctuates from application to application and from author to author. True, the topic *"What is the 'right' level of abstrac-tion?"* is widely discussed. But, in the grand scheme of things, which port-folio management certainly is, use cases generally wind up with a level of

---

[6] See Chapter 3, "Portfolio Management Methods: A Balanced Portfolio," section Points for Management to Ponder.

[7] This is also true of extreme programming stories, depending on the amount of detail in the story.

abstraction that is not so high as to obviate the effect of bottom-up estimation (better than marketing descriptions) nor so low as to make bottom-up estimation an overly cumbersome task (widget level).

Use cases also scale well in terms of level of abstraction and detail. It is not uncommon for a company's strategic plan to look out as much as three years; that is, after all, what strategic, long range planning is about. Given that the projects in a portfolio are the vehicle for implementing a company's strategic plan, we can expect to be dealing with projects that range from those already underway, to those just starting, to those that aren't scheduled to start for months or *years*. Use cases can start at a high level of abstraction and with as little as a name and just enough information to provide an expectation of what is intended for delivery—for instance, the use case goal, without scenarios—and through time grow in detail to be a fully dressed use case and/or expand into multiple use cases. In true rolling wave-style planning, use cases let us plan in detail for what is close and plan loosely for what is distant. For projects in the portfolio not due to start for a while, Extreme Programming's *story* may be a good model for a starting level of detail; it provides just enough to get the idea across, but not so much that it won't fit on an index card.[8] Leffingwell and Widrig's (2003) approach to picking the right level of abstraction for features can be applied here for use cases: for projects in the portfolio scheduled to start in the *future*, use a level of abstraction for use cases that is high enough so that the result is under some maximum number of use cases, such as 10.[9,10]

And finally, use cases are a lingua franca—a common language—of requirements, understandable by developers, testers, managers, marketing and customers alike, which facilitates contribution to, and review of, the effort estimates that are made.

But before we look at how to your leverage your investment in use case CM to help with project portfolio management, we need to lay some CM groundwork.

---

[8] See Chapter 11, Writing Stories (Beck and Fowler 2001).

[9] See the section "Managing Complexity by Picking the Level of Abstraction" in Chapter 9, "The Features of a Product or System" in Leffingwell and Widrig (2003).

[10] IBM Rational's RUP Director Per Kroll as "Dr. Process" fields various questions put to him on the IBM Rational Web site. In response to the question, "How many use cases is too many?" Dr. Process responds "...a project of [7 to 9 months] would involve roughly 10 to 30 use cases." For purposes of scoping a project in a portfolio that hasn't begun, I recommend fewer.

Use Case Metadata (Requirements Attributes)

Whether you buy a commercial tool specifically designed for requirements management or decide to use the same CM tool you use for source code, or even decide to roll-your-own database application, some thought needs to go into what *metadata* is needed to support use cases as configuration items (Hass 2003). That decision is driven, in large part, by the metrics you would like to have available for project management and process improvements activities (e.g., in this chapter we are interested in use case metadata in support of project portfolio management).

Metadata—a configuration management term—is the additional information that needs to be associated with a configuration item (e.g., a use case) to help manage it. It is information that helps a project team manage the use case, but is not part of the use case proper: *it's not of interest to the use case actor*.

For example, whereas the *steps* in a use case are part of the use case proper—the actor is interested in the steps—*effort to implement* is metadata of interest to the development team in managing the development of the use case, but the actor really doesn't know or care about effort to implement the use case.

In the requirements engineering and management literature, this information is also referred to for example as "requirements attributes" (Wiegers 1999), or "attributes of product features" (Leffingwell and Widrig 2003). I will use the CM term "metadata" to help emphasize the "up one level" nature of the data—it is data about data—specifically, data about the use case that is not part of the use case per se. The term "metadata" also tends to reinforce the configuration management theme by defining additional fields you need to set up in your CM tool to support use cases.

How Are You Currently Invested?

When you balance your investment portfolio, you are looking at the allocation of money across various investment instruments of different types (e.g., stocks, bonds, and cash). When you balance your project portfolio, you are looking at the allocation of resources—the efforts of your staff—across a set of projects of different strategic types (e.g., new product development versus extensions to existing "cash cow" products).

Say you walk into your local Fidelity Investment or Charles Schwab office and tell them you need help with your investment portfolio. Before they even begin to determine the mix of stocks, bonds, and cash you need based on your investment objectives and risk tolerance, the first question they are likely to ask is *"How are you currently invested?"* And, as Cooper et al. (1994) suggest, this is a good place to start with project portfolio management as well. So ask yourself, for all your projects that are already underway and for all your projects that are planned for the future—your *current* portfolio of projects—how is your staff effort currently invested by strategic project type?

This is the first fundamental question we will look at answering by leveraging use case CM.

Inventory of Projects

The first requirement for a balanced portfolio of projects is…a portfolio of projects! If your company has one of these, much of the work is already done. But you may find that the process described in this chapter is a very useful sanity check on your portfolio, comparing what you *think* your allocation of resources looks like versus what your use case CM data reveals.

If you don't have a portfolio of projects, you'll need to build a database that lists the inventory of *all* projects you want to manage. While conceptually simple—you make a list of all projects—it can be a politically charged activity. But, remember, this could well be one of the best investments in time you will ever spend in improving the quality of your staff's work environment and, consequently, the quality of the products they produce.

A project portfolio database need not be complicated. Here is basic information you can track for each project:

- **Project Code**: An alphanumeric code that uniquely identifies each project in the portfolio. This serves as the key in your project portfolio database.

- **Project Name**: The common name of the project. I recommend not using a project name as a key in a project portfolio database; names change too frequently and hence are not stable as a key.

- **Duration**: The amount of time that you expect the project to last. A common measure for duration is calendar work days. Because a portfolio database deals with both projects that are underway and those planned for the future, this will range from semi-accurate (former) to best estimates (latter).

- **Start Date**: The project's estimated start date.

Note that **Duration** and **Start Date** don't have any relevance to the *mix* of project types in your portfolio, but are key to pipeline management. We'll go into more detail about this later.

In addition to these fields, each project in the portfolio needs to be categorized however you want to balance the portfolio (e.g., the same way you balance your investments in terms of cash, bonds, stocks, and so on). There may, in fact, be several different ways you want to slice and dice your projects, risk and reward being two common ones (If a large percent of your resources is spent on high-risk, low-reward projects, you have a problem!). A field is added to the database for each dimension along which you want to categorize your project portfolio. For our example, we'll stay with one category, which we'll call **Project Type**. Each project in the portfolio will be categorized as one of the following types:

- **New Product Development**: Projects that establish new products for your company. This could be done as part of your expansion into new markets or to replace aging products.

- **Cash Cow Extensions**: Projects that develop new functionality for your existing, mature, cash cow products.[11]

---

[11] "Cash cow" is industry lingo for a typically mature product that is a main source of revenue for the company.

- **Custom Development**: Projects that involve custom work for a specific customer. Companies may be concerned about the amount of custom work they do because it is often not reusable with other customers and can drive support costs up.

- **Research**: Projects that experiment with new ideas. This is typically an internal release; we'll assume here that these do not generate any revenue for the company but are needed to pave the way for new product development, and so on.

Figure B.1 in Appendix B, "Bare Bones Project Portfolio Database and Use Case Metadata," shows a Microsoft Access table for a bare-bones portfolio database implementing these fields.

Having defined these project types, an obvious question is "What is the right balance?" Our goal is not to answer that question but to provide the tools to measure the *current* allocation. The process for deciding what is right for your company is literally a book in itself and has been thoroughly covered elsewhere. However, let us assume for the purposes of this example that you have a target mix in mind: your company strategy calls for the allocation of development resources shown in Table 8.1. If your company already has a project portfolio database in place, this could represent the mix that you *think* you have.

Table 8.1   *Target allocation of resource by project type*

Project Type	Percent of Resource Allocated
Cash Cow Development	50%
New Product Development	40%
Custom Development	5%
Research	5%

Now let's turn our attention to the role of the use case in project portfolio management.

Metadata Needed for Use Cases

Our goal is to measure the current planned allocation of development resources against each of the identified project types. To do this, we'll estimate the effort planned for each project in the portfolio, and then roll the results up by project type.

It is in the estimation of the planned effort for each project that the use case comes into play. By estimating the effort of each use case in a project, we get a bottom-up estimate of the overall project effort. We'll discuss this more later. For now, we just need to make sure that after the effort of a use case is estimated, we have somewhere to record it in the use case CM database.

Here's an example of metadata we need to associate with each use case (Figure B.2 presents this information in a Microsoft Access table):

- **Use Case ID**: An identifier that uniquely identifies the use case as a configurable item.[12]

- **Project Code**: Use case metadata specifying the project code of the project in which a use case is to be implemented. This field ties to the field of the same name in the project portfolio database.

- **Estimated Effort:** Use case metadata providing an estimate of the effort to implement the use case; for example, staff days: 3 staff working for 10 working days = 30 staff days. It could well be that one use case is implemented across multiple projects, which we'll discuss later.

Notice that the effort to implement a use case is ambiguous. This could either mean the effort of all roles associated with software development,

---

[12] If you are using a commercial requirements management tool or commercial source code CM tool an identifier is generally automatically generated for each configuration item. If you are building your own database for use case CM, you'll need some ID such as this. The use case name can't be counted on to uniquely identify a use case, nor is it a stable field (i.e., it is very likely to change over time) so it is not suitable as part of the key.

such as developers, testers, managers, marketing, and so on, or it could refer to just the effort of one role, such as developers (i.e., the ones who design and code). For our purposes, it doesn't really matter which interpretation you care to use, with one caveat: a portfolio balanced for *one role* might not be balanced for *all roles* unless your organization has the right ratio of staff for each role. This is particularly true for the ratio of testers to developers, the two biggest staffing requirements for most software development projects. If the ratio of testers to developers is not sufficient, the development organization can produce far more (unstable) code than a testing organization can test. Balancing a portfolio of projects based on development resources will do little to alleviate overloading on the testing group in this case. In short, if you want to do portfolio balancing for just one software development role, figure out which is your bottleneck and balance to that. It won't be perfect, but it's a good 20/80 heuristic.

Assign Use Case to Project and Estimate Effort

After metadata fields are set up in your use case CM database, all that remains is to assign each use case to the project it will be implemented in (i.e., assign it a project code) and provide an estimate for the effort required to implement it. It's important to keep in mind that this is not an activity a single person is likely to undertake (i.e., assigning use cases to projects and estimating effort for use cases across the company). With a CM framework in place, development teams will perform this task, enterprise wide, for the use cases of their projects. With a possibly wide variety of application types and a wide variety of staff doing the estimation, you could very well wind up with a variety of estimation styles and accuracies. But, luckily, for portfolio management, it's probably OK.

For project portfolio management, one doesn't necessarily need pinpoint accuracy in estimates. First, because we are working at the portfolio level, we are dealing with an aggregate of use cases, so underestimates in one use case will likely cancel overestimates in another: the *law of large numbers* from statistics is on our side.[13] In the worst-case scenario—where estimates

---

[13] Breaking a big task into smaller ones, and then estimating their effort to derive the estimate for the whole is a common project estimation technique. It works because errors made in the small tend to cancel one another out: you overestimate one, but underestimate the next. See (McConnell 1996) for more discussion on the Law of Large Numbers as an estimation technique.

are made via the *WAG[14]* method—we can almost be certain that any estimate for a project made by bottom-up *WAGs* on use case effort will be closer to the truth than a single WAG on the project as a whole.

Besides, if your project portfolio is really out of whack—and industry trends suggest there's a good chance it probably is—being off a bit on a use case estimate here and there is not going to make a significant difference.

Techniques for Estimating Effort

Though we don't need to necessarily take a rocket-science approach to use case estimation for portfolio management, it's still worthwhile to have some ideas on how to approach the problem in order to provide guidance to development teams. Here are some examples illustrating three common themes in estimation of effort: *effort based on size, historical data, and collective wisdom and experience.*

Use Case Points: Estimation Based on Size

When dealing with use cases where ample detail is provided and teams are inclined to be as accurate as possible, *use case points* are an option. Briefly, the estimate of effort is driven by an estimate of use case size in terms of number of transactions between user and system, number of scenarios making up the use case, and number of analysis classes (if available). The size estimate is then calibrated based on various factors, such as technical complexity of the application and team and environmental factors. The final calibrated use case point count is then converted to an effort estimate. Use case points were originally researched by Gustav Karner and are a derivative of Allan Albrecht's Function Points applied to use cases.[15]

Estimating XP Stories: Estimation Based on Historical Data

In Extreme Programming (XP), estimation relies heavily on historical data. A new *story*—XP's counterpart to the use case—is compared with one you've done in the past, the true implementation effort of which you now

---

[14] WAG stands for Wild A** Guess, a common software project estimation technique.

[15] See (Schneider and Winters 1998) for more detail, particularly the section "Estimating Work with Use Cases" in Chapter 8, "Use Cases and the Project Plan."

know. That historical data is then used to estimate the effort to implement the new story (e.g., it's twice as hard, or half as hard, as the previous one). For use cases that are briefly fleshed out because they are part of projects in the portfolio not scheduled to start for a while, this approach is a good option (Beck and Fowler 2001).

Wideband Delphi: Estimation Based on Collective Wisdom and Experience

A general group problem-solving technique that is often applied to project schedule and effort estimation is Wideband Delphi (Boehm 1981).[16] Briefly, a team, through an iterative process of making individual, anonymous estimates, followed by show-and-tell, and then group discussion, converges on an estimate all team members agree upon. In the process, tacit assumptions and information held by individuals is brought to the surface for the group as a whole to see. In a workshop setting, any number of streamlined variations on this theme can be used to allow a team to crank out a lot of use case estimates in a short amount of time.

What About Use Cases Implemented Across Projects?

You may have a use case that will be implemented across multiple separate projects. I have been involved in cross-company, multi-project programs where use cases were used to show how several products worked together in large cross-product workflows. The same would be true for a use case that crossed component boundaries and where the components were being implemented in separate projects by separate teams.[17] For these instances, in terms of CM, you can either introduce a separate project code for cross-project use case work, with effort representing all projects, or each project can have its own "version" of the use case—from its perspective—for which it is responsible for CM and which includes the effort for their piece of the use case.

---

[16] Originally described by Barry Boehm in the book *Software Engineering Economics* (1981), there are ample sources describing this technique.

[17] An example of use case-driven distributed development across separate component teams is presented in Chapter 2, "Aligning Decision Making and Synchronizing Distributed Development Horizontally in the Organization."

Checking the Mix

An inventory of projects has been made and categorized by project type. The use case CM database has been extended to include metadata about project code and effort. Development teams have allocated use cases to the projects in the portfolio and estimated the effort to implement each. We are now ready to run a report that measures the allocation of estimated effort—via use cases—against project types. Figure 8.1 illustrates the use of a pie chart for just this purpose. Figure B.3 in Appendix B provides the Access database query that totals the effort by project type used to generate this pie chart.

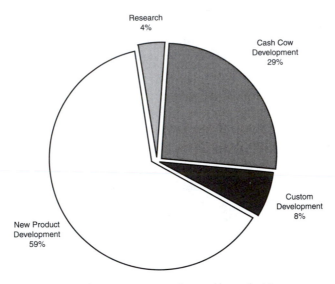

Figure 8.1   *Pie chart of effort to implement use cases allocated by project type.*

With a breakdown of effort by project type available, we can now compare the target portfolio mix against actual. A comparison of target goals for allocation from Table 8.1 is compared with actual contents of the portfolio in Table 8.2.

Table 8.2 *Comparison of target versus actual content*

Percent of resource allocated by project type in project portfolio

Project Type	Target—Percent of Resource Allocated	Actual—Percent of Resource Allocated
Cash Cow Development	50%	29%
New Product Development	40%	59%
Custom Development	5%	8%
Research	5%	4%

As the comparison shows, actual contents of the portfolio—as modeled by our inventory of projects and planned use cases—are not in synch with the target allocation of resource by project type. The current portfolio of projects has less effort in Cash Cow Development than we want and too much in New Product Development. Planned work in Custom Development and Research are pretty close to target allocations.

We started out this section asking the question "*How are we invested?*" i.e., how does our portfolio of projects allocate the company resources by strategic project type. By leveraging our investment in use case CM as a means to do bottom-up estimation of effort by project, we've identified a framework for answering this question on an ongoing basis. In Scott Ambler's Enterprise Unified Process, results such as those in Table 8.2 would be reviewed by the portfolio management team at its periodic meetings, probably quarterly or semiannually. For our example, the results of Table 8.2 indicate that some adjustments to the portfolio are probably needed. But before making changes—killing some projects and removing scope (use cases) from others—there are more questions a portfolio management team needs to answer.

Managing the Pipeline

To this point, we have been concerned with how to leverage use cases to measure the *mix* of projects in the project portfolio. But we also need to be able to measure if the projects in the portfolio are executable within the times specified by the portfolio given the finite set of development resources in the company. This is called *pipeline management,* taken from the analogy of software development being like a pipe with fixed through-put capacity. The problem of balancing the portfolio of projects has to take both these dimensions into account: the mix of project types and the quantity of projects that the organization can realistically take on at a given time.

Let's look at how the work we have already done to estimate use case effort and assign use cases to projects can help with pipeline management.

Full Time Equivalent (FTE) Models of the Project Portfolio

Full Time Equivalent (FTE) is a simplified measure of work that provides a quick way to get ball-park estimates of the number of staff needed to get a job done within a specified period of time. Let's walk through a simple example; see Table 8.3. Let's say we have five use cases to implement this month. Each use case is estimated to require 10 work days for one person to implement. That works out to be 50 staff days of effort to implement all use cases. If one FTE is counted as being able to work 20 days a month, to determine the number of FTEs we need to implement all use cases this month, we divide the total effort by 20 (the number of work days for one FTE), which yields 2.5 FTEs.

FTE models present us with a 20/80 solution to balancing project portfolios: they are a simplification of the complexities of real life projects, so they are quick and easy to apply to large aggregates of projects. And because they are a simplification of reality, they represent a best-case scenario: if your project portfolio doesn't balance using the FTE model, it most likely will not balance under the messy conditions of scheduling in real life!

Table 8.3   *Calculating FTEs needed to implement use cases*

5	Use cases to implement this month
10	Work days for one person to implement one use case
50	Work (staff days) to implement all use cases
20	Work days in a month for one full-time person
2.5	FTEs needed = Work divided by working days a month for one full-time person

Run Chart of FTEs Through Time

A good way to sanity check the project portfolio is to build a run chart of the number of FTEs required to do the work in the project portfolio through time. If the portfolio calls for all the work being done at the same time, say in six months, the run chart will show a large number of FTEs required to implement the work in that period of time. If the portfolio spreads the work out across two years, the run chart will show a quarter of the FTEs required, but for a longer period of time. The sanity check to perform is that the run chart should never call for more FTEs than we actually have available to work. That is the upper limit on our capacity to develop software: the number of FTEs we have available.

Microsoft Project has the capability to generate run charts of FTEs through time, called *resource graphs*. These are ideal for viewing the data in a project portfolio; your favorite scheduling tool probably provides similar functionality. The run chart in Figure 8.2 was produced by importing combined data from both the project portfolio database and from the use case CM database into Project (see Appendix C for details on how this is done).

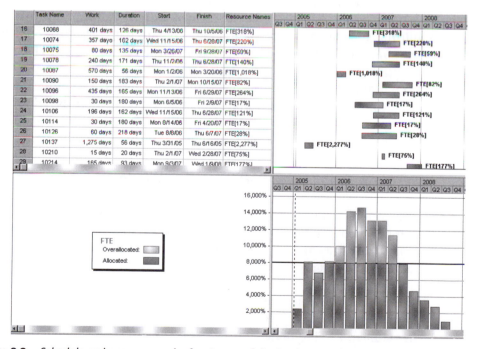

Figure 8.2   *Schedule and resource graph of project portfolio database generated by Microsoft Project with effort supplied by use case CM database.*

As a member of a use case development team, one of the first things you might notice about Figure 8.2 is the time scale: years. Your first reaction might be: *Nobody has use case-driven projects that last years!* Keep in mind that the time scales are not for one project, but rather *all* ongoing or planned projects. Portfolio management is about strategic, long-term planning, so a portfolio of projects typically reflects the company's three-year business plan, which is illustrated here. How do you write use cases for a project that won't start for another year? As already noted, use cases that are identified for such projects can be at a *very* high level of abstraction and with as little as a name and just enough information to provide an expectation of what is intended (refer to the "The Good Thing About Use Cases..." section).

Let's hit some of the highlights of what we see in Figure 8.2.

Gantt Chart: Top Half of Window

Figure 8.2 presents a split window; the top half provides a Gantt Chart view of the projects in the portfolio. The percentage that Project calculates for each project (each line of the Gantt chart) is the number of FTEs needed for that project. An entry like FTE[100%] means one FTE, the equivalent of one full-time person. An entry like FTE[50%] means half an FTE, or one person working half of the time. An entry like FTE[2400%] means 24 FTEs.

Even at this level, you can start spotting problems. For example, you spot what you know is a five-person project that shows up here as requiring, for example, 15 FTEs to accomplish the number of use cases assigned to it in the time allotted by the project portfolio.

Resource Graph View: Bottom Half of Window

The bottom half of the window shown in Figure 8.2 provides the resource graph, which is a rollup of *all* FTE calculations for *all* projects in the portfolio. In this way, we get a portfolio-wide look at the capacity being called for to execute all projects in the portfolio.

The Y-Axis of the resource graph is labeled from 2,000% to 16,000%. Again, these entries can be read as the number of FTEs required: 2,000% = 20 FTEs (remember, 1 FTE = 100%) and 16,000% = 160 FTEs.

Notice that the graph has a horizontal line drawn at 8,000% (80 FTEs). This line marks the upper limit of capacity for work of the company in FTEs. The area above this line indicates the extent to which the portfolio calls for more resources than are available. In our example, the capacity for work is exceeded by the portfolio of projects in a number of places by as much as 75%.

For the example here, the company's capacity for work has been set to 80 FTEs. You should set this to the number of FTEs you have to work on the projects in your portfolio.[18] If your estimates of effort for implementing use cases include all roles associated with software development—developers, testers, managers, marketing—use that as a basis for the number of FTEs you have available. If, however, your estimates of effort for implementing use cases include one role—for instance, the bottleneck in your development process—use the number of FTEs available for that role as your capacity limit.

Keep in mind that the number of FTEs available to work on projects in the portfolio probably does *not* equal head count. Let's say you have 50 developers, and in your company the same developers who will work on the portfolio of projects also spend 10% of their time doing maintenance, which in our example is not covered in the portfolio of projects. In that case, you really have more like 45 FTEs that are available to work on the portfolio of projects (50 minus 10%). In general, it is rare that 100% of a person's time at work is spent exclusively on projects. So remember to adjust the FTE limit to account for non-portfolio efforts, such as training, meetings that don't relate to the project, sick leave and vacation, and so on.[19]

Tracking the Status of the Portfolio via Use Cases

Just as periodic checks of your stocks and bonds are important to see if they are growing as hoped, so are periodic reviews of your portfolio of projects to see if they are progressing as planned. In this section, we'll look at a

---

[18] In Project, this limit is set via the resource sheet.

[19] Company-wide down time such as holidays and weekends can be accounted for by adjusting work time in the scheduling tool.

report you may find useful for tracking the progress of large numbers of projects in the portfolio. The report tracks the progress of projects in terms of the status of the use cases that make up each project.

Status of Use Cases

A type of metadata commonly associated with requirements is *status*. A good way to think of the status of a use case is in terms of the life cycle of a use case, progressing from conception to implementation and validation, at which time it is shipped to the customer in the form of implemented code. Table 8.4 provides *typical* values for tracking the status of implementation of a use case.[20]

Table 8.4   *Example use case status and descriptions*

Status	Description
Draft	Use case writing in progress
Proposed	Use case submitted for analysis and approval
Approved	Use case has been analyzed and approved for *some* release (metadata field **Project Code** will specify which)
Rejected	Not approved for any release
In Progress	Coding underway
Implemented	Coding complete
Validated	Use case shown to be implemented correctly in the product

Use cases—and their cousin, the Extreme Programming (XP) *story*—have a number of benefits as a basis for tracking progress in a project:

- First, use cases are a good size. A use case, as a basis for a project deliverable, provides a discrete unit of work that is not so big that you have to wait a long time to know if it's behind schedule and not so small that managing the project by them is overly tedious. As a project deliverable, they naturally

---

[20] These are only examples typical of those found in the literature, such as (Weigers 1999) and (Leffingwell and Widrig 2003). You need to identify status information that works for you.

encourage project management by "inch pebbles" rather than milestones. It is no coincidence that the Unified Software Development Process is both use case-driven and iterative/incremental. The former enables the latter to happen (the same can be said of XP stories).

- Use cases are customer focused. Futrell, Shafer, and Shafer (2000), in discussing project Work Breakdown Structures (WBS)—the blue print for running the project—argue that the best WBS is one organized around work products and deliverables that are linked directly to satisfying the customer's requirements. Use cases certainly fit this bill.

- Finally, use cases are always pertinent. Use cases are one of the few development artifacts that are pertinent as a basis for tracking project progress through all the core workflows of the Unified Software Development Process (requirements, analysis, design, implementation, and testing). In contrast, though defects are a wonderful basis for tracking product health—for example, in terms of open defects, arrival rates, and the rate at which they are resolved—they are only available for use very late in the game.

Figure D.1 in Appendix D shows an extension of the use case metadata to cover the status of use cases in your requirements management tool or source code CM system.

Now let's see how to leverage use case status for tracking the progress of large numbers of projects in the portfolio.

Tracking the Progress of Projects with the Status of Use Cases

One straightforward approach for tracking the progress of a project is to track the number of use cases by status type (e.g., the number in draft versus number implemented). As Wiegers (1999) has noted, tracking the number of requirements that are in discrete categories (e.g., draft versus implemented) is more realistic than trying to track, for example, percent completion of each individual requirement. Wiegers (1999) provides example run charts for tracking requirement status in this fashion.[21] But using the *number* of use cases has the drawback that not all use cases require the same effort to implement. For instance, if you implemented and validated all but 20% of your project's use cases that remaining 20% could well represent 80% of the remaining effort of your project.

An alternate approach is to use the sum of *effort* of use cases by status type; it is a more accurate indicator of project progress. Again, the work we have already done on estimating use case effort and assigning use cases to projects is just what we need.

Figures 8.3 and 8.4 present Excel-based reports that are useful for tracking the progress of large numbers of projects in your project portfolio; bars remain legible with as many as 100 projects. (See Appendix D, "Reports for Tracking Progress of Projects in Portfolio" for details on how to produce a report like this.) Figure 8.3 presents the Y-axis as total effort, which is useful for comparison of the sizes of projects. Figure 8.4 presents the same data but with the Y-axis showing % of total effort; this can be useful when comparing projects with widely varying efforts.

In this report, each project is shown with a single bar; if you have a very large portfolio of projects (such as more than 100), you may want to do separate reports for meaningful subsets, for example by project type (e.g., new product development versus research). Each bar provides a visual cue as to the readiness of the project to release in terms of the status of the use cases which make it up. Project 1, for example, has about 35% of its use case effort with status **implemented** and another 65% completely finished. Overall, Project 1 is nearly done. To the far right on the X-axis is Project 6, with a start date much later than that of Project 1. You can see that 100% of its use case effort is in **draft** status.

Notice that each project name (X-axis) is prefixed with the start date of the project (you can use completion date if you prefer). This allows us to sort the projects with time increasing from left to right along the X-axis. This orientation along the X-axis, from earlier to later, means that, in general, we

---

[21] Weigers (1999). See the "Requirements Attributes" section in Chapter 16, "Requirements Management Principles and Practices."

expect to see more advanced progress in projects as we scan left to right. This provides an additional sanity check on projects, allowing us to look for projects in the portfolio that don't appear to be progressing adequately.

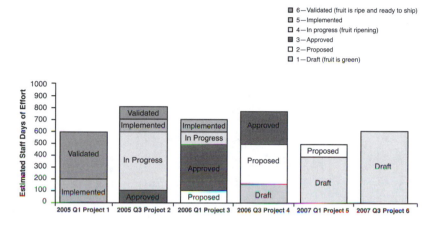

Figure 8.3   *Report for tracking status of projects in the portfolio by use case status and effort (staff days).*[22]

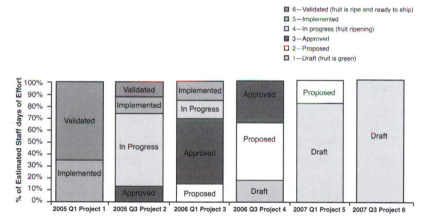

Figure 8.4   *Report for tracking status of projects in the portfolio by use case status and percentage of effort.*

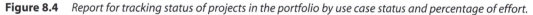

[22] Here's an idea you might want to try to improve the "at-a-glance" quality of the report. Assign each status a color along a continuum starting with bright green for draft to bright red for validated. This color scheme uses the metaphor of ripening fruit to further convey project progress at a glance; scanning from left (earliest dates) to right (later dates), one expects to see the "fruit" of the portfolio go from predominantly red (projects "ripe" for release) to predominantly green (projects still "green"; not ready to ship).

In all, the report is a good tool for getting a high level, "at-a-glance" look at the progress of large numbers of projects in your portfolio, as illustrated in Figure 8.5.

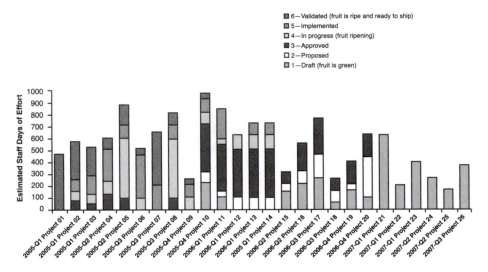

Figure 8.5   *Report allows "at-a-glance" review of progress of large numbers of projects in your portfolio.*

Chapter Review

In this chapter, we've looked at how to leverage your company's investment in use case configuration management (CM) to provide metrics and reports to facilitate project portfolio management. To review:

- Project portfolio management is the measured allocation of development resources according to some strategic plan, much like you measure your financial investment in stocks, bonds, and cash.

- An important component of portfolio management is pipeline management: determining whether a set of projects in the portfolio can be executed by a company in a specified time, given finite development resources in the company.

- Use cases provide a good basis for bottom-up measurement of the effort needed for projects. Metrics derived from the use case CM database, tied to the project portfolio database, allow a portfolio management team to:

  - Evaluate the mix of strategic project types in the portfolio

  - Evaluate whether projects are executable in the times specified by the portfolio

  - Track the status of large numbers of projects in the portfolio

- While theories of portfolio management are concerned with answering *What mix of project types is right?* a good first start is to ask the question *What mix do you already have?* For some companies, putting the measurement framework into place to answer this question may be all the project portfolio management they ever need.

- From a quality standpoint, not having a project portfolio management process means vital projects may drag on longer than they should because staff is spread thin. Vital projects suffer; staff suffers; quality suffers.

Part 5

Appendices

A

Sample Use Case

This appendix is in support of the "Using QFD to Align Decision Making Horizontally Across a Company" section in Chapter 2, "Aligning Decision Making and Synchronizing Distributed Development *Horizontally* in the Organization." It provides a sample use case to illustrate the combined use of three disciplines—geology, geophysics, and petrophysics—for oil and gas exploration. This use case is provided as motivation to the central problem of the section, (i.e., selection of a developer's toolkit for shared earth modeling company-wide across all components of O&G's product suite).

While providing a tutorial on oil and gas exploration is out of the scope of this book (never mind that I'm not qualified to do so), some explanation on what the use case is actually doing will be provided after each use case step.[1]

The name of this use case is Create 2D Cross Section. The goal is to gain a better understanding of where oil might be by producing a 2D display of a geologic cross section, augmented with measures made of wells (petrophysics) and data from seismic surveys (geophysics) for a line-of-section drawn on a basemap by an interpreter. Figure A.1 will be used as a visual reference in the use case. The steps for the use case follow:

---

[1] Thanks to John Fierstien and Gary Paisley for helping with the geoscience of this use case.

1. Log-in as an interpreter with valid ID and create new project or load existing project to be evaluated.

   Explanation: *Interpreters* are geoscientists that interpret data to determine the location of oil and gas. A *project* is just a bundle of work—models, data, notes, and so on—that gets saved. A given project may have a number of different interpreters, so logging-in not only prevents unwanted access to a project, but provides a way to keep separate the interpretations of one person from another.

2. Set stratigraphic column to be used for the project.

   Explanation: A *stratigraphic column* is a model of the sequence or layers of rock formations in an area. Different areas of the world have different geology: the strata that is exposed in Houston, Texas, is different from the strata that is exposed in Denver, Colorado. The interpreter is simply specifying the geology to be used for the project.

3. Review available well data and select wells of interest.

   Explanation: Wells are oil wells; actually wells drilled in *exploration of oil*: many are "dry holes." Wells—even dry holes—are important because they provide one of the few opportunities to get a direct "look" inside the earth, called well logging. If an interpreter looks at half a dozen wells in a field, and all had oil bearing rock at the same depth in the hole, the interpreter might make the leap of faith that oil bearing rock lies at that same depth in other parts of the field.

4. Select well log template or create new template with well template editor, then preview with well viewer.

   Explanation: A *well log* is a report of the data obtained from logging a well. An interpreter uses a *log template* as a starting place to specify what properties are to be displayed on the well log, such as *electrical resistivity*. Because oil is an insulator, it "resists" electricity. By viewing a well log of the electrical resistivity measured up and down the borehole, the interpreter can spot depths where there may be oil.

5. Review available 3D seismic surveys of the area and select one of interest.

Explanation: Whereas the geologic model of an area is based on observations of strata at the surface and what we know about geology of the earth in general, and whereas well logs are based on measures made at particular spots along the borehole of particular wells, *seismic surveys* are a way to remotely view inside the earth on a broader scale giving a fuller picture of the earth for the area of interest. *3D seismic surveys* allow the geoscientist to select an arbitrary section through the seismic data that matches any cross section (explained in step 7) that a geoscientist might construct.

6. Create basemap showing well locations.

   Explanation: A *basemap* is basically what most of us think of when we think "map": a view of the earth's surface from above. Of particular interest on the basemap are the locations of wells that have been drilled in the area. See basemap (center) in Figure A.1. Wells selected from step 3 are shown on the basemap.

7. Draw a line-of-section on basemap that includes wells to evaluate; View 2D cross section.

   Explanation: A *line-of-section* is a straight line, or series of connected straight lines, on a basemap. An interpreter usually draws a line-of-section connecting several wells in an area, as has been done in Figure A.1; see the dark line running northwest to southeast on left of basemap. The line-of-section specifies that part of an area for which the interpreter wants to view the cross section. A *cross section* is a view of the earth from the side. When you drive your car through a hill where the hill has been cut-away for the road, you are looking at a cross section of the hill. Having included wells in the line-of-section, the interpreter will get a view of not only the geologic strata that corresponds to the line-of-section but also a well log superimposed over each borehole in the cross section. The interpreter will also get a cross section of the seismic data along the line-of-section. In this way, the interpreter combines information from three disciplines—geology, petrophysics, and geophysics—to form a more complete idea of what actually lies beneath the earth and where oil and gas are likely to have been created and trapped in a reservoir.

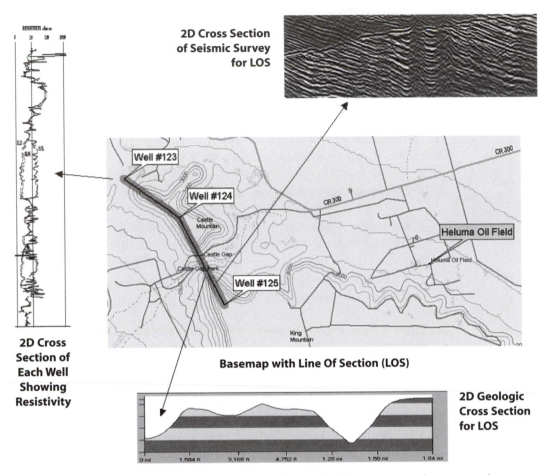

2D Cross Section of Seismic Survey for LOS

2D Cross Section of Each Well Showing Resistivity

Well #123

Well #124

Castle Mountain

Castle Gap

Castle Gap Park

Well #125

King Mountain

CR 300

CR 300

Heluma Oil Field

Heluma Oil Field

Basemap with Line Of Section (LOS)

2D Geologic Cross Section for LOS

0 mi   1,584 ft   3,168 ft   4,752 ft   1.20 mi   1.50 mi   1.84 mi

Figure A.1   *Basemap (center) with line-of-section (LOS)—the dark line running northwest to southeast on left of basemap—indicating that area for which the geoscientist wants a geologic cross section, well logs, and seismic survey displayed in 2D.*

B

Bare-Bones Project Portfolio Database and Use Case Metadata

This appendix provides tables and queries in support of the "How Are You Currently Invested?" section in Chapter 8 "Leveraging Your Investment in Use Case CM in Project Portfolio Management."

Bare-Bones Portfolio Database

If you don't have a portfolio of projects, you'll need to build a database that lists the inventory of all the projects you want to manage. A project portfolio database need not be complicated. Figure B.1 shows basic information you can track for each project. The database needs to include a field or fields by which every project can be classified and by which you can measure how the project portfolio database allocates development resources. Here field **Project Type** is used for this purpose. Fields **Duration** and **Start Date** are used for pipeline management of the project portfolio.

Project Portfolio database : Table			
Field Name	Data Type	Description	
Project Code	Number	Code that uniquely identies each project in the portfolio	
Project Name	Text	Name of the project	
Project Type	Text	Type of project: New Product Development, Cash Cow Development, Custom Development, Research	
Duration	Number	Work days planned for this project	
Start Date	Date/Time	Planned start date	

Figure B.1   *Fields needed for a bare-bones project portfolio database. Note the symbol indicating the field that forms the key for the table.*

Use Case Metadata

A goal of project portfolio management is to measure the allocation of development resources against each of the identified project types. To do this, you can estimate the effort planned for each project in the portfolio, and then roll the results up by project type. It is in the estimation of the planned effort for each project that the use case comes into play. By estimating the effort of each use case in a project, you get a bottom-up estimate of the overall project effort. Figure B.2 shows a table with a minimal amount of use case metadata needed to generate the reports of Chapter 8.

Use Case metadata - Project Code, Effort : Table			
Field Name	Data Type	Description	
Use Case ID	Number	Unique identification for each use case	
Project Code	Number	Unique code which identifies project in which this use case is to be implemented	
Estimated Effort	Number	Estimate of effort, in staff days, to implement this use case	

Figure B.2   *A minimal amount of use case metadata is needed to generate the reports of Chapter 8.*

Checking the Mix of Project Types

After an inventory of projects has been made and categorized by project type and development teams have allocated use cases to the projects in the portfolio and estimated the effort to implement each, you are ready to run a report that measures the allocation of estimated effort—via use cases—by project types.

The query shown in Figure B.3 illustrates the combined use of data from the project portfolio database (refer to Figure B.1) and the metadata of the use case CM database (refer to Figure B.2) to produce a table listing estimated effort per project type, illustrated in Figure B.4. Such a table can then be used in your favorite graphing package to produce a pie chart like that shown in Figure 8.1 in Chapter 8.

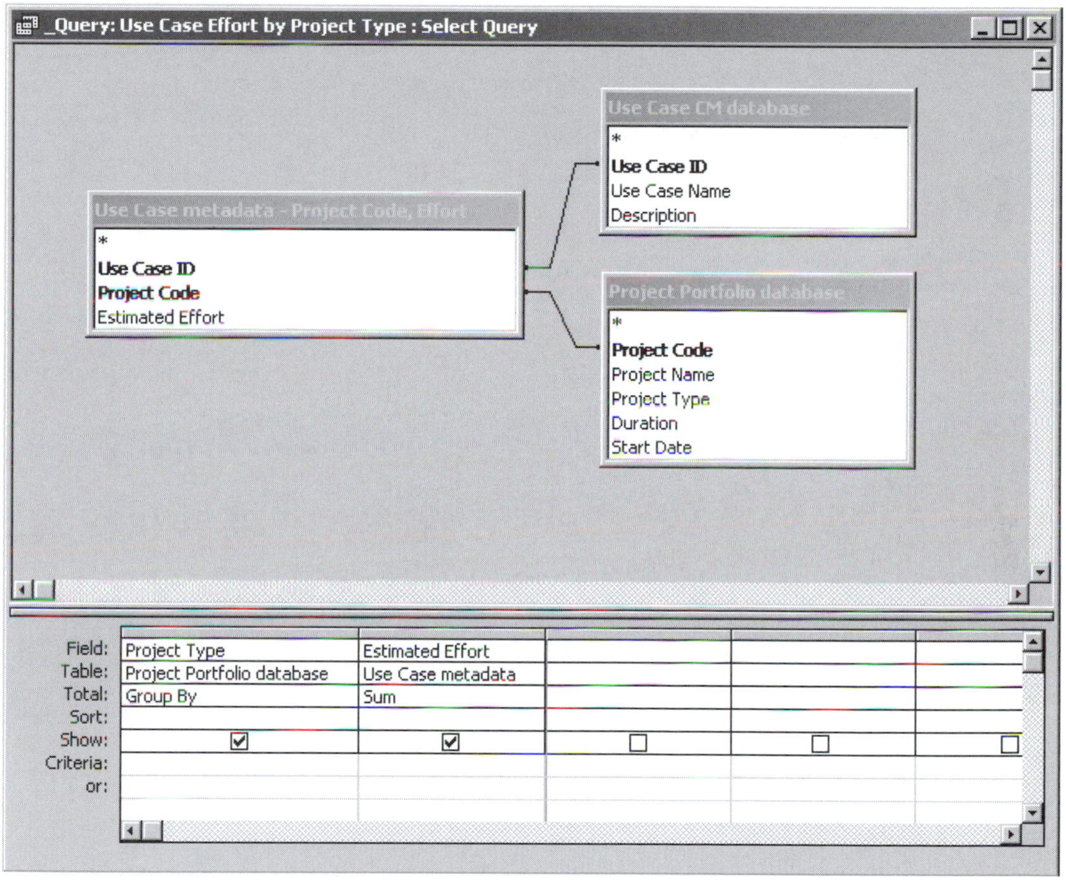

Figure B.3 *Query to calculate estimated effort by project type. Example results from this query are shown in Figure B.4.*

Figure B.4 *Estimated use case effort by project type.*

C

Run Chart of FTEs Required by Project Portfolio

This appendix provides tables and queries in support of the "Managing the Pipeline" section in Chapter 8, "Leveraging Your Investment in Use Case CM in Project Portfolio Management."

A good way to sanity check a project portfolio is to build a run chart of the number of FTEs required to do the work in the project portfolio through time. Microsoft Project has the capability to generate such run charts, called *resource graphs*. The run chart of Figure 8.2 (lower window) was produced by importing combined data from both the project portfolio database and from the use case CM database into MS Project.

Following are sample queries showing how to combine data from the project portfolio database and the use case CM database for importing into a scheduling tool, such as MS Project.

Query to Sum Use Case Effort by Project Code

We start with a query that estimates the amount of effort that each project in the portfolio represents. The work we did to estimate effort for use cases will provide just what we need for this.

Figure C.1 is a Microsoft Access database query to sum use case effort by project code. A sample of the results from this query is provided in Figure C.2. This query is similar to the one we used earlier to total effort by project type (refer to Figure B.3).

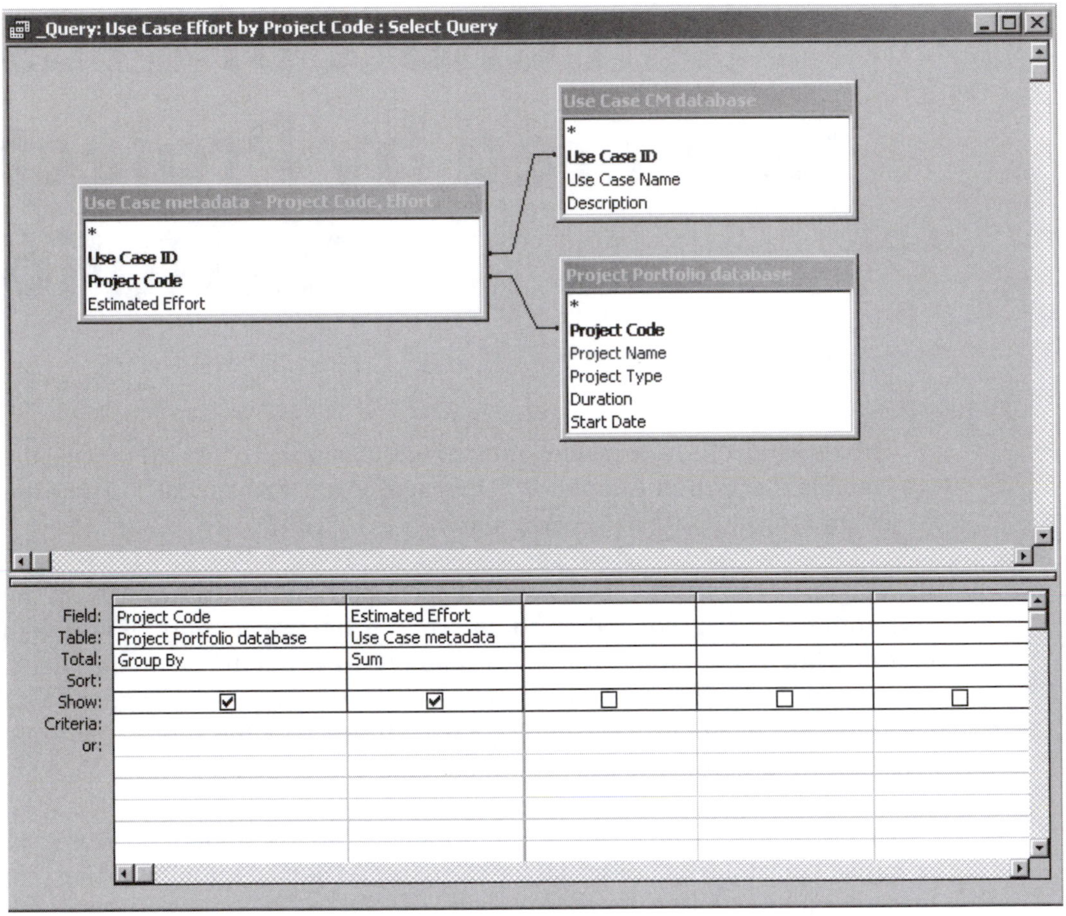

Figure C.1   *Query to calculate use case effort by project code.*

_Query: Use Case Effort by Project Code : Select Query

Project Code	SumOfEstimated Effort
10005	15
10017	564
10025	7049
10031	1935
10032	195
10033	225
10037	15
10039	744
10044	139
10049	15
10050	753
10052	780
10063	45
10066	71
10067	4100
10068	401
10074	357
10075	80
10078	240
10087	570
10090	150
10096	435
10098	30
10106	196
10114	30
10126	60
10137	1275
10210	15
10214	165

Record: 38 of 55

Figure C.2 *Sample results produced by query of Figure C.1.*

Query to Prepare Data for Import to Microsoft Project

Getting the combined project portfolio and use case information into Microsoft Project so that it can generate a resource graph is straightforward. A database query is written to build a table with the information needed for MS Project to generate a schedule. That table is then imported into Microsoft Project; MS Project does the rest, i.e., generates the desired run charts.

Figure C.3 shows the MS Access query that will generate a table suitable for import into MS Project; it uses the query just created to sum use case effort by project code (refer to Figure C.1).

A sample table created by this query is shown in Figure C.4. In the table, each row corresponds to one project in the portfolio database. Notice that the names of columns match the names of fields that MS Project uses for schedules, namely:

- Task Name—Each project in the portfolio becomes one task in MS Project. The project code is used for the task name.

- Work—This is the field MS Project uses for effort. For each project, we use the sum of effort of all use cases assigned to the project.

- Duration—This is the duration, in calendar work days, as per the project portfolio. See Figure B.1.

- Start—This is the date the project is scheduled to start as per the project portfolio. See Figure B.1.

To build a schedule, we simply import this table into MS Project. Figure 8.2 shows a schedule with resource graph generated from the import of the data of Figure C.4, which was produced by the query shown in Figure C.3.

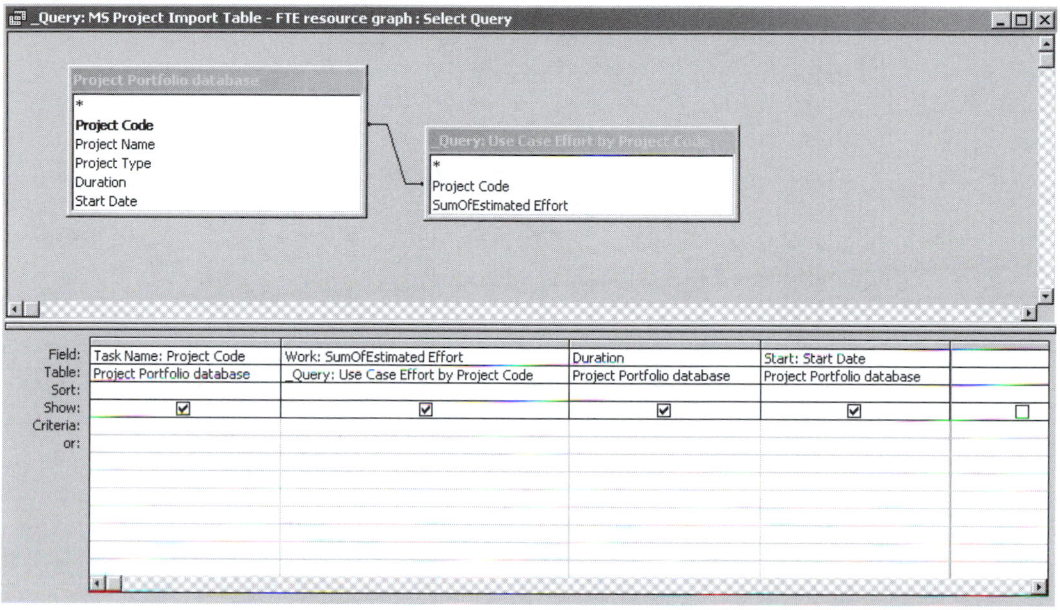

Figure C.3 *Query to calculate data for import to Microsoft Project. Notice that it uses the query previously defined in Figure C.1. An example of this query's results is provided in Figure C.4.*

_Query: MS Project Import Table - FTE resource gra...

Task Name	Work	Duration	Start
10005	15	20	2006-02-16
10017	564	188	2006-01-01
10025	7049	290	2007-04-20
10031	1935	525	2005-05-06
10032	195	525	2005-05-06
10033	225	470	2005-05-06
10037	15	25	2007-02-15
10039	744	249	2007-01-01
10044	139	97	2006-03-06
10049	15	20	2007-03-29
10050	753	121	2006-04-27
10052	780	151	2007-04-05
10063	45	82	2006-05-15
10066	71	60	2006-08-10
10067	4100	455	2005-12-31
10068	401	126	2006-04-13
10074	357	162	2006-11-15
10075	80	135	2007-03-26
10078	240	171	2006-11-02
10087	570	56	2005-12-31
10090	150	183	2007-02-01
10096	435	165	2006-11-12
10098	30	180	2006-06-04
10106	196	162	2006-11-15
10114	30	180	2006-08-14
10126	60	218	2006-08-08
10137	1275	56	2005-03-31
10210	15	20	2007-02-01
10214	165	93	2007-09-01
10226	198	161	2006-11-16

Record: 31 of 55

Figure C.4 *Table for import into Microsoft Project. This table was created by the query shown in Figure C.3.*

D

Reports for Tracking Progress of Projects in Portfolio

This appendix provides tables and queries in support of the "Tracking the Status of the Portfolio via Use Cases" section in Chapter 8, "Leveraging Your Investment in Use Case CM in Project Portfolio Management."

Just as periodic checks of your stocks and bonds are important to see if they are growing as anticipated, so are periodic reviews of your portfolio of projects to see if they are progressing as planned. This appendix provides information on how to produce reports, such as those shown in Figures 8.3 and 8.4, which are useful for tracking the progress of large numbers of projects in the portfolio. These reports track the progress of projects in terms of the status of the use cases that make up each project.

Metadata for Use Case Status

A type of metadata commonly associated with requirements is *status*. Figure D.1 shows how to extend the table of Figure B.2 in Appendix B, "Bare-Bones Project Portfolio Database and Use Case Metadata," to include tracking the status of each use case (e.g., Draft, Proposed, Approved, Rejected, and so on).

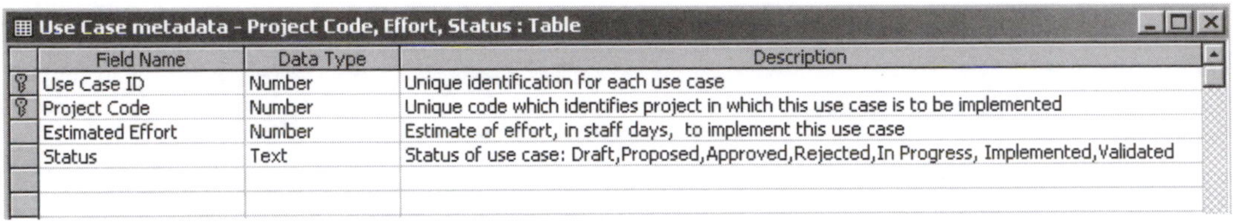

Use Case metadata - Project Code, Effort, Status : Table

Field Name	Data Type	Description
Use Case ID	Number	Unique identification for each use case
Project Code	Number	Unique code which identifies project in which this use case is to be implemented
Estimated Effort	Number	Estimate of effort, in staff days, to implement this use case
Status	Text	Status of use case: Draft,Proposed,Approved,Rejected,In Progress, Implemented,Validated

Figure D.1 *Use case metadata extended to cover status.*

Report for Tracking Status of Projects in the Portfolio by Use Case Status

An effective approach for tracking the status of a project in a portfolio database is to track the sum of *effort* of use cases in discrete categories (e.g., draft versus implemented); this is more realistic than trying to track, for example, percent completion of each individual use case, and more accurate than simply counting the number of use cases in each category. This section describes the process for generating reports similar to those shown in Figures 8.3 and 8.4.

Figure D.2 provides an MS Access query to join data from the project portfolio database with that of the use case CM database. The fields shown are those needed to generate project portfolio progress reports. Notice how the query prefixes the project start date to project code; this field forms the X-axis of Figures 8.3 and 8.4. The results of this query are used in the pivot table of Figure D.3 to organize the data for graphing in Excel or your favorite graphing application.

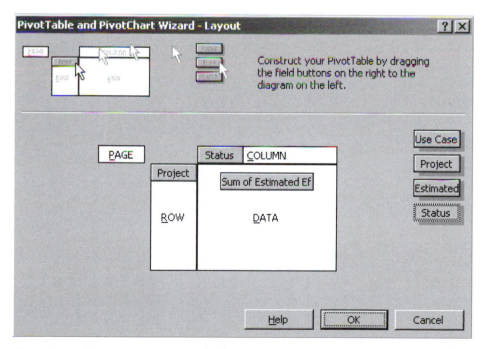

Figure D.2   *Query to generate data for reports like those of Figures 8.3 and 8.4. Field "Project" will appear on X-axis and is a composite of project start date prefixed to project code. Results of this query provide input to the pivot table of Figure D.3.*

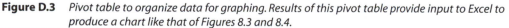

Figure D.3   *Pivot table to organize data for graphing. Results of this pivot table provide input to Excel to produce a chart like that of Figures 8.3 and 8.4.*

References

Ambler, Scott. "Enterprise Unified Process," Available at http://www.enterpriseunifiedprocess.info/.

Akao, Yoji. 1997. QFD: Past, Present, and Future. Presented at International Symposium on QFD.

Armour, Frank, and Granville Miller. 2001. *Advanced Use Case Modeling*. Boston: Addison-Wesley.

Beck, Kent, and Martin Fowler. 2001. *Planning Extreme Programming*. Boston: Addison-Wesley.

Beizer, Boris. 1990. *Software Testing Techniques*, 2nd ed. New York: Van Nostrand Reinhold.

Binder, Robert. 2000. *Testing Object-Oriented Systems: Models, Patterns, and Tools*. Boston: Addison-Wesley.

Boehm, Barry. 1981. *Software Engineering Economics*. Englewood Cliffs, NJ: Prentice Hall.

Broekman, Bart, and Edwin Notenboom. 2003. *Testing Embedded Software*. Boston: Addison-Wesley.

Charan, Ram, What the CEO Wants You to Know, Publisher: Crown Business; 1st edition (February 13, 2001).

Cockburn, Alistair. 2000. *Writing Effective Use Cases*. Boston: Addison-Wesley.

———. 2002. Use Cases, Ten Years Later. *Software Testing and Quality Engineering (STQE) Magazine*, March/April, vol. 4, no. 2.

Cohen, Lou. 1995. *Quality Function Deployment: How to Make QFD Work for You*, Boston: Addison-Wesley.

Coleman, Derek, Patrick Arnold, Stephanie Bodoff, Chris Dollin, Helena Gilchrist, Fiona Hayes, and Paul Jeremaes. 1994. *Object-Oriented Development: The Fusion Method*, Object-Oriented Series edition. Englewood Cliffs, NJ: Prentice Hall.

Cooper, Robert, Scott Edgett, and Elko Kleinschmidt. 1998. *Portfolio Management for New Products*, Boston: Addison-Wesley.

Date, C.J. 2000. *What Not How: The Business Rules Approach to Application Development*. Boston: Addison-Wesley.

Davis, Alan. 1995. *201 Principles of Software Development*. New York: McGraw-Hill.

———.1993. *Software Requirements: Object, Functions, and States*. Upper Saddle River, NJ: Prentice Hall.

Day, Ronald G. 1993. *Quality Function Deployment: Linking a Company with its Customers*. Milwaukee, WI: ASQC Quality Press.

DeMarco, Tom. 2001. *Slack*. New York: Broadway Books.

Futrell, Robert, Donald Shafer, and Linda Shafer. 2002. *Quality Software Project Management*, Upper Saddle River, NJ: Prentice Hall.

Gauss, Donald, and Gerald Weinberg. 1989. *Exploring Requirements: Quality Before Design.* New York: Dorset House Publishing.

Gelperin, David. "Precise Use Cases." Available at http://www.livespecs.com/.

Gluch, David P., Santiago Comella-Dorda, John Hudak, Grace Lewis, and Chuck Weinstock. 2002. "Model-Based Verification: Guidelines for Generating Expected Properties." Technical note, CMU/SEI-2002-TN-003, Carnegie Mellon, Software Engineering Institute.

Gries, David, and Fred B. Schneider. 1993. *A Logical Approach to Discrete Math,* New York: Springer-Verlag.

Haag, Stephen, M.K. Raja, and L.L. Schkade. 1996. "Quality Function Deployment Usage in Software Development." *Communications of the ACM,* vol. 39(1), January.

Hass, Anne Mette Jonassen. 2003. *Configuration Management Principles and Practices.* Boston: Addison-Wesley.

Highsmith III, James. 2000. *Adaptive Software Development.* New York: Dorsett House Publishing.

Jacobson, Ivar, Magnus Christerson, Patrik Jonsson, and Gunnar Overgaard. 1992. *Object-Oriented Software Engineering: A Use Case Driven Approach,* Boston: Addison-Wesley.

Jacobson, Ivar. 2003. "Use Cases: Yesterday, Today, and Tomorrow." *The Rational Edge,* March.

Johannessen, Per, Christian Grante, Anders Alminger, Ulrik Eklund (VolvoCar Corporation), and Jan Torin. 2001. "Hazard Analysis in Object Oriented Design of Dependable Systems." Presented at IEEE International Conference on Dependable Systems and Networks.

Jones, Cliff B. 2003. "The Early Search for Tractable Ways of Reasoning about Programs." *IEEE Annals of the History of Computing,* April-June, Vol. 25, No. 2.

Juran, J.M., and Frank M. Grynam. 1988. *Juran's Quality Control Handbook, Fourth Edition.* Texas: McGraw-Hill.

Lamia, Walter. 1995. "Integrating QFD with Object-oriented Software Design Methodologies." Presented at the 7th Symposium on QFD.

Leffingwell, Dean. 2003. "Calculating Your Return on Investment from More Effective Requirements Management." IBM/Rational tech report, June. Available at http://www-128.ibm.com/developerworks/rational/library/347.html.

Leffingwell, Dean, and Don Widrig. 2003. *Managing Software Requirements: A Use Case Approach.* 2nd. ed. Boston: Addison-Wesley.

McCarthy, Jim. 1995. *Dynamics of Software Development.* Redmond, Washington: Microsoft Press.

McConnell, Steve. 1996. *Rapid Development.* Redmond, Washington: Microsoft Press.

Meyer, Bertrand. 1988. *Object-Oriented Software Construction.* 1st ed. Upper Saddle River, NJ: Prentice Hall.

Moore, Geoffrey. 1991. *Crossing the Chasm,* New York: HarperBusiness.

Musa, John D., Anthony Iannino, and Kazuhira Okumoto. 1990. *Software Reliability: Professional Edition.* New York: McGraw-Hill.

Payne, Jeffery E. 1999. "Quality Meets The CEO: How To Get Management Buy-In." *Software Testing and Quality Engineering (STQE) Magazine,* May/June, vol. 1, issue 3.

PMBOK Guide. 2000. *A Guide to the Project Management Body of Knowledge.* Newston Square, PA: Project Management Institute.

Rumbaugh, James, Ivar Jacobson, and Grady Booch. 2005. *The Unified Modeling Language Reference Manual.* 2nd. ed. Boston: Addison-Wesley.

Runeson, Per, and Björn Regnell. 1998. "Derivation of an Integrated Operational Profile and Use Case Model." Proceedings of 9th International Symposium on Software Reliability Engineering (ISSRE'98).

Schneider, Geri, and Jason Winters. 1998. *Applying Use Cases: A Practical Guide.* Boston: Addison-Wesley.

Sommerville, Ian. 2000. *Software Engineering, 6th Edition.* Boston: Addison-Wesley.

Storey, Neil. 1996. *Safety-Critical Computer Systems.* Boston: Addison-Wesley.

Warmer, Jos, and Anneke Kleppe. 1999. *The Object Constraint Language: Precise Modeling with UML.* Boston: Addison-Wesley.

Weinberg, Gerald, and Daniela Weinberg. 1988. *General Principles of System Design.* New York: Dorset House Publishing.

Weller, Ed. 2002. "Calculating the Economics of Inspections." Available at http://www.stickyminds.com/.

Wiegers, Karl. 1999. *Software Requirements.* 1st ed. Redmond, WA: Microsoft Press.

———. 2000. "Karl Wiegers Describes 10 Requirements Traps to Avoid." *Software Testing and Quality Engineering (STQE) Magazine,* January/February, vol. 2, no. 1.

Wyder, Todd. 1996. "Capturing requirements with use cases." *Software Development Magazine.* February. Available online at http://www.sdmagazine.com/.

Index

Page numbers followed by *n* signify footnotes.

Page numbers followed by n signify footnotes.

Page numbers followed by *n* signify footnotes.

Page numbers followed by *n* signify footnotes.

Page numbers followed by *n* signify footnotes.

Page numbers followed by *n* signify footnotes.

Page numbers followed by *n* signify footnotes.

Page numbers followed by n signify footnotes.

Page numbers followed by n signify footnotes.

Page numbers followed by *n* signify footnotes.

Page numbers followed by *n* signify footnotes.

Page numbers followed by *n* signify footnotes.

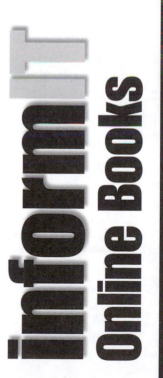

informIT